Women's Rights
in
France

Recent Titles in
Contributions in Women's Studies

Women's Rights in France

Dorothy McBride Stetson

CONTRIBUTIONS IN WOMEN'S STUDIES,
NUMBER 74

GREENWOOD PRESS
NEW YORK · WESTPORT, CONNECTICUT · LONDON

Library of Congress Cataloging-in-Publication Data

Stetson, Dorothy M.
  Women's rights in France.

  (Contributions in women's studies, ISSN 0147-104X ;
no. 74)
    Bibliography: p.
    Includes index.
      1. Women's rights—France.   2. Women—Legal status,
laws, etc.—France.   3. Feminism—France.   4. France—
Social conditions—1945–   . I. Title. II. Series.
HQ1236.5.F8S74   1987   305.4′2′0944   86-14988
ISBN 0-313-25403-6 (lib. bdg. : alk. paper)

Library of Congress Catalog Card Number: 86-14988
ISBN: 0-313-25403-6
ISSN: 0147-104X

First published in 1987

Greenwood Press, Inc.
88 Post Road West, Westport, Connecticut 06881

Printed in the United States of America

The paper used in this book complies with the
Permanent Paper Standard issued by the National
Information Standards Organization (Z39.48-1984).

10 9 8 7 6 5 4 3 2 1

To Virginia McBride Altman

CONTENTS

TABLES

PREFACE

France has always seemed to lag behind the United States in the march toward equality of the sexes. French women, weighed down by an authoritarian legal system, hierarchical church, and absolutist traditions, have endured long periods of marginality and inferiority. For 100 years, women's rights activists in Paris looked across the Atlantic to see what the Americans were doing and read what the Americans were writing. The call for women's liberation that sounded in New York, Chicago, and Berkeley rallied militants to the Mouvement de Libération des Femmes in Paris and Lyon. French women learned about their own bible, *The Second Sex* by Simone de Beauvoir, long after it had inspired American feminists.

Then, between 1981 and 1986, the French government seemed to take a giant step forward with the creation of a new ministry for women's rights, the Ministère des Droits de la femme. At long last, feminists were inside the government, part of the political executive, with a chance at real influence. The ministry consisted of a small group of energetic feminists led by Yvette Roudy with an agenda to wipe clean the residue of centuries of patriarchy. At a time when the spirits of American feminists were wilting under Reaganism, France became the bright spot for women's rights.

In 1983 I began a study of the Ministry of Woman's Rights, intending to describe and analyze its impact on the policy and status of women. My initial investigation showed that these government feminists and their program were not newly born in 1981 but part of a massive overhaul of the legal and economic status of women that had been underway for decades. The project quickly expanded to include all the changes in public policy and the role played by feminists both inside and outside the government. Between 1965 and 1985 every policy affecting women, from reproduction to retirement, was rewritten. This has meant, among other things, that equality of the sexes has replaced the patriarchal family law code. Instead of criminal prosecution for using contraceptives or seeking abortions, the state provides family planning services. Women who were restricted to ten percent of the openings for job training now have preference in state-sponsored programs of "positive" discrimination. Assaults on the male-dominated culture have threatened pornography, prostitution, and sexism in school textbooks.

My interest in policy involves the exploration of the way issues develop and change and the influence of various actors and groups in the policy process. The process surrounding women's issues is especially intriguing because feminist demands strip away the conventions of policymaking and reveal the core of political conflict, the struggle over the meaning of political issues. Whether it is rape, abortion, job training, family allowances, divorce, or high school curricula, a public problem inevitably leads to conflicts about its meaning and resolution. Feminists strive to define issues so they will change traditional patriarchal sex roles and the values that perpetuate them. Theirs is only one of the many points of view competing to hold sway over the description of public problems. To have any influence feminists must gain control of the issues and change the way they are defined, replacing the conventional logic with a feminist one. The outcome of this conflict is crucial because changes in the laws are likely to further women's rights only if the policymakers agree that the problems they are designed to fix are derived from patriarchal sex roles.

Despite growing interest in feminism and women's studies in American universities, only recently have we looked at the women's movement in the United States in comparison with women's rights in other countries. This book portrays the developments in the public fortunes of French women from the perspective of similar issues in the United States. After the great activity in law reform in both countries, who is ahead? Ten years ago, from our impressions of French sex kittens on the screen and impossibly abstract theories on the intellectual fringes, we would have concluded that the status of most French women had changed little. Now we find that the energetic feminists in the government have presided over the adoption of several policies that are more feminist than those in the United States. This study examines the effect of these changes on the lives of French women as citizens, their legal status, and opportunities available to them through state action. It does not cover the changes in the personal lives of French or American women in such areas as consciousness raising; sex role socialization; their representation in the arts; or their personal relations with men in the kitchen, the office, or the bedroom. For some feminists these are the true political issues because they involve the major problems of power facing the majority of women. To me, however, formal policy is important because it sets the public standard for sex roles which shape our private lives and relationships.

This study was made possible by research grants under the Fulbright program of the Council for International Exchange of Scholars, the Franco-American Commission, and the Division of Sponsored Research at Florida Atlantic University. I am indebted for the friendly and capable assistance of the staffs at several libraries and documentation services in France: Bibliothèque Marguerite Durand; L'Agence femmes information; Ministère des Droits de la femme; Fondation Nationale des Sciences Politiques; and the Bibliothèque national. I am especially grateful to several French colleagues for their help, friendship, and, most of all, for their genuine interest in women's rights: Janine Mossuz-Lavau, Mariette Sineau, Liliane Kandel, Genevieve Acker, Anne-Marie Chauvraud, Janie Deveze, and Serge Hurtig. I also wish to thank Bernard E. Brown, Jan W. Hokenson, Leslie Derfler, Anita Bluestein, and the staff of the Wimberly Library of Florida Atlantic University.

ABBREVIATIONS

AFI	L'Agence femmes information
ANEA	L'Association National pour l'Etude de l'Avortement
BVP	Bureau de Vérification de la Publicité
CFDT	Confédération Française Démocratique du Travail
CGT	Confédération Générale du Travail
CLRA	Collectif Lesbian de Recherche et d'Action
CNRS	Centre National de la Recherche Scientifique
CSW	Commissions on the Status of Women
CUARH	Comité d'Urgence Anti-Répression Homosexuelle
CWE	Committee on Women's Employment
EEC	European Economic Community
EEOC	Equal Employment Opportunity Commission
EP	European Parliament
ERA	Equal Rights Amendment
FMA	Féminin, Masculin, Avenir
FR	Féministes Révolutionnaires
GIS	Groupe Information Santé
INED	Institut National d'Etudes Démographiques

LDF	Ligue du Droit des femmes
MFPF	Mouvement Français pour le Planning Familial
MIEL	Mouvement d'Information et d'Expression des Lesbiennes
MJF	Mouvement Jeunes Femmes
MLAC	Mouvement pour la Liberté de l'Avortement et de la Contraception
MLF	Mouvement de Libération des Femmes
MWR	Ministry of Woman's Rights
NOW	National Organization for Women
PC	Parti communiste
PS	Parti socialiste
Psych et Po	Psychanalise et Politique
RPR	Rassemblement pour la République
SFIO	Section Française de l'Internationale Ouvrière
SPRS	Services publics de reinsertion sociale
UDF	Union pour la Démocratie Française
UFCS	Union Française Civique et Sociale
UFF	Union des Femmes Française
WAP	Women Against Pornography
WAVAW	Women Against Violence Against Women
WLM	Women's Liberation Movement

Women's Rights
in
France

1

INTRODUCTION

WOMEN'S RIGHTS are public rights conferred by a variety of government policies. During the past twenty years, the French government has changed most of the policies affecting women's rights, thereby greatly altering the legal status of French women and improving their economic and social position. The process that led to these changes engaged politicians and interest groups in investigating the problems facing women and deciding how they should be addressed. When turning their attention to women's rights, French authorities confront no new issues; instead they try to settle conflicts over the definition of the old issues. Feminists challenge conventional approaches to policy by advocating a new logic that furthers the opportunities, dignity, and equality of women. In trying to convince the policymakers to change their traditional perspectives, feminists meet resistance from those who quarrel with their ideas about women. Feminists themselves often do not agree on the meaning or the importance of issues. The result is conflict over what conditions, actions, and language will be best for women. The resolution of these conflicts constitutes the story of women's rights in France.

A recent dispute over sexism, pornography, and the image of women in media in France illustrates the politics of women's rights. In the spring of 1985, posters plastered all over the Paris *métro* stations compelled commuters' attention to a film called *Rendezvous*. The pale naked body of a woman was drawn to a standing position, her arms held in the steely grip of a man dressed in black. Her head was bowed and hidden, her body in back view. The man, apparently interrupted in the midst of a cruel act, was invisible, save for his hands, his grim face, and his eyes staring directly at the viewer. Without blood or bruises, whips or chains, the image told of male dominance and female submission. On a few posters were glued tiny printed signs: "Down with pornography."

Someone, a feminist perhaps, had quietly signaled to others that this display was more serious than the usual film ads that blanket Paris every week. Images of sexual bondage used to be hidden from view, reserved for the fans of the Marquis de Sade. Now sexual liberty has lowered the barriers that once kept such pictures hidden. Some feminists charge that sexism thrives behind the face of free speech: "Liberty of expression, they say. For whom? Certainly not for the women who bear the cost [of male sexual fantasies]. Liberty of expression for some must stop where it attacks the integrity and dignity of others."[1] Feminists see what their foremothers were ignorant of: a culture of sexual oppression that is perpetuated through media images. Some believe that women's emancipation depends on their right to fight against those images. They want a new law that will permit them to sue advertisers and filmmakers for sex discrimination.

The result is a new approach to an old problem. The proper dissemination of sexually explicit materials has long been a public issue in both France and the United States. The public debate has been framed conventionally in terms of freedom of speech versus public morality. What is new is the attempt by some feminists in both countries to change the meaning of pornography and in so doing affect government's reaction to it. For these feminists, pornography is not immoral because it reveals sexual behavior, it is dangerous because it fosters violence against women. Freedom of speech is not limitless; by defining pornography in terms of violence they hope to push it beyond free speech limits. Other feminists, however, fear that despite degrading images of women in some sexually explicit material, censorship will ultimately hurt women more. Only since the lifting of moral taboos, they argue, have women been able to learn about their own sexuality.

The current controversy about pornography and women's rights represents the heart of all political conflict: the battle over the meaning or definition of an issue. The development of a new subject for government action is rare, even revolutionary; policymaking usually concerns new conflicts about the meaning of old problems. For a long time, determining the proper place for sexually explicit pictures, books, and films has meant finding a balance between public morality and free expression. Feminists now propose a new view of the issue. They define pornography not as sexual expression but as the representation of an ideology of oppression and violence against women. If their view of pornography prevails, they hope to attract support from large sectors of the law-abiding public. If pornographers and poster makers allowed their issue to be defined in feminist terms, they would find themselves defending oppression and sexual violence, a battle they would very likely lose. Thus they doggedly stick to language defending the free expression of harmless sexual fantasies, while challenging research that links violence to pornography and charging that feminists are just modern prudes. So far, policymakers have avoided taking a stand on this controversial issue.

There is a lot at stake. "The definition of alternatives is the supreme instrument of power."[2] Every debate over policy, every policy question, is itself part of a larger conflict over which question will be selected for action and how it will be posed. The way choices are presented determines the content and effect of policy, including the distribution of benefits, rights, privileges, and other resources. To understand a particular policy, therefore, it is essential to examine how those involved in making it choose to view it—what Charles Anderson calls the logic of public problems.[3]

The definition of the meaning of policy issues has been especially important to the women's rights movements in France and the United States. An array of policies and practices had functioned in both countries to assign women to traditional female roles in public and private life. Every campaign for reform of these laws has involved a battle to redefine an old problem—be it birth control, family law, labor law, political rights, or education—in a new way that will change economic, social, and political opportunities for women. There is no unified view of these issues that all feminists everywhere share, but their general goals are the same. "The feminist ideology is based on the recognition that women constitute a group that is wrongfully oppressed by male-defined values and male-controlled institutions of social, political, cultural, and familial power."[4] To achieve equality and improvement in women's place depends on a change in patriarchal sex roles and the values that perpetuate them. In their campaigns for public policy, feminists seek to redefine issues in order to advance changes in traditional sex roles and their cultural supports.

Despite their agreement on long-term goals, feminists face many obstacles in winning acceptance for their view of the world. Advocates of women's rights, like all others who attack the policymaking process, face what Peter Bachrach and Morton Baratz describe as the bias of the pressure system: "The dominant values and the political myths, beliefs, rituals, and institutions which tend to favor one or many groups, relative to others."[5] Feminists usually encounter a bias that considers their perspective unimportant and their concerns of low priority. In the United States such opposition has often forced feminists to accept old definitions in return for any government action at all, or disguise laws intended to help women as furthering other goals.

Recent studies of policymaking and women's rights show that American feminists have more success when they ask for reforms that are narrowly drawn. Ellen Boneparth argued that the definition of women's rights issues affects their acceptability to lawmakers.[6] Joyce Gelb and Marion Palley found that proposals that are least threatening and most incremental have the greatest chance of success.[7] If an issue has low visibility, fits with prevailing policy, and involves limited concerns, it will have a better chance of passing, whatever the subject. Incremental issues make groups proposing them appear more legitimate. In the area of women's rights, issues usually involve either *role equity*, the legal equality of the sexes without changing sex roles, or *role change*, proposing a basic reorientation of the roles of men and women in all respects. Most issues framed in terms of role equity conform to the acceptable criteria of low visibility, limited change, and narrowness, and thus are those that have the greater success. Role-equity proposals attract the support of many more groups than role-change proposals. For example, when the Equal Rights Amendment (ERA) was presented as a matter of simple equality before the law, it enjoyed widespread support of both liberal and conservative groups. However, soon after Congress passed it, the issue was redefined to include the promise or threat (depending on your point of view) of changes in family and sexual relations. As an issue of role change it accumulated a formidable and effective opposition. The ERA lost its acceptability.

Jo Freeman found that the major federal women's rights legislation of the 1960s and 1970s passed with relative ease through Congress because it was defined in narrow and individualist terms.[8] The equal pay law did not threaten men; rather it prevented employers from using women's low wages to undermine male workers. Equal opportunity policy was applied to individual employers and educational institutions, and enforcement was based on the logic of individual grievances. In no way was this legislation seen either as an attack on male prerogative or as a massive boost for the female sex.

Is it always necessary to accept the prevailing definition of issues and settle for incremental yet ineffective policy? Some researchers have observed that groups that challenge the bias system have often been successful in gaining control of the definition of issues and have won the critical conflict over the conflict itself. Roger Cobb and Charles Elder describe various ways that groups can attract support outside the dominant system.[9] An expanded, interested public can bring political resources to bear in the battle over issues. They propose that, contrary to the narrow, incremental, and technical issues that American feminists have found less threatening to elites, it is the proposals that are more ambiguous, less complex, brand-new, emotional, and socially significant that attract the most support from mass publics. By presenting issues in new ways, an interest group such as feminists, outside the dominant system of bias, can expand the conflict to larger publics, gain control of the definition of issues that affect them, and redefine those issues in feminist terms.

In the United States, for the most part, feminists have not succeeded in mobilizing mass publics and convincing the government to define women's rights issues in broadly feminist terms that come anywhere near role change. Most policies they favor have a narrow logic of role equality. Defeat of the ERA and partial success on economic and family issues have reinforced a conscious strategy based on the assumption that broad issues involving role change are dangerous and threatening. It is no wonder that American public policy falls far short of the feminist vision of women's rights.

The problem is that narrow definitions portend limited effects. Role equity has an individualist logic, especially in the United States. It removes legal classification by sex, leaving the cultural, economic, and social biases intact. In the nineteenth century, when ideas of a divinely ordained separation of the sexes prevailed, a demand for equality seemed to be radical. Experience with the vote and the equal pay laws, however, shows that legal equality alone does little in the absence of other changes. While an individual faces no legal discrimination and may succeed in gaining political and economic power, legal equality alone has little effect on the status and participation of women as a group.

Mary Ruggie's comparative study of employment legislation in Great Britain and Sweden shows the importance of such issue definition on policy output.[10] Labor policy has been much more beneficial for the status of working women in Sweden than in Britain. The wage gap is narrower, unemployment lower, and day care facilities more accessible. Ruggie argues that the difference is traced to the prevailing conception about the policy in the two countries. In Great Britain, the problem of women workers is seen as the status of the individual, pertaining to those women who happen to work. Authorities rarely stray from traditional ideas of sex roles, nor from the view that women are a marginal labor force. In Sweden, on the other hand, women's work issues are defined in much more general terms—in fact, not as women's issues at all. Rather, women workers and their problems are incorporated as part of a conscious effort to use labor policy to reduce social and economic inequality. This comparison reminds us that the fate of women's rights policy in the United States is not inevitable in all countries. The challenge to feminists is the same, that is, to define policy issues in feminist terms. But their success will vary according to their tactics and resources and the political and cultural context in which they operate.

At first glance one might expect little success for feminists in France, where the barriers to women's rights are as formidable as those in any country. France is a Latin country with a centrist bureaucracy unsympathetic to equality and decentralization. Napoleon's civil law code weighed heavily on French women, and they didn't get the vote until 1944. The culture that produced, sustained, and even praised the Marquis de Sade and *L'Histoire d'O* (*The Story of O*) exploits women's bodies for art's sake. Feminist historical tradition is spotty and chimerical. Even pronatalism has been a more organized movement than feminism and has enjoyed a stronger historical tradition and more support among the elites.

Since publication of *New French Feminisms* in 1980 and several articles in *Signs*, French feminism is known in America for its theoretical and intellectual battles. While in the United States there is concrete and pragmatic action to achieve legal and economic rights, the French seem to be concerned with dissecting unfathomable theories (Lacan) and playing word games only remotely translatable into English. Whatever stories of political action drift across the Atlantic seemed romantically unconventional—meetings attacking international crimes against women, left-wing doctors performing abortions in public, and prostitutes occupying churches. The limited knowledge we have of these fringe activities has done little to dislodge the image of sexually contented French women who, unlike American women, prefer to remain feminine and exercise their influence behind the throne, over the pillows, and between the sheets.

Reality, of course, is much more complex than any of these stereotypes. The politics of women's rights is as complex and varied in France as it is in the United States. There are women from all parts of the political spectrum, Left and Right, acting to change the status of women in all aspects of French society. Feminism has been institutionalized in the government where most ministries have offices for women's affairs. Between 1981 and 1986, a prominent feminist as Minister of Woman's Rights enjoyed authority and resources unmatched by any feminist in American government. Intense pressure for modernization has produced major reforms in every policy area in the last twenty years. Add to that the tradition of state intervention in a society in which policy is viewed as an instrument of social change, and it appears that the French government may be more, not less, active than the American government in pursuing feminist goals.

THE FEMINIST MOVEMENT

This story of women's rights in France begins with a description of the feminist movement. The contemporary advocates of women's rights in France are heirs to a long tradition. Organized protest dates from 1789 and the French Revolution. Feminist writings began in the fifteenth century with Christine de Pisan. Individual women have been seeking economic and political power in French society since the beginning of recorded history. More recent accounts show that political action for women's rights parallels that in the United States, with some important differences. French women attained an earlier consciousness of their position, yet endured a longer period of legal and political inferiority. During the French Revolution women demanded total equality, yet until the 1880s their political protest was stymied by a series of authoritarian governments. In the meantime, French feminists took advantage of short-lived periods of liberalization in 1830, 1848, and 1871 to agitate for change. Between 1880 and 1945 French and American activists had similar goals: equality in the family and education, the vote, moral equality, equal pay, protection for mothers, and birth control. American women frequently enjoyed the support of other political action groups, whereas potential allies of French women, including liberal republicans, workers, and socialists, gave them little help. They did not receive the vote until 1944, more than two decades after American women gained equal political rights.

After World War II feminism seemed dormant. Nevertheless, this period spawned *The Second Sex* by Simone de Beauvoir, which became the most influential feminist book in both the United States and France. The work meticulously and poetically traced the experience of women in society. The thesis that sex differences are due to social conditioning and not biology was not new. Poulain de la Barre had said as much in the seventeenth century.[11] De Beauvoir packaged the message in one elegant and quotable phrase: "One is not born, but rather becomes, a woman." Her message to feminists was that since sexual inequality is man-made, it can change, although change will be extremely difficult.

At first *The Second Sex* had a greater impact in the United States. "One must not be afraid to say that all contemporary feminism proceeds from *The Second Sex*—American women who have read it with passion know it and often owe their radicalism to it—; in France, admired or criticized, the work made a scandal; minds were not ready, without doubt, to receive this masterful lesson given by a woman."[12] It took twenty years before de Beauvoir and her book became part of a successful feminist movement in France. Among the political offspring are three distinct trends, all with historical roots: radical feminists, egalitarian and reform feminists, and socialist feminists. In this study these groups and more will appear and reappear as participants in the process of promoting women's rights. The intent in this section is to give the general outlines and chronology of the contemporary feminist movement in France.

The year 1965 was *l'année rupture* (watershed year) in both the United States and France. That year the demand for liberation was first heard at the convention of Students for a Democratic Society. Hundreds of American women were drawn together to study evidence of their oppression provided by reports of the Commissions on the Status of Women and the sentiments of *The Feminine Mystique*. In France one book was the magnet that brought the first feminist action group together in 1965:

One day, while passing a bookstore, a title attracted my attention: *La Condition de la française d'aujourd'hui* by Andrée Michel and G. Texier. A book about women. I went in and bought it. It had been a long time since I had read a book with so much enthusiasm. No doubt a feminist book! Nothing published since Simone de Beauvoir was as radical. In the midst of the official chorus of "the emancipation of women has occurred; what are you complaining about?" finally a different sound, finally the truth, argued, on the real condition of women in France. My morale rose. All hope was not lost for feminism.[13]

At first a group including both men and women met to discuss the book and its findings. They called themselves Féminin, Masculin, Avenir (FMA). As the women learned more about the oppression of traditional sex roles, they sought out other women in universities and in leftist political groups.

Radical feminists were mobilized by the events of May 1968. The May movement arose from the politics of the Left, which nurtured long-lasting hostility to feminism. Many women were caught up in the struggle against social and political oppression waged by the students and workers. In the two decades since World War II the numbers of women at universities and factories had increased tremendously. Their experience with the protests of 1968 revealed deeply felt sex discrimination not unlike that found by women in the student and civil-rights movements in the United States. The upheaval brought men and women together, but when women wanted to talk about their situation and their oppression they were ridiculed and told to be quiet.

After things calmed down, FMA sponsored a debate at the Sorbonne on women and revolution; a passionate crowd gathered to protest their treatment during the May movement. "The atmosphere was joyful, I had never seen a gathering like that. I floated . . . When the time came to stop the debate, no one wanted to leave. We would spend our whole lives there in this encounter, beyond the decorum, the coldness, the deficiencies of ordinary life."[14] Although the student activism of 1968 subsided, the women were just getting started. Some of the most active were at the University of Vincennes in the Paris suburbs. They struggled with issues of organization, strategy, and ideology in hundreds of small-group sessions. In May 1970 a debate at Vincennes brought open insults and heckling. Soon after that the Mouvement de Libération des Femmes (MLF) came into being, christened by the male-dominated press.

On 26 August, during a slow month for news in Paris, twelve women approached the Tomb of the Unknown Soldier at the Arch of Triumph, the site of frequent patriotic ceremonies. They carried a wreath and banners that read: "One man in two is a woman," and "There is only one person more unknown than the soldier, his wife." They intended to show solidarity with American women on the fiftieth anniversary of the right to vote. Before they could reach the Arch, however, the police confiscated the wreath and the banners. Journalists called them a "women's liberation group" because they resembled Women's Liberation Movement (WLM) activists in the United States. In October, *Partisans* magazine published a series of articles entitled "Libération des femmes: Année Zero." The movement was launched.

In the next few years activity increased, at first inspired by the American radical feminists. Discussion, writing, and action built a complex web of radical feminist groups under the rubric of the MLF. These women broadened their analysis of the status of women from complaints about structure to examination of the basic relationships between men and women and, finally, to the study of sexuality itself. The MLF gave first priority to the issue of woman's body. "It was at the center of exchanges among women in consciousness-raising groups. It was the basis of the radicalization of many women who had never 'done politics' and for whom daily oppression was a problem that was strictly private." [15] Their experience with the men of 1968 taught them to separate from men, to concentrate on the particular nature of women, and to develop that apart, not to try to integrate into man's world. They demanded specificity and identity for women, denouncing all oppression by patriarchal society. They shunned formal organization, preferring spontaneous action by small *groups-femmes*. "The movement of Women is neither an organization nor a political party, there is neither election, nor delegation nor members, nor dues, nor chiefs nor militants, nor program: the Movement is the antithesis of a political organization, a reaction against political organization."

The M.L.F. it's you
> it's all the women in revolt who take the floor
> it's when two or three women meet and speak together of their experience and their malaise
> it's us, all those who revolt together against the society of men, made by men and for men. [16]

The dynamism and excitement of their experiences spread and attracted women from the Left and Center, students, intellectuals, and
professionals. Eventually, women workers took up the cause of wom-
en's rights. Since organization was discouraged, the MLF for the first
few years was like a wave, attracting, forming, and re-forming groups
for campaigns, meetings, and demonstrations.

In the mid-1970s three tendencies began to develop out of the free-
form action of the radical feminists. These are easier to identify looking back than they were at the time.[17] The leftist tendency stayed
closest to the original pattern of small groups and preserved the decentralized structure. Animated by militant women from extreme leftist
parties, they sought out workers in the neighborhoods of Paris. They
concentrated on radical anticapitalist class analysis, trying to accommodate it to the idea of sexual oppression. This meant relating reproduction by women and their work in the home to Marxist ideas of
class oppression, property, and the work force. They maintained that
the exploitation in reproduction and the home is the true basis of capitalism. Women must organize, they argued, because capitalists use
male power to control all workers.

The Circle Elisabeth-Dimitriev in 1972 emphasized the need for collective solutions to the special discrimination against women. These
militants refused to separate the battle against patriarchy from the struggle
against capitalism. In 1974 a group called Lutte de Classe launched a
leftist feminist movement on a national level with a journal, *Pétroleuses*, named for the female incendiaries of the Paris Commune. "The
sexual manipulation (submitted to by men and by women) is func-
tional in relation to the needs of capitalism at different moments in its
development."[18] The leftist tendency shunned separatism of others in
the MLF and tried to bridge the gap between women's rights and other
radical political movements by insisting that the situation of women,
although critical, was part of a larger system of exploitation.

The oldest continuous MLF group, Politique at Psychanalyse (it was
Psychanalyse et Politique from 1970–73 and is still referred to by
many as Psych et Po or Psychépo), made up the second branch of
radical feminism and rejected just about all of the goals of the leftists.
From the first, Psych et Po was primarily a theory group, exploring
the Freudian concepts of psychoanalysis using the new perspective of
women's sexuality. "If capitalism rests on the sexual division of labor, the battle of women is founded on the differences of the sexes.

The only discourse on sexuality is the psychoanalytic discourse. The women's struggle must be based on the dialectics of historical and psychoanalytic materialism.''[19]

Led by the mercurial and mysterious Antoinette Fouque, this group has consistently rejected the label *feminism*, which they considered a way of inserting women into the patriarchal culture. Feminists are like men, accepting the phallocracy that is only too happy to receive them. Psych et Po especially denounced American feminists, accusing them of having "a phallus in their heads."[20] They concentrated on the liberation of women from patriarchy, not their integration into it. They replaced the phallic and misogynous symbols and language of patriarchy with symbols from female sexuality, *"pouvoir matriciel"* (lit. power of the uterus, from Latin *matrix*, or womb), clitoral power, and ideas plumbed from long-oppressed singular female consciousness. They came to be known as proponents of essentialism and *néo-fémininité*, amplifying and elaborating the female biological characteristics. Psych et Po founded the publishing house and bookstore Des Femmes. Despite the radical nature of their writings and their insistence on a woman-centered movement extolling the power of *la différence*, this most radical of groups remained flexible in practice. They participated with less theoretical and more moderate women in campaigns for law reforms. They followed the creative spirit of their leader not only to do the unpredictable and the extreme, but also to remain an important factor in women's rights politics.

The third tendency arising from the MLF were the Féministes Revolutionnaires (FR). This group was influenced by the writings and activities of Simone de Beauvoir and is the most similar to the Women's Liberation Movement in the United States. From this tendency, the gay women formed their own group, Les Gouines Rouges in 1971, criticizing the heterosexual perspective of many feminists. For them, homosexuality was the essential political choice for women, not only because it rejects men, but because it replaces male definitions of female sexuality:

The homosexual act between two women . . . constitutes in itself a potential of revolt and, I add, of conscious and political revolt; . . . Who preaches a sexuality of pleasure is revolutionary, for to preach a sexuality finally of woman's body is to AFFIRM a sexuality of women, is to RECOGNIZE finally the female sex completely denied by men, our sex and the sexuality of reproduction. It is to DESTROY by a female practice all the male theories on the alleged desires and the alleged bodies of women.[21]

Although Les Gouines Rouges ceased to exist in 1972, lesbians have continued to be active in the MLF, forming other groups, such as Lesbiennes Feministes and the Mouvement d'Information et d'Expression des Lesbiennes, and publishing newsletters and magazines such as *Quand les femmes s'aiment*, *Désormais*, and *Espaces*.

From the beginning the Féministes Revolutionnaires took direct action to promote the cause of women and to attract other women to the effort. The FR was a driving force behind several actions in the early 1970s: the Foire des Femmes, the women's strike, the days of denunciation of the crimes committed against women. In 1974 a group of the FR led by de Beauvoir formed an organization called the Ligue du Droit des femmes (LDF). These women were militants and shared MLF ideas regarding the centrality of female sexuality to the rights of women. They tried to avoid both Marxism and *néo-fémininité* by holding to the position that it is men who oppress women through pervasive sexism and sexist practices. The LDF chose to register as a formal association and seek concrete changes in the laws that were perpetuating sexual oppression. They wanted a new *droit* (right) for women in the largest sense of this term. Key to their goals was the struggle against the ideology of sexism and male dominance over women.

The various factions of the MLF participated in the several women's rights campaigns of the 1970s, maintaining a vigorous debate over strategies, goals, and tactics. Then in 1979 Psych et Po made a move that shattered the movement. On 18 October, this group, which had shunned patriarchy and all its trappings, became a formal association registered with the state. In France the law of 1901 permits citizens' groups to gain legal status that gives them exclusive legal right to their name, to sue in court, and to make contracts. The name that Psych et Po won exclusive right to use was Mouvement de Libération des Femmes, the informal name that had sheltered all the diverse groups since that day at the Arch of Triumph in 1970. They went on to claim exclusive commercial right to the MLF name and the feminist symbol, a clenched fist inside a female sign. This meant that only Psych et Po and its press Des Femmes could use what had been the common logo of all.

Feminists in France were appalled, then frustrated, but not surprised by this challenge. Antoinette Fouque had always separated her group from the rest. Former allies in the women's movement now found themselves facing each other in court, with suits and countersuits over the use of the MLF name and logo. The resulting battle meant the end of the MLF as a movement. Only a few separate organizations remain: various groups of radical feminists who cluster around the Maison des femmes in Paris and other cities; MLF-*déposé*, as Psych et Po is now called, which runs its bookstore and press on the Left Bank; and the Ligue du Droit des femmes, which continues to lobby as an association of the law of 1901.

During the 1970s the LDF provided a bridge between the radicals of the MLF and the growing strength of egalitarian and reform feminists. The moderates first gathered in November 1970 at the Etats-Généraux de la Femme, sponsored by the women's magazine *Elle*. *Elle* invited readers and various celebrities to discuss the status of women at an open meeting, based on a study the magazine had made of changes in women's lives and attitudes. The forum focused on the attitudes of French women toward careers outside the home, problems of accommodating work and family responsibilities, birth control, and the treatment of women in French society. The general session passed motions on a wide range of issues.[22] The Etats-Généraux also inspired a number of existing women's organizations to work for equality and women's rights.

The Mouvement Jeunes Femmes (MJF), for example, had been organized after World War II by women who were trying to maintain some of the gains in the family and economy they had made during the war. Until the 1970s, the MJF had always been referred to as a "female protestant organization." As such, they attracted women who were less tied than most to Catholic patriarchal traditions. One of their early projects was for legal contraception. Later, they concentrated on civic education to enable women to fight for their rights. Local chapters sponsor seminars and training sessions. Since 1970 MJF has declared itself to be feminist and has participated in the various campaigns for law reform in many policy areas. They see themselves as less aggressive than newer feminists but equally committed to the goals of women's rights.

The early 1970s gave rise to a major new reform group: Choisir. The organization was composed of women from the MLF who were active for abortion reform. Simone de Beauvoir was the first president, but the leader has always been attorney Gisèle Halimi. Choisir is the feminist group most like the American National Organization for Women (NOW), although it is not nearly as large. Their goals are to refashion the relations and status between the sexes in every aspect of society, from family to politics. Choisir has a pro-woman, egalitarian vision of shared family duties and shared power in the legislature. It is well-organized, with a national bureau and a newsletter. Halimi's personality dominates, as do her tactics for promoting change. She focuses on the law—through filing suits and using trials for public relations. Choisir has drafted reform bills and persuaded political parties, usually the Socialists, to introduce them. In 1978 Choisir drafted the Common Program for Women, a manifesto of demands for the legal and social transformation of sex roles. That same year it publicized these demands by running 100 women as candidates in the parliamentary elections (they got 1.5 percent of the vote). Choisir and the Mouvement Jeunes Femmes are the most vigorous of the moderate egalitarian feminist organizations.

Activities of the MLF and the moderates gave feminist issues public attention and individually and collectively stimulated women who had been quietly involved in leftist political parties. Feminism and socialism had had a problematic relationship since the nineteenth century. Women moved to support socialist causes against class oppression had been forced to reject feminism because it was promoted by bourgeois women opposed to major social and economic change. On the other hand, men dominated the labor unions and leftist parties and clung to traditional patriarchal attitudes about sex roles. It seems that Proudhon, rather than Marx, had been most influential among the French workers; Proudhon thought women should not be allowed to work outside the home. In 1936 Leon Blum, the first Socialist premier, had maintained that the ideal society was one in which a man earned enough to support his wife and family. Intellectuals of the Left, even Simone de Beauvoir, had thought the equal status of women would evolve with the achievement of the socialist society. Thus, women workers had no place in either feminism or socialism.

Socialist feminism, the third force in contemporary feminism in France, resulted from attempts by women in leftist circles to reconcile socialism and feminism. One of the most active leaders was Jeannette Laôt of the Confédération Française Démocratique du Travail (CFDT). Laôt had worked her way up the union organizational hierarchy from the assembly line. When she joined the union's Commission féminine, she found that most members believed that home was the proper place for women and their roles as workers were an exception and an aberration. Although the union supported the equal-pay idea, it did not challenge the traditional division of labor. During the 1960s the members of the commission began to study the problems of women workers based on their own experiences as well as through the consultation of feminist writings. They concluded that socialist class analysis must incorporate the problem of the relation between the sexes and that the situation of women workers was due not only to exploitation in the enterprise but also the role imposed on them in the home, dominated by men. "A socialist society can only be constructed by all the workers together, men and women. The liberation of women from all that alienates them in the contemporary society is an indispensable condition for the passage of socialism."[23] This analysis led to support by the CFDT for feminist causes. Laôt was personally active in lobbying for contraceptive freedom, abortion rights, and equal legal status in marriage and the family.

A woman who inspired Laôt was Colette Audry. Audry had worked in and out of leftist organizations for decades. She was a close associate of de Beauvoir and Jean-Paul Sartre and wrote for their journal *Les Temps modernes*. In 1963 she created a collection of women's studies for Denoël-Gonthier, which brought works by Betty Friedan and Evelyn Reed to France several years before the MLF appeared. Of Audry, it was said, "She has the passion of intelligence and logic, but also the tenacity of political conviction. A woman of ideas, the strength of her influence comes from what the love and knowledge of literature gives her—the sense of the concrete, the desire to look in life for the substance itself which justifies the idea and nourishes it. Thus has she informed politics and feminists, and Yvette Roudy, for example, admits owing much of her thought to her."[24]

Introducing Yvette Roudy to feminism was important for the future of women's rights in France. Audry engaged Roudy to translate *The Feminine Mystique*, and in working closely with the text, Roudy found it answered many of her questions about women's status and made her a committed feminist. She was also an active member of the Section Française de l'Internationale Ouvrière (SFIO), the socialist party, and joined a group of women supporting the candidacy of François Mitterrand in the 1965 presidential elections. Their Mouvement Démocra-

tique féminin was led by Marie-Thérèse Eyquêm—who had been active
in promoting women's sports. When Mitterrand formed the new Socialist party in 1971, these women were prominent in promoting feminist goals. The Socialist party responded to their demands by install-
ing a permanent secretary for women's affairs and enacting a
comprehensive program for women's rights in 1979–80.

The cornerstone of their proposal was employment. Women suffer
more from capitalist exploitation than men: they have higher unemployment, lower pay, worse training. Socialist feminists, such as Yvette
Roudy, tend to criticize the patriarchal system more vehemently than
the capitalist. This sets them apart from women in the Communist
party, who still contend that the classless society will liberate women
as well as the proletariat. Both agree feminist goals will not be achieved
apart from socialism because only Socialists and Communists will accept the changes needed to liberate women. Two things are necessary
for the alliance to proceed. First, feminists must ''denounce simultaneously the economic exploitation of women and their situation of
dependence with respect to men.'' Second, ''Socialists must be convinced that feminism and socialism are indissolubly tied and that the
society for which they fight cannot be called socialist as long as women
remain oppressed.''[25]

For eleven years, between 1970 and 1981, from the laying of the
wreath to the election of Mitterrand, feminists in France had their hey-
day. It was a fragmented yet dynamic movement, filled with all the
drama that characterizes French politics. Feminism was more intellectual in style than in America; it was also a movement of workers and
housewives. There was much conflict over various goals and personal
antagonisms. But there also were moments of great solidarity, as tens
of thousands marched for abortion or in celebration of International
Women's Day. Women's status changed as a direct result of their
activities, and many of the victories are described in this book.

By the end of the decade the movement had run its course. The
bitter dispute over Psych et Po's legal appropriation of the symbol of
the movement drained militancy. The energy was further dissipated by
the victory of the Socialist party in 1981. Ideology for change became
institutionalized, both prisoner and ally of the government. There was
neither a socialist Left nor a feminist Left free to criticize the power
structure. By March 1982, when the government for the first time
officially recognized and celebrated International Women's Day, the

press recorded the crumbling of militant feminism. Psych et Po closed its magazine, keeping the press and bookstore. Feminist and women's organizations began to enjoy the leadership and sustenance from the Ministry of Woman's Rights. The militants quieted down as moderate feminists went about trying to get more women into jobs, organizations, and politics.

FEMINISTS IN GOVERNMENT

The first government agency assigned exclusively to women's issues was the Committee on Women's Employment (CWE) (Comité du Travail Féminin) in the Ministry of Labor in 1965. Patterned after the Women's Bureau of the United States Department of Labor, the committee was advisory, charged with studying issues relative to the training and employment of women and recommending legislation and rules. The members included experts in law and family concerns and representatives of unions, employers, and women's organizations. The committee drafted legislation and explored ways of improving training and work conditions for women while helping them reconcile family responsibilities with requirements of employment outside the home. The CWE was inconspicuous and nonpolitical. Committee leaders believed that the best way to change policy was not to set aside a separate office for women, but to place people conscious of the woman's perspective inside each ministry.

President Giscard d'Estaing wanted everyone to know about his commitment to women. In 1974 he persuaded Françoise Giroud, a well-known editor and writer, to accept the new post of Secretary of State for the Status of Women (Secretaire d'Etat à la Condition féminine) in his Center Right coalition government. The post of Secretary of State was not new; presidents have frequently assigned persons to special projects by designating them secretaries within a certain ministry, in this case the Prime Minister's office. But this was the first such secretariat devoted to women and gave the first official publicity to women's issues.

The appointment generally met with scepticism from feminists. Women's liberation groups interpreted all of Giscard's efforts to improve women's status as feeble attempts to capture the women's vote. Most appeared to be for publicity, with little substance or effect. The fact that the secretary for women would have no budget, staff, or power seemed ample evidence for their charge. Giroud's own style sent the message that, despite all the whoopla about women's rights, she was still a savvy lady, a loophole woman who had "made it in a man's world" on her wit, charm, and intelligence. In one of her first interviews after being appointed, Giroud denied being a feminist "because I am not a sexist." Although her actions showed her advocacy of a moderate pro-women's rights position, she seemed to try to separate herself from other politically active women.

Most moderate feminists now acknowledge, however, that Giroud made important contributions by laying the groundwork for policy changes in favor of feminist goals. Since she found it necessary to invent the job, her decisions formed the framework for subsequent government agencies for women.[26] She assigned task forces to study specific policy areas: rural women, legal discrimination, employment, sports, women in politics. She recruited twenty-three regional delegates to gather information and represent her throughout the country. Since she had no separate budget, she relied on her personality to gain government approval of *Cent mesures pour les femmes*, a list of precise changes in laws and administrative procedures to be made by the executive. She also represented the government in debates in the legislature.

In 1976, Giroud resigned and Giscard temporarily downgraded the women's advocate to the status of delegate. After a near loss of his majority in the 1978 legislative elections, Giscard named Monique Pelletier Minister-delegate to the Prime Minister for the Status of Women. Unlike Giroud, Pelletier had close political ties with the president and his party. She was assured that she ranked sixth in the Council of Ministers hierarchy.[27] Still without a separate budget, the minister nevertheless increased the staff, published a monthly newsletter, and headed the first interministerial committee on women's affairs. In 1980 the portfolio on the family was formally added to Pelletier's responsibilities. And, although there was a Secretary of State for women's employment in the Ministry of Labor, Pelletier led government action on all policies having to do with women. She was responsible for securing legislative action on rape, abortion, and marriage laws and preparing major overhauls of both employment and family policy. After Pelletier's tenure, women's issues were no longer viewed as idiosyncratic notions of a president who wanted to look like a modern innovator. They became a legitimate part of the program of the entire government.

Although Pelletier's boss lost the 1981 elections, the winner, François Mitterrand, had promised to do even more for women.[28] In June 1981, President Mitterrand appointed Yvette Roudy as Minister of Woman's Rights (Ministre des Droits de la femme).[29] Her legal status was the same as Pelletier's, a minister-delegate in the office of the Prime Minister. But there were to be two major differences. First, the MWR would have a separate budget with a tenfold increase in funds. Second, Roudy would trade the family portfolio for the employment committee. Despite its fear of being isolated in a women's ghetto, the CWE was moved to the Ministry of Woman's Rights. Mitterrand appointed a separate secretariat for family, population, and immigrant workers in the Ministry of National Solidarity and Social Affairs.

Each of the agencies established for women has expanded upon the one before it. The first committee specialized in employment. Then, Giscard's cabinet-level appointments were charged with improving all aspects of the status of women. Finally, the Ministry of Woman's Rights had the ambitious assignment of eliminating discrimination and making society accept the rights of women. Their powers, which at first were advisory to one minister, also increased to include leadership of an interministerial committee and, with Roudy, the responsibility of countersigning all governmental decrees affecting women. In 1985, Roudy became a full minister with cabinet status.

What accounts for France taking the lead among modern states and investing an executive agency with responsibility for women's issues? History gives contradictory evidence. French culture has been receptive to ideals of equality. After all, France led the world with the Declaration of the Rights of Man; it could also lead in guaranteeing the Rights of Woman (Roudy and Giroud share this opinion). Further, French women have a strong literary tradition and have enjoyed privileges and influence; the battle of the sexes has been less intense in France than elsewhere.[30] Yet France also has a lot of catching up to do. Modernization has lagged. The Napoleonic Code was especially repressive, and women didn't even get the vote until 1944.

More immediate reasons can be found in the events of the 1970s. Between 1960 and 1975 there was a dramatic increase in the number and percentage of women in the work force. This coincided with the rise of an effective feminist campaign for abortion reform. In the 1974 election, women were perceived for the first time as an autonomous voting force. Giscard's campaign included a full program for improving women's status, especially for women workers. In the second tour, he clearly owed his victory over Mitterrand to the female vote (which he lost in turn in 1981).[31] After victory, Giscard went ahead with an ambitious plan to modernize French society. The appointment of Giroud brought needed allies from the Left to counterbalance the conservatives in his own coalition. Political action of feminists in the Socialist party made the establishment of a ministry for women's rights an important promise in the 1981 campaign. The Socialist party lost its majority in the 1986 legislative elections and with it the Ministry of Woman's Rights. The long-term role of feminists in government remains in doubt.

ORGANIZATION OF THE BOOK

This overview of recent feminist politics in and out of government in France is an introduction to the massive changes in public policy affecting women's rights that have occurred in the last twenty years. Laws touching every aspect of women's lives have been affected, and, for most of them, feminists have pushed to abolish traditional patriarchal values and redefine issues in ways that would improve the position of women. In general, these new definitions are based on a vision of shared rather than separate sex roles.

The following chapters explore the changes in women's rights in France by focusing on the conflict about the definition of issues. By examining reforms in the context of policy development since the French Revolution, policy in six areas will be surveyed: politics, reproduction, family, education, work, and sexuality. For each, the following questions will be considered:

1. Do feminists agree on how to define the issues in each policy area so that they will improve the rights of women?
2. Have some or all feminists been successful in gaining control over the issue conflict so that government policy changes are based on feminist logic?
3. What has been the importance of the government feminists, especially the Ministry of Woman's Rights, in the policy-making process?
4. What have been the policy outcomes? How has the way the issues are

defined affected the content of government policy? What has been the effect on resolving the problem, the distribution of influence and benefits, and popular support?

5. In general, how do changes in French policies compare with reforms in the United States?

NOTES

1. *Le Figaro* (23 mai 1985). Advertisement placed by the Ligue du Droit des femmes.

2. E. E. Schattschneider, *The Semisovereign People* (Hinsdale, IL: Dryden Press, 1975), 66.

3. Charles Anderson, "The Logic of Public Problems," in *Comparing Public Policies*, ed. Douglas Ashford (Beverly Hills: Sage, 1978), 19–42.

4. Claire Goldberg Moses, *French Feminism in the Nineteenth Century* (Albany: State University of New York Press, 1984), 7.

5. Peter Bachrach and Morton S. Baratz, "Two Faces of Power," *American Political Science Review* 56 (December 1962), 950.

6. Ellen Boneparth, *Women, Power and Policy* (New York: Pergamon, 1982).

7. Joyce Gelb and Marion Palley, *Women and Public Policies* (Princeton: Princeton University Press, 1982).

8. Jo Freeman, *The Politics of Women's Liberation* (New York: Longman, 1975).

9. Roger Cobb and Charles Elder, *Participation in American Politics* (Boston: Allyn & Bacon, 1972).

10. Mary Ruggie, *The State and Working Women* (Princeton: Princeton University Press, 1984).

11. François Poulain de la Barre, *De l'égalité des deux sexes* (1673).

12. Maïté Albistur and Daniel Armogathe, *Histoire du féminisme français, du moyen age à nos jours* (Paris: Des Femmes, 1977), 414.

13. Annie de Pisan and Anne Tristan, *Histoires du M.L.F.* (Paris: Calmann-Lévy, 1977), 32–3. Observation by "Anne."

14. Ibid., 39.

15. Danièle Leger, *Le Féminisme en France* (Paris: Editions Le Sycomore, 1982), 13.

16. A leaflet signed "MLF partout" reprinted in Sylvie Coquille, *Naissance du Mouvement de Libération des Femmes en France 1970–1973*. Memoire de Maîtrise (Nanterre: Université de Paris X, 1980), app.

17. Naty Gaudilla Garcia, *Libération des femmes: Le M.L.F.* (Paris: Presses Universitaires de France, 1981).

18. "Maternité-politique-sexualité-libération," supplement to no. 2 of *Pétroleuses*.

19. A. Muchnik, "Le MLF c'est toi, c'est moi," quoted by Coquille, *Naissance du Mouvement*, 98.

20. Ibid.

21. Quoted from *Le Torchon brûle*, no. 5, p. 11, by Coquille, ibid., 98.

22. Albistur and Armogathe, *Histoire du féminisme français*, 453.

23. Jeannette Laôt, *Stratégie pour les femmes* (Paris: Stock, 1977), 241.

24. Michelle Coquillat, *Qui sont elles?* (Paris: Mazarine, 1983), 86.

25. Parti socialiste, "Féminisme-Socialisme-Autogestion" Supplement au. no. 71 de *Combat socialiste* (février 1979).

26. Françoise Giroud, *La Comédie du pouvoir* (Paris: Fayard, 1977), 77.

27. Interview with Pelletier, November 1983.

28. Choisir, *Quel président pour les femmes?* (Paris: Gallimard, 1981).

29. Yvette Roudy's first action as minister was to refuse to sign the decree giving her authority as minister because, according to protocol, it referred to her as *le ministre . . . il*. After her objection, the pronoun was changed to the feminine gender *elle*. However, she lost two other battles over terminology. She wanted the name of the ministry to be Ministère des Droits *des femmes* to stand for solidarity with the rights of all women. She also wanted to be called formally *la ministre* rather than *le ministre*. Although Roudy remained *le ministre* throughout her tenure, her staff and publications referred to her with the feminine article.

30. Michèle Sarde, *Regard sur les françaises* (Paris: Stock, 1983).

31. Wayne Northcutt and Jeffra Flaitz, "Women and Politics in Contemporary France," *Contemporary French Civilization* 7 (Winter 1983), 183–98.

2

POLITICS

WOMEN HAVE ALWAYS been marginal to conventional political life in France. The law deprived them of basic civil rights long after their husbands, brothers, and sons were enjoying liberty, equality, and fraternity. From the first glimmerings of democracy, every effort made by French women to break into public life met with repression or indifference. Women were kept out of political action, not only by their traditional roles in marriage and family life, but by specific laws denying them the most rudimentary civil rights. Their frantic struggles for relief were opposed by men on all sides. Left and Right alike refused, ignored, or manipulated women's demands for access to public life. French women, excluded from the franchise until 1944, endured their inferior status even longer than women in the United States, Britain, and most of Europe.[1]

Despite the evidence of their inferior legal status, the tantalizing theory persists that women have shaped French destiny by their direct influence over powerful men. Stories of romance and intrigue in court politics during the Ancien Régime sustain the myth that French women, more than women in other countries, have enjoyed their real power in the boudoirs of the kings, ministers, priests, and generals. Purveyors of this myth intimate that such influence continues today in the sway each woman holds over her man. Accordingly, they contend that data on voting turnout, political party membership, and elected offices will not measure the true power of women.

Disagreements about female political influence arise from the contentious problem of defining power. Frameworks dominant in political science divide the arenas of power into public and private domains. They direct all attention to the public domain of formal governmental power and not only undervalue, but virtually ignore, the private world of family and reproduction where women exert their influence. According to these frameworks, whatever influence a few privileged women enjoyed through pillow talk meant little to most women, who remained severely oppressed.

Feminists are faced with the problem of how best to define the issue of politics so as to promote the cause of women's rights. They agree that isolated reforms, such as the suffrage, have done little to change women's situation or further women's rights. Legal equality has merely allowed women into the political arena as an extension of their traditional role in the family, without disturbing the male-dominated democratic system. They disagree on the best way for women to gain power in the political arena in their own right. Should women accept prevailing frameworks that undervalue their private domain or try to replace the basic definitions of power? Should women seek equality and participation through established political channels or strike out on their own in a separate battle? Should women settle for an equal share of conventional political action through voting, running for electoral office, joining political parties, forming interest groups, and lobbying? Or should they dare to create a rival female political world where the private becomes public, confronting and permanently altering the male version?

Moderate feminists choose integration: Women will gain power by entering the public arena and winning the offices in political parties and government now occupied by men. Choisir, for example, would like to mobilize women's votes behind feminist candidates.[2] Then, as more and more feminists join the government at all levels, their issues, such as equal opportunity in employment and eliminating sexist stereotyping in the schools, will move up on the public agenda. Old policies such as rape, prostitution, and pornography will be redefined in feminist terms. The suffering of women subject to illegal abortions and family violence and shackled by ignorance and privacy will finally get public attention. Moderate feminists believe that the myth that politics has a sex—male—must be destroyed. But changing attitudes is slow work, and sometimes behavior must be changed first. They support rules requiring parties to include a certain percentage of women as officers and on the party candidate lists. They hope these quotas will help women shake off the effects of centuries of disabilities that continue to handicap their chances of power.

While agreeing that quotas may push more women into political office, feminists of the Left await social and economic change to provide the basis for political equality.[3] Without social change in the family, property, and the economy, political rights will never further women's rights but will serve to co-opt their energy and the energy of their struggle to sustain bourgeois capitalist patriarchal democracy. The suffrage, for example, did not translate into female power; all it did was change the rhetoric at election time. Women were enticed into voting for men of the Left or Right; after the election any thought of real improvement in women's status was immediately forgotten. Only a socialist blueprint for an egalitarian society will truly open doors for women. Women must enlist the help of men to be freed from both patriarchy and capitalism, the dual chains holding them back.

The radical feminists with their theories about *la différence* take another approach and separate women's politics from men's.[4] The battle that women face is to liberate themselves from patriarchal society and develop their own politics through segregation, not integration. "Women who want to be constituted as a political force can only do it beginning with themselves; this is because to 'do politics' for women cannot be separated from their lives."[5] One would not expect to find radical leaders voting or joining political parties, much less running for office. They contend that women can do nothing from inside the male political arena but must form their own "inside." Through affirmation of the female self they can free themselves from male domination. Then they can fight the entire patriarchal system.

Radical feminist political goals arise from their own female sexuality: control of the body, of course, but also control of the meaning of the female body. For the most part, taking control is a matter of psychology and language rather than laws and elections. Liberation politics takes place in the consciousness-raising groups and in the self. Women are special—they can make their own politics. If they need action from the patriarchy to achieve full control of their lives, as has been necessary on the issues of rape, abortion, pornography, and prostitution, then women must defy authority with daring political acts.

Only the moderate feminists have accepted the logic of the existing system as a way of improving women's political rights. Their success can be charted using data on laws and female participation in male-dominated politics. While socialists and radicals may occasionally get involved in conventional political activities, they insist upon broader definitions of politics. Socialists include power relationships in economy and society. Radicals diverge toward the politics of psychological and linguistic sexuality. Some of the evidence pertaining to women's power, according to these wider conceptions, will be found in the chapters on reproduction, family, education, work, and sexuality.

The rest of the chapter includes information on rights and participation of women in the political system of France according to the conventional definitions of the moderates. The data on women is presented with full recognition of the persistent conflict among feminists not only over the definition of politics but also over the support of women for political office regardless of affiliation. Many find no joy in victories of women on the Right or women who assume office disclaiming all connection with feminism. France has no equivalent of the bipartisan National Women's Political Caucus and, with the exception of support of election quotas, even moderate feminists are interested in political rights for women in order to promote their demands and programs, not simply to increase the number of females in public life.

LAWS

France may have been one of the last countries to give women the vote, but a French man was among the first to ask for it.[6] Condorcet, who affirmed the idea of social progress, is credited with making political rights an essential part of the woman question in France.[7] In 1787, this *philosophe* argued that it was impossible to deny political rights to women because they were equal in mind and reason to men. This equality would be apparent to all if women and men received the same education. Since women enjoyed the same natural rights they should also have the same political rights. In America, by contrast, the first formal demand for the vote was not heard until sixty-one years later at Seneca Falls. Yet, despite the head start in developing theories of equal rights for women, French feminists enjoyed few victories.

The early upheavals of the French Revolution brought women of all classes into public life. A prominent component of *le peuple*, they became increasingly active on their own behalf. A lively female press advocated participation in juries and assemblies, the vote, divorce reform, and even sexual freedoms. They formed many clubs, among them an especially radical egalitarian organization called the Club des Citoyennes Républicaines Révolutionnaires. Issues of women's rights, including the vote, surfaced during revolutionary assemblies in 1789–90.

Olympe de Gouges is the most famous female martyr of the Revolution. When the Declaration of the Rights of Man ignored women, Olympe countered with her own "Declaration of the Rights of Woman and the Female Citizen" in 1791.[8] De Gouges called for freedom of association, legal and political equality, and "free communication of thoughts and opinions."[9] She said that the Revolution could not be successful without full participation by women. She also showed how women can redefine politics and how private concerns become public when women seek power. Freedom of speech "is one of the most precious rights of woman, since that liberty ensures the recognition of children by their fathers."

The curtain of darkness that fell on the Revolution in 1793 was nowhere more smothering than on women. In the spring the National Convention confirmed that "children, the insane, minors, women, and prisoners, until their rehabilitation, will not be citizens."[10] In the summer, the Constitution of the First Republic granted universal male suffrage and specifically excluded women from all political rights, including citizenship. In the fall, all women's clubs were prohibited. From then on, women could legally attend no political assembly. By 1795 all political rights and revolutionary reforms for women had been completely removed. The National Convention cracked down on public activity by women: "Be it decreed that all women should retire as formerly it was ordained, into their respective homes; those who one hour after this decree are found in groups of more than five persons will be dispersed by armed force and then arrested, until public tranquility is again restored in Paris."[11]

The French Revolution abolished the feudal caste system and proclaimed equality; it promised freedom for women, then crushed their rebellion and completely excluded them from the polity. The fate of French women who wanted equal rights was more final than the neglect and indifference the American women faced. Women who fought in the American Revolution did not seek equal rights for themselves.

It was almost as an afterthought that Abigail Adams asked her husband to "remember the ladies," a request he, with humor, gently set aside. Not until 1848 did feminists draft their own version of the Declaration of Independence. They did not face the cruel repression encountered by French women mobilized by the dramatic social upheavals of 1789. By this repression, bourgeois France declared politics to be a man's concern. Women were not to be a part of the polity or the society, they were part of what belonged to man: "The *citoyen* holds political meetings, takes part in parties, solicits votes from his fellow *citoyens* or elects his representative, legislates, delivers justice, holds public office. In short, he holds and exercises power. And the *citoyenne*? Well, she is the wife of the *citoyen*." [12] The wife's fate was sealed by the Napoleonic Code. This code entrapped woman in the institution of marriage, where her only right was the duty to obey her husband.

Thus the stage was set for the struggle for political rights in the nineteenth century: repression and silence of generations of women broken only by cyclical bursts of activity. Each time the active women renewed their demands for political equality they were suppressed by the state and swindled by the Left, just as they had been in the first revolution. Between 1816 and the beginning of the Republican Era in 1870, political activity for women's rights paralleled the cycle of repression and revolt in the political system. Under the monarchies (1816–30, 1830–48, 1852–70) conservatives dominated the government, censored the press, forbid open meetings, and discouraged public speaking. Democrats were often in exile or prison or just trying to survive. In this context demands for women's votes made little sense apart from the broader democratic reform movements. So women concentrated on presenting their arguments for education and work, for better treatment in the family, and for moral improvement. When controls were lifted and the feminists organized, their demands paralleled the larger movements for change. [13]

In the 1830s the feminists surfaced, influenced by the utopian social ideas of Saint-Simon. His vision of a society based onequality and freedom from exploitation promised many improvements in women's lives. Rather that working for specific and limited changes in the law or political rights, the feminists used their newspaper to present theories of female oppression that were to inspire activists for the next forty years. Their views differed from the simple concepts of equality of mind and reason that moved Condorcet and de Gouges. These early socialist feminists elaborated a theory of sexual equality based on complementarity. Man's reason must be completed by woman's sentiment: the combination fulfills human potential.

The most famous feminist of the period, Flora Tristan, also made few specific demands for political rights. She concentrated on wooing support from the fledgling worker movement for the general improvement of women's lot. Tristan accepted the idea of complementarity, but departed from the Saint-Simonians by focusing on the specific problems of the workers. Many of their ills, she argued, could be blamed on the behavior of unemancipated poor women. Men must free women and give them education and work in order to claim their own political and social rights. "The law that enslaves woman and deprives her of education oppresses you, working man. I have just shown that the ignorance of working-class women has the most disastrous consequences. . . . —They arrest all progress." [14]

The Second Republic was established in 1848 and gave rise to fresh demands for political rights for women. New freedoms stimulated the growth of feminist clubs and newspapers. When the republican provisional government declared universal male suffrage, the feminists wanted votes for women, too. They also hoped to run female candidates for office. The feminists of 1848 perpetuated ideas of complementarity. They glorified woman's role as mother; the concept became the "linch pin of the feminist rationale for sexual equality." [15] When the first election brought to power conservatives who repressed the worker revolt, clubs and newspapers shut down and women were again forbidden to participate in public gatherings.

Efforts to link the oppression of women with the class struggle had failed. After the Second Empire was established in 1852, antifeminism increased, especially on the Left, resulting in the severing of ties between the women's movement and the worker movement. A few feminists, such as Louise Michel, remained with the revolutionary Left and cast their lot with the revolt of the Paris Commune (1871). Their defeat meant that many radical women ended up in exile, physically excluded from the battle for political rights for several years. This left the field to bourgeois feminists with close ties to the republicans and liberals who designed the Third Republic. The constitution of a liberal republican government in France prepared the way for the suffrage campaign. Laws of 1881 finally guaranteed the political freedoms that had been proclaimed a century before: freedom of the press, freedom of assembly, and freedom of speech. Feminists were able to organize, publish newspapers, and campaign for women's rights. Their campaign focused on law reform and the suffrage. Even these limited demands faced formidable opposition from politicians of both the Left and Right.

Bourgeois feminists did not always agree about the value of the franchise. The moderate feminists, the first to organize in the 1870s, concentrated on the *droit civil*, that is, reforms of the civil law code of Napoleon to make women equal in marriage. For them, to demand the vote was premature, even radical. Women were not ready to vote; they needed more education. Men were certainly not ready to give them the vote; their attitudes would have to change. In short, the people of France, who had endured so many upheavals, were not ready to absorb another shock.

The small band of suffragists, led by Hubertine Auclert, disagreed. Auclert argued that political rights, especially the vote, was a precondition for getting any other changes for women. "For her, the vote for women would bring about everything: equal marriage laws, good moral practice by all, and even the flowering of women's beauty, because oppression stifles and degrades their complexions!"[16] Auclert understood the workings of the new representative government. Legislators would begin to heed the concerns of their voting constituents throughout the country and turn away from the upper class notables in Paris who had been so influential under the monarchies. Women would have to win their cause through the ballot box, not in the Parisian salons. The suffragists concentrated on trying to present women candidates in local elections (although illegal), making speeches and publishing their writings.

Opponents were everywhere. The Right distrusted democracy and the Centrists wanted to wait until women were "ready." Socialists thought the franchise was bourgeois and not worth their effort. Why did women need the vote when all political rights would be granted after the workers' social revolution? Feminists themselves were heavily influenced by divisions in French political life. Even among the suffragists there were conflicts over religion, republicanism, socialism, tactics, organizations, and personalities. Suffrage politics rarely achieved enough cohesion to qualify as a movement.

Between 1900 and 1910 demands for the vote finally began to take hold. At the time, French feminism was essentially bourgeois republican and thoroughly respectable. Most advocates rejected militant tactics, refusing to join Auclert in the burning of the Napoleonic Code at the foot of the Vendôme column or the storming of the election urns on the Left Bank. They feared violence would offend French public opinion and hurt their cause. They also had ample evidence of the willingness of the French police to treat demonstrators harshly. The feminists continued a moderate strategy for the most part: posters, lectures, large meetings, rallies, and presenting female candidates in elections. Gradually women in various occupations were allowed to vote for governing councils: teachers (1880), small shop-keepers (1898), workers (counseils des prud'hommes) (1907). Bills for limited suffrage were introduced in 1890, 1901, and 1906. Votes for women attracted increasing support, especially from members of the Chamber of Deputies, the lower house of parliament.

Women's rights leaders recognized that the suffrage was an important means to other goals. Many defined the issue as good not only for women but for society as a whole. Still influenced by ideas of complementarity, the argued that votes for women would improve the family, France—indeed—all of humanity. Women would use their vote to bring concern for children, hygiene, and morality to public life; to prevent war; and to fight debauchery and alcoholism. This logic resembles the pitch made by some branches of the suffrage movements in the United States and Britain. There, too, arguments for justice and equality frequently gave way in order to focus on the good that women, as homemakers and mothers, would do in politics and government.

By 1914 the stage was set in France, as well as in the United States and Britain, for victory of the suffrage movements. The campaign may not have been as continuous or unified in France as in the other countries, but it was older and had strong theoretical foundations in democratic and revolutionary ideologies. Then, during World War I, women served in many capacities, finally "earning" their rights. In January 1918 a French deputy proclaimed on the floor of the Chamber:

The war has shown in full light the immense value of female cooperation in national life. . . . Women were nearly all mobilized in the fields, in the factories, in the ambulances, in the administrations. They have proved that they could be, in nearly all domains, our precious collaborators; let's not treat them like slaves![17]

Yet while women won precious political rights in the United States and Britain, French legislators never gave women the right to vote. A universal suffrage bill passed the Chamber of Deputies four times: 1919, 1925, 1932, 1936. It came to a vote only twice in the Senate and was defeated both times (1922, 1933). Women served in ministerial positions in Leon Blum's Popular Front government in 1936 before they could cast a ballot for Blum's socialist party. Why were suffragists denied their victory in France?

It is tempting to focus on the inadequacies of the French suffrage movement: too little, too late, too fragmented, no support. But the context of the movement is also important, especially the antidemocratic and antifemale sentiment. Unlike their counterparts in Britain or the United States, French politicians were absorbed for much of the nineteenth century with the problem of finding a legitimate form of government. Republican democracy came unexpectedly. Even when the Third Republic was declared in 1870, many considered it an interim government until the monarchy could be restored. There was little time to adjust to the idea of suffrage for anyone before women began demanding it for everyone.

Opposition to the suffrage was stronger in France than the United States. It came from all sides of the political spectrum, even the natural allies of women's rights, the liberals and socialists. Many of the opponents' arguments are found in the debates in the Senate in 1922 and 1933. There were three types: traditionalist, sexist, and republican. The traditionalists extolled the virtues of woman's role in the home. Politics, being man's work, would brutalize woman, dirty her, drag her from the exalted position of "angel of gentleness" in the home. "In reality, the role of woman is to shape man; it is in the home that she accomplishes this great work." [18] Women would lose their sex and would cease to be appealing to men. Senators threatened women that men would no longer love them if they got the vote. "They risk losing the secret power that they possess over men."

The sexists maintained that the female sex is naturally inept at politics. A chasm separates the intelligence and education of men and women; women are not able to exercise political responsibilities. Their qualities of gentleness, passivity, and sexual desirability are completely incompatible with needs in government for leadership and strength. Since the majority of women rejected the vote, only the undesirables, like prostitutes, would vote, contributing even further to immorality. "And the feminists? They want things like mixed education, free maternity, abrogation of all matters relating to morals with sexual liberty, that is, the right of a woman to replace a lover she has grown tired of."[19]

The republicans, on the other hand, were afraid that too many women would vote. Since women were uneducated and religious, they would be led around by the Catholic church. The Radical party shuddered before the prospect of millions of new voters following dictates of Pope and priest. The fragile republic could not survive a massive infusion of female voters. Despite their democratic rhetoric extolling universal suffrage, leading Centrist politicians made no move to help overcome the opposition of the Senate. There, the Radical party of republicans voted four to one to defeat votes for women.

Opponents were thus successful in defining the issue of women's political rights in such a way that they threatened everyone. Their logic asserted the differences between the sexes and the unsuitability of females to public life. Proponents also accepted the assumption of sex differences. Even sympathetic legislators wondered whether the culture was "ready" for political rights for women. They tried to make the issue as undisturbing as possible. Thus, little effort was made to shift the debate toward ideas of equality or to persuade politicians that female citizens in a democracy should have exactly the same rights as males. Instead they responded that sex differences would improve politics because women would bring family values into politics. All-male politics was wrong; it needed the goodness of women. Women also needed the vote even more than men, since they were more vulnerable and oppressed. They would be concerned with womanly policies such as education, health, and morality and not disturb man's monopoly over finance, military, and foreign policy. In addition, a strong case was made immediately after both world wars that women deserved the vote for their service. Others claimed that since many other countries were passing suffrage measures, votes for women were à la mode.

In the end, neither suffragists nor their opponents had much to do with establishing equal political rights for women. The conventional wisdom is that women were given the vote to pay them for their heroism and suffering during World War II. Not only had they run much of the economy while men were in prison or labor camps, but they were extremely active in the Resistance. Many women martyrs, such as Danièle Casanova, died in concentration camps. Equality for women was one of the issues stirred up by the social turbulence of the Occupation and Resistance and gathered in by Charles de Gaulle at the end

of World War II as part of his mission to transform France and modernize French institutions. The right to vote was slipped in as part of
the administrative ordinance outlining plans for governing France after
the Liberation issued 21 April 1944 by de Gaulle in his capacity as
head of the Provisional Government. A constitutional assembly was to
be elected: "Women are electors and eligible in the same conditions
as men."[20]

As easy as that, the battle was over. The preamble to the Constitution of 1946 formally recognized the equal political status of men and
women: "The law guarantees to the woman, in all domains, equal
rights to the man." It further specified the right to vote: "All French
citizens of both sexes who are of age and who enjoy civil and political
rights may vote under the conditions determined by law." The 1958
constitution proclaimed "attachment to the Rights of Man and to the
principles of national sovereignty as defined by the Declaration of 1789,
confirmed and completed by the Preamble to the Constitution of 1946."
It also repeated the guarantees of voting rights.

These provisions and the additional references to equality sprinkled
through the document are not a guarantee of equal legal status and are
an inadequate basis to challenge legislation based on discriminatory
sex classifications. Judicial review is much more limited in France
than in the United States. The Constitutional Council, established by
the Fifth Republic in 1958, rules only on new legislation referred to it
by government leaders, not on administrative rules or laws already in
effect. Thus the constitutional equality meant no change in the Napoleonic Code nor in the myriad of other laws that classified according
to sex. Parliament or the ministries must change these. Only once has
the council ruled a law unconstitutional for violating the requirement
of sex equality. This case will be discussed in the next section.

POLITICAL PARTICIPATION

The moment that women cast their first ballots there was a gender
gap in France. Women showed little interest in politics; a majority
believed political activity to be the business of men. Opinion polls in
the 1950s found sixty percent of women with no interest in politics
compared with twenty-eight percent of the men.[21] Lacking education
in political matters, they were far more likely than men to express no
opinion in polls. Fewer women turned out to vote. Nonvoting is often

viewed as a measure of how alienated citizens were with the constitution of the Fourth Republic. According to that measure, twenty percent of the women were completely outside the democratic processes,
having never voted, compared with only eight percent of the men.
When they did vote women favored conservative parties rather than
the Left. A survey by UNESCO in 1953 showed that thirty-four percent of the men versus twenty-eight percent of the women supported
the socialist or Communist parties.[22]

The gender gap has narrowed over the years along with the modernization of the culture and the constitution. In the 1980s, although women
are still more likely to express no opinion, the figure is rarely more
than fifteen percent.[23] Party preferences and the party system have
changed over the past thirty years. The Fifth Republic established a
strong president who is directly elected and a single-member district
electoral system for the National Assembly. These constitutional changes
encouraged a simplification of the party system. Although many parties still exist, they find it necessary to form electoral coalitions or
coalitions supporting or opposing the president and his government. In
their studies of women in politics, Mossuz-Lavau and Sineau describe
the party system as quadripolar with bipolar tendencies.[24] There are
two Left parties, the Parti communiste (PC) and the Parti socialiste
(PS); and two Right parties, the Union pour la Démocratie Française
(UDF) and the Rassemblement pour la République (RPR). Table 1
shows the trends in party preferences of men and women in presidential runoff elections between candidates from the Left and Right.

The figures show several things. De Gaulle and Giscard owed their
victories in 1965 and 1974 to the majority support they received from
women. The women's vote was especially crucial to Giscard's narrow
win in 1974. After that the Left continually made gains with women.
By the 1978 legislative elections half the female voters chose parties
of the Left. As one journalist pointed out, all Mitterrand needed to
win in 1981 was to attract two percent more of the female voters than
he had gained in 1974. Wooing the women who made up fifty-three
percent of the electorate was high stakes in the political battles. In
1981 forty-nine percent of the women voted for Mitterrand; this, with
the strong support from men, gave the Left their foundation for victory.

The gender gap in political party voting has narrowed from fourteen
percent to six percent. Women, more often than men, still tend to vote

Table 1
Left-Right Voting, by Sex, in Three Presidential Elections

	Women	Men
1965		
Mitterrand (L)	38%	52%
deGaulle (R)	62%	48%
1974		
Mitterrand (L)	46%	51%
Giscard (R)	54%	49%
1981		
Mitterrand (L)	49%	56%
Giscard (R)	51%	44%

for conservative candidates. This difference continued in the 1984 elections for the European Parliament (EP). Based on data from exit interviews, there was nearly a ten-percentage-point difference in the female-male support of the Center Right list headed by Simone Veil.[25] Women, more so than men, avoided extremist parties, showing less support for both the Communists and the ultraright list headed by Jacques LePen.

Mossuz-Lavau and Sineau have published several studies analyzing trends in the political behavior of women. Their work reinforces conclusions drawn by Duverger and Dogan in the 1950s that socioeconomic factors are responsible for the gender gap. In the 1950s, age, education, and religion were important in explaining female conservatism and lack of interest in politics. Women, marginal to society, had fewer opportunities for education and work. They were also more likely to be active Catholics and this religion, strictly separate from politics, reinforced the traditional private roles of women.

Recently, Mossuz-Lavau and Sineau have examined the effects of employment on political behavior.[26] Housewives conform to the stereotypical views of women in political life. They are less interested, vote less often, and are more conservative than both employed men and employed women. The importance of employment on politicization is underscored when looking at women who had once been active in the work force but were housewives at the time of the survey. These ex-actives more closely resembled workers of both sexes than women in the home who had never worked. Thus, changes in political behavior of women in the last thirty years can be accounted for in large part by their entrance in massive numbers into the active work force.

Both housewives and workers took part in associations long before they could vote. Through the law passed in 1901, anyone can form an organization of "two or several persons putting together their knowledge and activities for a purpose other than profit." Participation in organizations has rarely translated into political clout. It has long been the conventional wisdom that strong individualism, alienation, and tradition have prevented the growth of voluntary associations as a vehicle for political participation in France. Despite this stereotype the number of associations has increased greatly since the 1960s. In 1965, 17,450 were registered. By 1978 they had doubled to 34,696. Estimates of informal groups go as high as 600,000. Accurate data on the percentage of women participating in voluntary associations and interest groups are difficult to come by.[27] A survey in 1978 showed that forty-one percent of French women belonged to at least one association, compared with fifty-three percent of men.[28]

Although many associations, such as syndical, professional, philanthropic, and campaign organizations, admit members of both sexes, women rarely reach leadership positions except in the all-female bodies. Many of these are dedicated to education, social aid, charity, or family concerns. They vary from single-interest and professional groups such as the Association of Midwives (*sagesfemmes*) to large community clubs. Every town has its women of the *accueil* group, a sort of welcome wagon, and its family assistance group. Some associations are entirely removed from public life, while others are occasionally consulted by some government agency. A few have a regular role in government and politics.

Along with the feminist groups discussed in chapter 1 there are partisan and neutral women's associations that are active in politics. The partisan groups either are found closely connected to political parties or can be definitely placed onthe political spectrum. The largest association is the Union des Femmes Françaises (UFF) with 180,000 members. Since its origin in the Resistance it has been identified by all with the Communist party (except by its own leaders who stoutly deny all political affiliation). On the Right, Femme Avenir, founded by de Gaulle, admits its close ties with the Gaullist party, the RPR, but not identity with the often-traditional patriarchal leanings of the party's current leader, Jacques Chirac. Non-Communist women of the Left have been active in the Mouvement Démocratique féminine and the Club Louise Michel, both led by Socialist women.

There are several large nonpartisan associations that are also politically active. Foremost among them now is the Union Française Civique et Sociale (UFCS) with 10,000 members. The UFCS resembles the United States League of Women Voters because of its interest in educating women to enable them to take part in civic life. Many people still consider it one of the old Catholic women's organizations, but this connection has done little to still its active support of women's rights issues. Other nonpartisan groups include the Conseil National des femmes, which incorporates a number of women's clubs; the Fédération Nationale des femmes; and the Soroptomistes, who define themselves as a "female Rotary."

Women are less enthusiastic about joining political parties, but their membership has grown. They still remain underrepresented when it comes to holding party office. Table 2 shows the percentage of women among the rank and file and the executive councils of the four major party groupings. These figures on general membership are based on frequently unreliable reports from the parties themselves. If they indicate anything, it is the lower membership of women in the parties of the Left than the Right. On the other hand, the Gaullists, with the largest proportion of female members, have the lowest representation of women in the executive.

More reliable is the almost unanimous opinion of women political activists that parties are the major obstacle keeping women out of elected office. The parties of the Right are considered to be the worst. There, women face open opposition from many men who cling to the notion that politics is a man's game. Women are less directly discriminated against from the Left, but they face indifference or long-standing masculine traditions that are equally disabling. To their credit, the parties of the Left have done the most to overcome discrimination. Pressured by its own committee on female action, the Socialist party adopted a quota requirement for female representation on all its governing bodies. Starting at ten percent in 1972, it was raised to twenty percent in 1979, although clearly the party has not met this goal. Party elections in 1985 brought female representation on the political bureau to twenty-five percent, but it declined to only fourteen percent for the secretariat.

Table 2

Proportions of Women Holding Office in the Governing Organs of the Political Parties, June 1982

Party	Members	Legislative Organs	Executive Organs	
			Broad	Select
Communist Party	36%	Central Committee 21%	Political Bureau 18%	Secretariat 17%
Socialist Party	21%	Steering Committee 18%	Executive Bureau 15%	National Secretariat 14%
Republican (UDF)	40%	National Council 32%	Political Bureau 20%	"Secretariat" 6%
Gaullists (RPR)	43%	Central Committee 8%	Political Council 6%	Executive Committee 8%

Source: Jeanine Mossuz-Lavau and Mariette Sineau, "Women in the Political World of Europe," The Situation of Women in the Political Process in Europe, Part II (Strausbourg: Council of Europe, 1984) 111.

There is a sharp drop from the percentage of women among the rank and file or even on governing boards to the percentage of women presented as candidates by the major parties. Only the fringe parties have offered women as presidential candidates (one in 1974, three in 1981). The pattern will probably persist in 1988, although polls show a majority would not oppose a woman president.[29] The overall percentage of women running in national parliamentary elections did rise sharply in 1978, to 15.9 percent from 6.7 percent in 1973, and 3.3 percent in 1968. This spurt was due mostly to the candidates presented by the minor parties. Table 3 shows that the pattern of representation by women as candidates of the major parties for the National Assembly changed little between 1978 and 1981. They have done better in the elections for the European Parliament.

Some resourceful women on the Right have sought to circumvent the political parties and form new political associations. Dialogue—villes de France, led by Monique Pelletier, and Association femmes libertés formed after 1981 to attract women opposed to the Socialist government. These groups are especially interested in increasing women's political clout among Center Right politicians. Femmes libertés is a group primarily composed of young professional women in Paris. The Dialogue recruited 10,000 members in nearly 200 cities in just three years, and its leader is indefatigable in organizing symposia all over France. The annual meeting in 1984 assembled 300 delegates from 175 towns and cities. Pelletier has described the group as a dialogue to ''show it is possible to defend ideas without personal attack,

Table 3
Percentage of Women Candidates, by Party

	National Assembly 1978	1981	European Parliament 1984
RPR	2.9	2.0	16
UDF	5.0	3.2	25.6
PS	5.9	8.0	25.9
PC	13.3	13.5	27.2

to be adversaries without being enemies.'' This is a potential political movement for women who find parties discriminatory or unfriendly yet want to participate. In addition, the organization provides political resources for women on the Right that they do not find within the male-dominated elite in the RPR and the UDF.

Women in Political Office

Small numbers of female candidates mean even fewer in national elected office. The largest number of women ever to serve in the National Assembly were the 38 of 542 (7 percent) elected in 1946. After that, there was a steady decline until 1973, when only 7 (1.4 percent) of 496 representatives were female. Then women climbed back to 21 in 1978 and 29 in 1981. Of the 577 deputies elected in 1986, 34 are women. The percentage of women in the lower house is still less than it was in 1946 (5.9 v. 7.0), and the average for the postwar era is just 3 percent. Women in the Senate, which is elected by the local councils, have shown a decline from 7 percent in 1946 to fewer than 3 percent (9 of 304). Dismal as these figures are, they are almost identical with those in the United States national legislature. After the 1984 elections, 4.7 percent of the House of Representatives and 2 percent of the Senate were female. Both countries rank with Belgium, Spain, Greece, and Great Britain as having the lowest representation of women in national elected office among Western democracies.

There are the usual social, economic, and cultural barriers that prevent women from achieving elected office in France. A gender gap persists in attitudes and in access to the education and professions that lead to political power. Mossuz-Lavau and Sineau's study of women and politics in all European countries suggests that laws and practices, especially the electoral system for the lower house, add height to these barriers in the United States, United Kingdom, and France. All three countries have had single-member or uninominal voting, whereas most other countries have multimember districts and proportional representation. When the system was changed from proportional to uninominal voting in 1958 in France, there was an immediate drop in the percentage of women as both candidates (from 9.2 percent in 1956 to 2.2 percent in 1958) and in the National Assembly (from 3.6 percent in 1956 to 1.3 percent in 1958). Uninominal winner-take-all voting focuses attention on individual candidates and their relation to the localities. Parties are reluctant to risk all-or-nothing on a woman.

This is further aggravated in France by the time-honored practice of the *cumul* (accumulation of mandates). Holding both local and national elected office has always been permitted. In recent legislative elections, twice as many male candidates as female held at least one local office. People often believe that the local official will do more for their own district than someone with no formal status. Men have dominated local politics and thus have been more attractive as candidates to parties and voters. The single-member district system "encourages the creation of electoral 'strongholds' and the rule of local dignitaries." [30] Proportional representation, on the other hand, focuses attention on the battle between parties and their programs and ideologies rather than personalities. Women, especially those with less experience, may find running for office less intimidating. Proportional representation, however, increases the influence of the parties over the selection and placement of candidates on the ballot.

The French Socialist government restored proportional representation for the 1986 legislative elections, allowing a test of the hypothesis that the electoral system affects political opportunities for women. They have also proposed to limit the number of offices a person can hold simultaneously to two. Yvette Roudy was hopeful that the new electoral system would give an added boost to women seeking national office: "Next step: the legislative elections. Why would movement stop? Why not encourage it? The proportional system invites us to do it. Women will gain. Democracy too. Modernization equally." [31] Changes will not appear immediately, however. The parties of the Left which have always offered more women candidates, find their electoral support dwindling. Their motive in changing the electoral laws was to improve their own chances for retaining strong representation in the legislature rather than improving the chance for women. Competition in 1986 for party lists was fierce, and women with less clout in the party organization remain the underdogs. Socialists selected women to make up twelve percent of their candidate lists (raised from eight percent after a protest from Roudy). As it turned out, women improved their position on the Socialist *bancs*, winning nearly ten percent as against seven percent in 1981.

Despite the expected swing to the Right, neither the RPR nor the UDF opened new opportunities to women. Only two women were at the top of the RPR lists. Of the ninety lists, the UDF placed only one woman at the head. Prominent women united in protesting the parties' dismal record in selecting female candidates. Gaullist women of Femme Avenir called their party's nominations of women "cruelly insufficient." Monique Pelletier lamented the absence of women from crucial party positions: "We are now well-established on the political terrain. In spite of this strength, at the time the lists were put together, we were not there."[32] The 1986 legislative elections brought female representation in the National Assembly to nearly six percent. The parties of the Left have the most female representation: 9.85 percent of the Socialists and 3.57 percent of the majority UDF/RPR coalition are women. They make up three percent of the right-wing National Front as well.

The direct election of the European Parliament has given additional opportunities to French women to hold legislative office. Under the old system of indirect election only one woman (in 1958) had ever served in the French delegation to the EP. Most male politicians showed little interest in the first direct election in 1979 and left more openings for women. For the EP, candidates run on party lists proportioned according to the national vote. Twenty-one percent of the first French delegation was female (18 of 81), including a number of women who had been defeated in National Assembly campaigns or who had been unable to get their party's nod in a district. Although the European Parliament has little lawmaking power, it does go through various policymaking processes. For those who seek it, there are opportunities for experience and visibility. Edith Cresson, who was appointed Minister of Agriculture in the first Mitterrand government and then held the external trade portfolio, was chair of the Committee on Agriculture for the EP. Yvette Roudy chaired a European commission on women's rights. Christiane Scrivener, a secretary of state under Giscard, gained valuable experience as head of the budget committee, a post rarely given to a woman in any national legislature. After the 1984 ballot, female representation remains at 21 percent; women are 19.5 percent of the Center Right—including Simone Veil and Christiane Scrivener—30 percent of the Socialists, 20 percent of the Communists, and 1 of 6 deputies of the National Front.

Women also have gained some posts in the national executive. Although Roosevelt and Eisenhower bested their French counterparts by appointing women to full cabinet offices, the French have quickly caught up. Leon Blum had included women in his 1936 government, but Giscard in 1974 was the first to appoint a woman to a ministerial post—Simone Veil, Minister of Health.[33] Any French president has numerous quasi-cabinet positions that he can create and fill at will. Giscard appointed three women to such subministerial posts, including Françoise Giroud, secretary of state to the prime minister for the status of women. In January 1985 Mitterrand and Reagan each had three women in their cabinets holding regular departmental portfolios: External Trade, National Solidarity, Health and Social Service, and Environment in France; Transportation, Health and Human Services, and United Nations Ambassador in the United States. Since then, Mitterrand promoted Yvette Roudy to full cabinet rank, increasing female representation in the French executive to four of nineteen. In 1986, Premier Jacques Chirac's first government included four women out of forty-one appointments, but none at full ministerial rank: a minister-delegate for health and secretaries for education and *Francophonie*. Meanwhile, Jeane Kirkpatrick's resignation and Margaret Heckler's "promotion" to ambassador to Ireland brought the United States figure to one of fourteen.

In most countries, women have been more successful in local politics than national. Participation by women in state government in the United States has increased from five percent in 1971 to nine percent in 1977 and thirteen percent in 1983. These offices are not strictly comparable to local government in France, but the data show that women in both countries have begun to improve their representation at the local level while major barriers remain in access to national elected office. The French government took the unusual step of proposing a sex quota to give women some additional help in municipal elections. Following a suggestion by Françoise Giroud, Giscard asked Monique Pelletier to prepare the legislation. There are nearly 36,500 communes in France, each with a council and a mayor: 400,000 positions elected through proportional representation are at stake during the municipal elections. Many of the communes are so tiny or sparsely populated, that a quota would be impossible to implement. The Pelletier bill required that twenty percent of the candidates for each political party be female in communes of more than 3,500 inhabitants. It passed the National Assembly in late 1980, but no further action was taken prior to the presidential election.

Mitterrand and Roudy brought up the issue again, claiming that the idea originated among feminists of the Socialist party. This second bill set a twenty-five percent quota in communes over 3,500 and easily passed in time for the 1983 municipal elections. Then the plan hit a snag—the Constitutional Council. This council must rule on the constitutionality of all laws affecting the organization of the state. In the early years of the Fifth Republic, the council rarely voided anything wanted by the Gaullists, but it has been flexing its muscles in recent years. The sex quota was declared incompatible with the constitutional provision of equality for women and men "in all the domains." Despite the invalidation of the quota, the municipal elections of 1983 brought many more women to office. In those larger communes that would have been subject to the quota laws, twenty-two percent of the councillors are women, almost the same percentage as the quota. Overall, fourteen percent of the 400,000 councillors are women, a dramatic increase from eight percent in 1977 and four percent in 1971. The female share of mayoralties, however, at four percent, remains low.

DEFINITION OF THE ISSUE OF POLITICAL RIGHTS

France has been both innovative and conservative when it comes to political rights for women. The issue of political rights was born in the French Revolution, when it was defined as a simple matter of equality. In the nineteenth century it was adapted to assumptions of the complementarity of the sexes. Most suffragists justified their campaign for the vote by insisting that feminine values were needed in politics, rather than arguing that shared humanity meant political equality. They posed the issue in the least threatening way. Granting political rights was a way of preserving and integrating the traditional sex role division of labor into the modern polity. Finally, after little debate, the sparse language of the constitution gave women the right to vote, with no resolution of the conflict over what the vote would or should mean.

The effect of the logic of women's political rights is that politics in France remains the most masculine of worlds. Men and women have the equal right to seek positions of power in government and political parties. But the law leaves undisturbed the unequal distribution of political resources. Women encounter the widely held cultural attitude that, regardless of voting rights, politics is and should be a man's

world. Women will be let in occasionally when they concern themselves with traditional women's issues of family, health, and education. Thus, although men feared the result of giving women rights and
postponed it as long as possible, they have effectively contained female politicians and preserved the national party and elected offices
for themselves.

Women have made strides by increasing their participation in activities that may bring them influence. They have joined associations and
political parties. As feminists they have demonstrated and lobbied,
achieving policies furthering women's rights and equality in many areas,
as the bulk of this book will indicate. Their position as swing voters
between the Left and the Right assured that their issues received attention in party programs. From now on every cabinet will by convention
include women in some ministerial or subministerial posts. They also
have begun to make inroads at the local level. And changes in restrictive election laws may increase women's opportunities at the national
level.

Feminists see political rights in a larger socioeconomic and cultural
context. Simple legal equality will never translate into equal political
power without major social and cultural change. What women have
achieved is not power itself, but access to those who have power. In
a way, this access is an extension and a redefinition of the influence
women have always exerted over men. In the past women used their
''secret power'' over men through family connections and in the bou-
doir.[34] Now their access is more open and democratic and less overtly
sexual, but it still depends on the goodwill of men who have power.
The possibility that women in substantial numbers can wield power in
their own right awaits social, economic, and cultural conditions permitting women to compete on more equal terms with men.

NOTES

1. Among European countries, only Italy (1945), Greece (1952), Switzerland (1971), and Portugal (1976) granted women the vote more recently. Of
them, only Switzerland had democratic traditions as old as those in France.

2. Gisèle Halimi, *Le Programme commun des femmes* (Paris: Grasset, 1978),
27–58.

3. Odile Dhavernas, *Droits des femmes, pouvoir des hommes* (Paris: Seuil,
1978), 5th pt.; Yvette Roudy, *La Femme en marge* (Paris: Flammarion, 1975;
1982).

4. Michele Blin-Sarde, "L'Evolution du concept de différence dans le mouvement de libération des femmes en France." *Contemporary French Civilization* (Fall/Winter 1982), 195–202.

5. Quoted from *Le Torchon brûle* by N. Garcia Gaudilla, *Libération des femmes: le M.L.F.* (Paris: Presses Universitaires de France, 1981), 32. Despite their disdain for regular electoral politics the MLF-*déposé* took the unusual step of endorsing Mitterrand for president in 1981. American feminist Kate Millet advised them to avoid making the mistake American feminists made in 1980 when they refused to endorse Jimmy Carter and wound up with someone far worse in the presidency.

6. Steven C. Hause, *Women's Suffrage and Social Politics in the French Third Republic* (Princeton: Princeton University Press, 1984), 3–5. Looking at French history over the long haul, Hause finds evidence of women enjoying political rights in the Middle Ages. Such practices varied from region to region and affected only a tiny group of property owners and heads of families. This evidence adds further weight to the conclusion that the status of women in France has only recently regained the level enjoyed 700 years ago.

7. Maïté Albistur and Daniel Armogathe, *Histoire du féminisme français, du moyen age à nos jours.* (Paris: Des Femmes, 1977), 222.

8. Olympe de Gouges, "The Declaration of the Rights of Woman," reprinted in Darlene Gay Levy, Harriet Branson Applewhite, and Mary Durham Johnson, eds. *Women in Revolutionary Paris, 1789–1795* (Urbana: University of Illinois Press, 1979), 89–92. De Gouges wanted the King to preside over the revolutionary government; she was executed as a royalist in 1793.

9. Article II: The purpose of any political association is the conservation of the natural and imprescriptible rights of woman and man; these rights are liberty, property, security, and especially resistance to oppression.

Article IV: The law must be the expression of the general will; all female and male citizens must contribute either personally or through their representatives to its formation; it must be the same for all; male and female citizens, being equal in the eyes of the law, must be equally admitted to all honors, positions, and public employment according to their capacity and without other distinctions besides those of their virtues and talents.

Article XI: The free communication of thoughts and opinions is one of the most precious rights of woman, since that liberty assures the recognition of children by their fathers. Any female citizen thus may say freely, I am the mother of a child which belongs to you, without being forced by a barbarous prejudice to hide the truth; [an exception may be made] to respond to the abuse of this liberty in cases determined by the law.

10. Quoted by Albistur and Armogathe, *Histoire du féminisme*, 235.

11. Quoted by Michèle Sarde, *Regard sur les françaises* (Paris: Stock, 1983), 535.

12. Odile Dhavernas, *Droit des femmes*, 302.

13. Jean Rabaut, *Féministes à la "Belle Epoque"* (Paris: Edition France-Empire, 1985), 102. The term *feminist* was not used publicly to refer to activists for women's rights in France until 1892, according to Rabaut. Feminist is used here to refer to those women in earlier years who sought to better their status vis-à-vis men.

14. Quoted by Claire Goldberg Moses, *French Feminism in the Nineteenth Century* (Albany: SUNY Press, 1984), 113.

15. Ibid., 133.

16. Rabaut, *Féministes à la "Belle Epoque,"* 52.

17. Albistur and Armogathe, *Histoire du féminisme*, 381.

18. *Journal Officiel*, Sénat, Débats parlementaires (7 novembre 1922), 1354.

19. Ibid., 1345.

20. Dhavernas, *Droits des femmes*, 312.

21. Maurice Duverger, *The Political Role of Women* (New York: UNESCO, 1955), app.

22. The data are not conclusive because the fragmented party system has made it difficult to compare party choices over time.

23. SOFRES, *Opinion publique* (Paris: Gallimard, 1985). In the United States there is a similar pattern.

24. Janine Mossuz-Lavau and Mariette Sineau, "France," in *The Politics of the Second Electorate*, ed. Joni Lovenduski and Jill Hills (London: Routledge & Kegan Paul, 1981) 112–33.

25. L'Agence femmes information, *Bulletin* 113 (25 juin 1984).

26. Janine Mossuz-Lavau and Mariette Sineau, *Enquête sur les femmes et la politique en France* (Paris, Presses Universitaires de France, 1983); *Les Femmes françaises en 1978* (Paris: CORDES, 1980).

27. Helga Marie Hernes, "The Role of Women in Voluntary Associations and Organizations," *The Situation of Women in the Political Process of Europe*, pt. III (Strasbourg: Council of Europe, 1984) 21. In her study of women in associations in Europe, Hernes found figures ranging from 17 percent to 57 percent for France.

28. Ministère des Droits de la femme, *Citoyennes à part entière* (novembre 1984).

29. SOFRES, *Opinion publique*, 314. Sixty percent of the French, fifty-six percent of men and sixty-three percent of women, were favorable to the following: Would you be favorable or opposed that a woman become president of the French Republic in the coming years?

30. Janine Mossuz-Lavau and Mariette Sineau, "Women in the Political World of Europe," *The Situation of Women in the Political Process in Europe*, pt. II (Strasbourg: Council of Europe, 1984), 64.

31. "La Proportionnelle: Une chance pour les femmes," *Le Monde* (16 avril 1985), 2.

32. L'Agence femmes information, *Bulletin* 172–4 (5–27 octobre 1985).

33. The women in Blum's cabinet were undersecretaries: Education, Cecile Brunschwicg, an active suffragist; Child care, Suzanne Lacore, leader of socialist women; Scientific research, Irene Joliot-Curie, Nobel prizewinner and daughter of Marie Curie.

34. Michelle Coquillat, *Qui sont elles?* (Paris: Mazarine, 1983).

3

REPRODUCTION

WHATEVER THE COLOR of a French feminist's ideology, she will agree that the right to *disposer de soi*, to "self-determination in childbearing," is the most basic right of woman. The cornerstone of the legal repression of women had been the prohibition of access to birth control information and techniques and the punishment for their use. Liberation depended on the right to decide when to give life. Feminists united in their campaign to overturn repressive laws and obtain reproductive services. Their goal was nothing less than to wrench control of fertility from the Catholic church, the politicians, and men in general and place it firmly in women's hands. They would set women free by penetrating their veils of privacy, secrecy, and ignorance. They succeeded: in the 1980s French women have access to an array of family planning services, including abortion in the first trimester, subsidized by the state.

This was no easy task. Feminists confronted a legacy of two centuries of pronatalist policy backed by a dominant ideology that viewed a woman's childbearing not only as a service to her husband and family, but as a duty to the state. It was, however, two centuries of failed policy. Although the penal code of 1810 made abortion a crime, contraceptives were not mentioned in the law, and family limitation became increasingly popular during the nineteenth century. People gradually settled into a long-standing pattern, a sort of informal contract with the government. The government kept its official pronatalist stance, while French men and women used any available means to limit the size of their families. Men took the least risk because male contraceptive techniques—condoms, withdrawal, and rhythm—were legal and readily available. Women used homemade contraceptive concoctions and relied on abortion or abandonment as a backup.

Until the 1890s any problems caused by the prohibition of abortion were rarely discussed. Health professionals occasionally received reports on the effects of illegal abortions by *faiseuses d'anges* (literally, the makers of angels). But the public debate centered less on the legality of abortions than on the proper way to care for unwanted children. Early in the 1800s the state had taken official responsibility for children left anonymously by mothers who could not or would not care for them. "Abandonment was a socially acceptable means to cope with an unwanted child in an era without safe birth control or abortion, and without an effective program of aid to dependent children."[1] In the Third Republic political leaders became more concerned about slow population growth. Since there was also new interest in keeping families together, they concentrated on providing alternatives to both abortion and abandonment.

Birth control was a radical issue introduced by neo-Malthusians in the 1890s and made little dent on the growing pronatalism among republican politicians. Birth control, privately practiced, was publicly condemned by Catholics and socialists alike.[2] Although little mention of birth control was made in women's rights circles at the time, a few feminist pioneers have been identified. Marie Huot in 1892 made the first call for *libre maternité*. Nelly Roussel considered the issue a basic goal of the movement: "Of all the liberties woman seeks and demands, the one which seems to me to have the greatest influence on her destiny is this sexual liberty—or more exactly this reproductive freedom—for which we fight here."[3] According to feminist writer and doctor Madeleine Pelletier in 1911, birth control was the mark of civilization:

The birth rate is decreasing in France slightly more than elsewhere, it is true. But it is declining all over Europe. Voluntary restriction of births and civilization move forward together. Whatever the country may be, as soon as a man is sufficiently developed intellectually and morally to have feelings for his wife other than animal desire, he refuses to weigh her down with pregnancies, and the woman, becoming conscious of her value, seeks to be more than just a procreator.[4]

Perhaps the fact that the birth control issue stimulated little interest among political activists is evidence of the success of the informal contract between the people and the government. Margaret Sanger visited Paris in 1913 to observe the effects of French family limitation. She praised not only the special advantages in education and attention the children enjoyed in families of workers and political activists, but the importance of the knowledge and ability to regulate family size: "All individual French women considered this knowledge their individual right, and if it failed, abortion which was still common."[5]

Sanger used the information on contraception she learned in France to launch her crusade to bring the secret of birth control to women in America. Back home she quickly ran afoul of United States law. American legislators, not burdened with worries about birth rates, conceived of the problem of contraception in moral language with a sprinkling of eugenics and racism. The Comstock Act and its state counterparts defined contraceptives as obscene materials and banned them from commerce. Abortions were prohibited by the states primarily to protect maternal health. When Sanger made birth control a public issue, American feminists shared the reluctance of their French counterparts to get involved. Sanger approached a few prominent leaders of the suffrage movement, but had to rely on her contacts in socialist circles for support in her crusade.

In France, any moral questions about contraception were overridden by the chronic concern with population growth. After World War I, this concern grew to an overpowering fear of depopulation. Reproductive health care had improved dramatically at the end of the nineteenth century. With anesthetics and the D & C, abortions had become "thinkable" as a medical procedure. New and more effective female contraceptive techniques (called neo-Malthusian devices and propaganda) had appeared. The improvement in contraception and abortion practice, however, threatened the recovery of the French nation from the devastation of the war. The parliament was prepared to break the unspoken contract between the government and the people and act to deter women from the practice of their cultural ideal of the two-child family. They were going to force parents to have more children.

New laws were needed to prohibit the use of the new contraceptives. Changes in the abortion laws were also required. Under Article 317 of the penal code of 1810, abortion had been a felony and both a woman and her abortionist could be imprisoned for long periods. But enforcement was lax, reflecting the general public tolerance of abortion. Courts and juries, sympathetic to the plight of poor mothers, were reluctant to convict. As political scientist Robert Michels observed: "abortion is so widely practiced today [1914] by married people of all social classes, and is justified by so many excuses that, as far as may be, the legal authorities shut their eyes to the commission of the offense."[6] Pronatalists reasoned that by reducing the seriousness of the crime of abortion and the penalties, the chances of conviction would improve. Contraception and abortion both would be *délits*, a middle-level criminal offense. The new laws would also serve to suppress all public discussion of birth control on the assumption that women, denied knowledge, would be forced to accept motherhood. Men were not the object of the 1920 law; their contraceptive, the condom, was defined as a prophylactic and not prohibited.

The law of 31 July 1920 repressed all incitement to abortion (whether or not abortion occurred) by spoken word or in writing, including documents about abortion procedures and the sale of any instruments or substances used in performing abortions (three to six years in prison plus a fine). This law also punished anyone who sold, gave, or revealed contraceptive techniques to others (one to six months in prison plus a fine). In 1923 another statute set penalties for performing abortion procedures at one to five years in prison and at six months to two years for a woman who had an abortion. Fines and professional suspensions were also meted out to abortionists.

The 1920 and 1923 laws are remarkable in several ways. At a time when other Western countries were weathering challenges from birth control movements, French legislators enacted a new set of severe laws. Whereas, in other countries, regulations were defended in moral or religious terms, French policy made family limitation a crime against the national interest. In the United States, contraception was being promoted as a deterrent to abortion; in France they were both subject to criminal penalty. Finally, since the public discussion of contraception and abortion was banned, all protest against the laws was itself subject to criminal prosecution. For the next thirty-five years, the laws remained undisturbed. They were incorporated into a 1939 law on the family entitled, "The Decree Law relative to the family and French natality." A slight reform in that law permitted therapeutic abortion to save a mother's life. But to improve enforcement doctors were required to report all diagnoses of pregnancy to the government. "Thus, the problem of abortion was always posed from the point of view of the State and the family; maternity remained a social duty, never a free choice." [7]

REFORM OF THE LAWS ON CONTRACEPTION

Efforts at overturning the repressive 1920 and 1923 laws did not start until the 1950s, long after Sanger's birth control movement. The stories of reform in France and the United States are very different with one exception: neither government defined the legalization of contraceptives as an issue of women's rights. Although Margaret Sanger had dreamed of a women's revolution based on voluntary motherhood, the American laws were changed to further medical goals, not feminist ones. In the 1930s the Supreme Court removed all bans on therapeutic uses of contraceptives. Moralists had dictated the ban, but doctors removed it. First, doctors acted to protect men from venereal disease. Later, they prescribed contraceptives to limit the health risks of pregnancy. Some states, motivated by race and class bias, not only legalized contraceptives but urged birth control upon poor minorities. In 1965 and 1972 the Supreme Court removed all legal restrictions by prohibiting states from interfering with private use of and access to family planning. [8] At no time was the law on contraception defined officially as part of a woman's right to reproductive choice.

In France between the world wars, opposition to the contraceptive laws came primarily from the leftists, who were concerned about the limits on free speech, and from renegade doctors like Madeleine Pelletier. The first serious challenge to the French law was launched by Dr. Marie Lagroua Weill-Hallé, the 1950s French counterpart of Margaret Sanger. Just as Sanger had had to go to France to learn about techniques of family limitation in 1913, so Weill-Hallé found herself in 1947 at the Margaret Sanger clinic in New York, gaining knowledge about modern contraception absent from her own medical training in France. Later, during her hospital residence in Paris, she was shocked to find doctors regularly and gleefully performing D & C procedures without anesthetic on women they suspected of self-induced abortions: "So they won't do it again." [9] First, she protested the situation in a series of articles in medical journals. Then, in a speech before the Académie des Sciences Morales et Politiques in 1955, she denounced the 1920 law for forcing unwanted pregnancies on women despite social, economic, or biological factors. Thus she made the first public demand in France for voluntary motherhood.[10] In 1956 Weill-Hallé formed an organization, La Maternité heureuse, which in 1960 became the Mouvement Français pour le Planning Familial (MFPF). At first they struggled alone against adverse Catholic opinion, opposition of the Communist party, and disinterest from the medical profession. But the MFPF campaigned on all fronts, and gradually younger doctors and reformers joined the cause. Their most effective tactic was the establishment of "orthogenic" family planning centers in direct violation of the pronatalist statutes.[11] By 1966 there were 200 centers all over France. Condoms, the male contraceptives, were already openly available as prophylactics. The MFPF smuggled diaphragms and pills for women from abroad, and sympathetic doctors prescribed them, using the therapeutic pretense. It can be safely said that this campaign forced the government to reform the contraceptive law. In doing so, however, the state did not accept the notion that contraception was a woman's right. With the orthogenic centers, violations of the laws had become so flagrant that the government acted only to remove a potentially embarrassing situation.

In fact, many of those supporting reform did not agree with MFPF's pro-woman position. Lawyers, demographers, and economists pointed out that the 1920s laws had lost their effectiveness and that they were incapable of stopping either use of or information about birth control. Some thought legal contraception would be a deterrent to rising abortion rates. Public opinion polls were showing that the law was out of date and out of favor. Sensing a potential election issue, the socialists included family planning in their platform in 1960. By 1965 even the Communists came to accept family planning.

After the 1967 elections the government of President de Gaulle allowed a private-member reform bill, drafted by a moderate Gaullist named Lucien Neuwirth, to be passed. The government's reluctance to sponsor the bill stemmed from the opposition of conservatives, Catholics and pronatalists within the Gaullist party itself. At this point, the medical profession, also dominated by the Right, refused to get involved in the issue at all: Contraception is "a problem essentially non-medical and the doctor must refuse the monopoly that they want to offer him."[12]

The 1967 law legalized contraceptives and gave the state the power to regulate their sale and distribution. Any medicines had to be prescribed by a doctor and purchased in a pharmacy. A woman was required to present a user card each time she purchased pills. This card, not unlike that of a drug addict, had to be punched for each prescription. A minor had to have parental consent. There would be no reimbursement from public health funds. Contraceptive information was to be available only through specially designated centers and they were forbidden from dispensing any devices. Legal bans on antinatalist propaganda, such as advocating a woman's right to limit her family, remained in place.

Despite these rigid controls, contraception quickly gained general acceptance as a social good in furthering family and child health and in preventing abortion, and in 1974 the law was once again reformed. In the seven years between 1967 and 1974, changes in the political environment, especially the political reawakening of feminism, had been dramatic. Radical feminists made the liberation of female sexuality from patriarchy their basic principle and reproductive freedom a central issue. Abortion was the key battle, but activists from the feminist-sponsored Mouvement pour la Liberté de l'Avortement et de la Contraception (MLAC) linked the two issues: "Avortement d'accord, Contraception d'abord" (Abortion, of course, Contraception, first). Choisir circulated a bill for abortion on demand and free distribution of contraceptives. Reform feminists meeting at Etats-Généraux de la Femme in 1970 demanded the right to contraception. But it was the call for legal abortion sparked by radical feminists that changed official attitudes on the contraception issue. The government, relentlessly prodded to settle the controversial abortion question, took refuge in the public opinion favorable to contraception. Officials began to present it as a deterrent to abortion and shifted their own role from regulator to provider of services.

In fact, in the early 1970s, only ten percent of French women were using modern contraceptives because of the refusal of hostile Gaullist ministers to implement the 1967 reform. Under the constitution, neither members of parliament, like Lucien Neuwirth, nor small private-interest groups, such as the MFPF, could force a reluctant government minister to act. Only the president could exert the necessary pressure. The election of May 1974 bought Valéry Giscard to the presidency with promises to modernize French society. He appointed Simone Veil Minister of Health and charged her with the responsibility to resolve the conflict over abortion. Giscard's administration welcomed a consensus issue like contraception. It was finally acceptable to give support to the small evil of contraception when faced with the giant evil of abortion.

The 1974 law, again a private bill by Neuwirth, simplified the distribution of contraceptives, eliminated the "addicts" card, and abolished the parental consent requirement for minors. Contraceptives were to be reimbursed by social security and distributed free at government family planning centers. In 1976 the government established a Centre d'Information sur la Régulation des Naissances, la Maternité et la Vie sexuelle to provide information to organizations and clinics, and Dr. Weill-Hallé has been chair ever since.[13] Finally, and quickly at the end, the government along with the medical establishment had changed their position on family planning from strict avoidance to acceptance as a means of improving family health. It was not at this point viewed as a matter of women's rights, and feminists did not insist on gaining control of the issue and making it one of their own.

In France as in the United States, changes in repressive contraceptive laws were not made to further women's rights. In France, contraception had been prohibited to force women to have children. It was legalized to save the state embarrassment when it was clear the laws had been flagrantly violated. The government soon revised this position with positive action for contraception as a deterrent to abortion and a means of improving family well-being. The American government banned contraceptives as obscene materials but later permitted them for health purposes, to limit population growth among the poor, and finally to ensure family privacy. In both countries the story of reform of contraceptive laws is incomplete without recounting the story of abortion reform. In the United States and France, feminists have been much more interested in abortion, perhaps because opposition to it is so much stronger. They have insisted that governments recognize a woman's right to choose. Only in France have feminists been successful in convincing government to define abortion as a women's rights issue.

ABORTION REFORM

In a way French women have always had control of abortion: They have practiced it regardless of the official government policy. The 1920 and 1923 laws denied women access to safe contraception and added the risk of criminal prosecution to the health risks of infection, hemorrhage, and death from abortion. Despite the odds, their determination was striking. Between 1923 and 1939 illegal abortions averaged 400,000 per year. They rose to 700,000 to 800,000 by the 1960s. Surveys by the Institut National d'Etudes Démographiques (INED) in 1950 showed that half the women who had abortions were poor and married and induced the miscarriage on themselves.[14] Despite several show trials and one execution, the latter under the Vichy regime, very few cases were prosecuted. There was little public interest in the question and authorities happily ignored the private anguish of women with unwanted pregnancies.[15]

In the 1960s the abortion issue first came to public attention in connection with the MFPF's campaign to legalize contraceptives. In 1969 Dr. Weill-Hallé formed the L'Association National pour l'Etude de l'Avortement (ANEA). At the same time, feminists hatched their radical ideas about sexuality and patriarchy. Abortion-on-demand quickly became the concrete expression of the liberation of women from patriarchal oppression.

These two groups saw the abortion issue in different terms and this led to different proposals. Family planners wanted to eliminate the dangers of clandestine abortions. Certain problem pregnancies threatened mothers to such an extent that they were willing to go abroad or submit to unsafe procedures from *faiseuses d'anges* to end them. The ANEA proposed a new bill similar to most of the abortion legislation in Europe at the time, and Dr. Claude Peyret, a moderate Gaullist, introduced it in the National Assembly in 1970. Abortion would be legal to protect the mother's health, if the fetus were deformed, if the pregnancy were the result of rape or incest, or if the family were too poor to support the child. Feminist groups, on the other hand, wanted abortion to be recognized as a basic right for women. When Choisir was formed in 1971 by lawyer Gisèle Halimi and author Simone de Beauvoir it was a pressure group with the single cause: woman's right to choose. They drafted a bill that covered both contraception and abortion. It provided for free family planning services and abortion on demand through the twelfth week of pregnancy, after consultation with a doctor through the twenty-fourth week, and, under conditions of health or deformity, after the twenty-fourth week.

In 1973, some Socialist deputies agreed to introduce a version of

Choisir's bill. Socialists had been the first large party to advocate reform. In 1965 François Mitterrand had included the issue in his program during his first campaign for the presidency. In 1971 the Communist party, agreeing that legal abortion would remove some health and economic burdens from the poor, officially advocated legalization of abortion and started introducing its own private bills into the parliament. Even so, the leftist parties tended to see abortion in social, economic, and health terms rather than in feminist terms.

The Center Right parties, especially the Gaullists, were divided on the issue. Several prominent leaders were conservative Catholics and pronatalists who feared abortion would increase trends toward immorality and depopulation. The conservative Ordre des Medecins formally ruled that abortion violated medical ethics and doctors would not perform them. These traditional opponents of abortion were joined by a new group that has a strong counterpart in the United States, advocates of *respect de la vie*.[16] Laissez-les-vivre is the most prominent "right-to-life" organization. To them, abortion is the same as murder and they define the fetus as a human life from conception. Like the American "right-to-life" groups they support their demands with both religious and scientific/genetic arguments.

Most of the first bills for abortion reform, therefore, came from the leftist opposition parties that lacked political resources to get them passed. Only the government could push a reform through the legislature. The challenge to advocates was to make abortion reform a priority issue for the Center Right government. Feminists led this campaign with a series of acts that rank with the best of French political theater. They made abortion reform not only the most prominent demand of feminists, but for several years a hot item of public discussion and debate that the government could not ignore.[17] The problem had been the public silence surrounding the ineffectiveness and suffering caused by the 1920–23 laws. The solution was to stage some dramatic scenes and call in the press.

Media stars and crime attract attention: The "Manifeste des 343 femmes" published in the *Nouvel Observateur* in 1971 combined both. Women of all classes publicly admitted having broken the law. Heading the list were the stars: actresses Catherine Deneuve, Delphine Seyrig; writers Simone de Beauvoir, Françoise Sagan, and Christiane Rochefort; lawyer Gisèle Halimi; and Socialist Yvette Roudy:

[Women obtain abortions] under dangerous conditions due to the secrecy to which they are condemned. I declare that I am one of them. I declare that I have had an abortion.

The Manifesto was the work of the Mouvement de Libération des Femmes. The 343 women who signed it shattered the silence surrounding clandestine abortion by daring the police to arrest them. It was the sort of spontaneous protest the MLF preferred. Some MLF women who wanted to continue to work for law reform formed the Mouvement pour la Liberté de l'Avortement in 1972 (that added *Contraception* to the name and became MLAC in 1973). The MLF itself had neither the organization nor the inclination to file law suits or lobby the legislature. The MLF women were ready to go to the streets for liberation of women's bodies but not to the legislature or the courts. It fell to Choisir, which was organized for legal conventional political action, to take on the legislature and the courts.

Choisir staged the next production at Bobigny in the fall of 1972. Gisèle Halimi defended a poor teenager pregnant from a rape, her mother, and two other women who were being prosecuted under the 1923 law. Seventeen-year-old Marie-Clare had ended up in a hospital after hemorrhaging at the hand of a *faiseuse d'anges*. Halimi and her clients collaborated to make the trial a political event:

When the accused realize they are fighting to defend a cause that goes beyond their own case, then the trial is political. And it is political because the accused turn themselves into the accusers, decide to use the court as a platform and go over the heads of the judges to address themselves to the whole body of public opinion.[18]

Again, media stars and crime combined as Halimi called de Beauvoir and Nobel-prizewinner Dr. Paul Milliez to the witness stand to denounce the law. The MLA and other militants staged demonstrations and marches outside the court and in Paris. Newspapers published dramatic photos of the anguished family, on trial because they could not afford to go abroad to have a safe, legal abortion. The court acquitted the girl, noting that her age, marital status, and condition of dependency were extenuating circumstances, and gave the other women light, suspended sentences. By then abortion had become a popular subject for discussion in the press and on the radio and television. It was a taboo no longer.

In 1973, radical feminists of the MLAC moved to the third act of their drama. Taking a page from earlier campaigns for contraception by Planning Familial, they went all the way in defying the law by setting up abortion clinics. Several groups participated in these "orthogenic" centers, aiding women in finding doctors to perform abortions. Physicians of the leftist Groupe Information Santé (GIS) affirmed that the right to control her body and her life belonged to a woman and to her alone. The MLAC held meetings throughout the country, organized trips to England and Holland, and openly performed vacuum aspirations, the so-called Karman method. They disobeyed the legal ban on abortion information by showing a film detailing the abortion procedure called "L'Histoire de l'A" (the title is a parody of the pornography classic *L'Histoire d'O*). Support was growing for reform, and, more important, for the idea that abortion was a woman's right.

Choisir concentrated on getting its bill through the deadlocked legislature. In 1973 the government produced its own proposal for conditional abortion similar to the Peyret bill of 1970 and wholly unacceptable to the feminists. Choisir was one of many groups that testified before the Cultural, Family, and Social Affairs Committee of the National Assembly. The committee rejected the government bill in favor of one like Choisir's for abortion on demand. But that was unacceptable to the government. The stalemate was broken when Pompidou's death in 1974 brought early presidential elections. All candidates promised reform, and the winner, Giscard, acted. According to Bruno Frappat of *Le Monde*, Giscard sought a liberal image for his new government and responding to women's demands for reform was one way to do that. Besides, he had just received a majority of the female vote. "No politician whose destiny is tied to universal suffrage can neglect the weight of the female vote, especially when it has just counted in his victory." [19]

Giscard appointed the first woman to a full ministerial post—Simone Veil, Minister of Health. Then he turned the abortion mess over to her to resolve. When she took up her new duties the outgoing minister warned her that something must be done about abortion "de toute urgence!" [20] Veil and Giscard agreed to a new bill that would recognize a woman's right to decide on abortion in the first ten weeks of pregnancy regardless of the condition of the pregnancy. They admitted that the only way to reduce the number of illegal abortions was to allow free choice: "This is why the government has preferred to recognize that finally the decision can be made by the woman." [21]

The feminists had, through conventional and unconventional means, convinced the government to guarantee abortion as a woman's right. Nevertheless, the authorities did not legalize abortion to improve the position of women. Instead, the Veil bill represented a sort of grudging acceptance of their powerlessness to prevent abortion in the face of women's determination. There was further evidence of the government's reluctance to make it a women's rights issue: the cabinet Secretary for the Status of Women, Françoise Giroud, was nearly invisible during debate on the reforms. In the United States, too, the justification for legal abortion declared in 1973 was not primarily to help women control their own lives. True, *Roe v. Wade* prohibits all government regulation of abortion in the first twelve weeks of pregnancy. In this, however, the justices gave doctors the right to decide a matter of medical practice. Additionally, they considered the decision an extension of the right to privacy granted to citizens to practice contraception without government interference. [22]

Unlike the United States policy, the Veil bill included some restrictions on access to abortion in the first ten weeks. This was a political compromise among the parties of Giscard's Center Right coalition to reduce the opposition of the influential medical profession. The intent was to reinforce the idea of abortion as an extraordinary medical procedure, a last resort for the woman distressed by an unwanted pregnancy. There were the dissuasive measures: Abortions would not be reimbursed by public health services; the doctor would have to inform the patient of the risks of abortion; the woman must consult a family counselor who will offer solutions to her distress; after all this the woman must wait a week after making her final request. Veil also included protective measures requiring that the abortion be performed in a hospital. The conscience clause would permit doctors and hospitals to refuse to accept women seeking abortions. After the tenth week, abortion would be legal only on condition of the danger of the pregnancy to a woman's health. The government gave the law a provisional character: It was to be reviewed after a five-year trial.

The debate in both houses of the legislature was sensational and extreme. It went on for days, and at one point Veil fled the National

Assembly under a barrage of personal attacks. But the compromise held, and the bill passed with a healthy majority that included all the leftist deputies and nearly half of those of the Center Right. None of them was entirely happy, but the feminists and the Left agreed that the *Loi* Veil was better than no change at all. Most of the activists moved on to other campaigns and issues and did not reconvene until the act came up for review in 1979.

By then, Giscard was still president, but Giroud had resigned and Veil had left the government and was presiding over the European Parliament. After a reminder in the 1978 legislative elections that the female vote was still important to him, Giscard appointed Monique Pelletier as Minister for the Status of Women. While Giroud had shown little overt interest in the abortion issue and had played no role in the parliament, Pelletier, the president's official advocate of women's rights, represented the government as floor manager for the extension of the law. The 1974 law, she said, provided social and medical protection while assuring individual responsibility for women. She presented the issue in a clear and coordinated fashion, mentioning its importance to women's rights while refusing to accept the radical feminists' conception of abortion as a symbol of liberty. Abortion was always a failure, a tragedy, but it must remain legal to prevent even further tragedy. Most of the supporters of the 1974 law, including the moderate feminists, agreed with the government's official view that a woman could retain the right to choose but that abortion must not become an ordinary means of family planning and a substitute for contraception.

The legislative debate was again lively and opponents of extending the law brought up the usual arguments. The government firmly rejected the pronatalist logic that had inspired the 1920 law: "In a free modern society, it is no longer possible for a nation to increase its population by forcing women to have children they do not want. It must find other incentives."[23] Pelletier promised the pronatalists an extensive debate on developing a policy that would encourage couples to have children. She argued that abortions, which had remained at about 150,000 per year, could not be eliminated by repealing the law.

The favorable vote in 1979 extended the abortion reform indefinitely. Again Giscard had to rely on the votes of the opposition parties of the Left—the Socialists and the Communists. The Left took every opportunity to remind the president that his image as a reformer was due to their votes, not those of his own party. Many were dissatisfied

with the law. Choisir's Gisèle Halimi insisted that further liberalization was essential: Extend the unrestricted period from ten to twelve
weeks; permit abortions in doctors' offices; eliminate parental approval. The Left continued to demand that abortions be paid for by
Social Security health programs.

By 1979 the content of abortion policy in France was similar to that
in the United States. There were no conditions in the first weeks of
pregnancy and few public funds were available to help pay for the
procedure. There were more administrative hurdles for the patient in
France, yet in the United States the woman's right to choose seemed
less secure. The French reform provoked wider and deeper support.
After serious debate, the legislature in a bipartisan vote accepted the
proposal from the political executive that a woman be allowed to choose
abortion. When they did it all again five years later, the executive gave
them its full support, declaring abortion to be an issue of women's
rights. In the United States the conflict over abortion has never been
adequately resolved. The reform came about when the Supreme Court
took the matter away from the legislatures and set guidelines for state
policy. Only this one court has recognized that the decision of whether
to bear a child properly belongs at least in part to the woman. The
conflict was not fully addressed in the legislatures, nor has the policy
enjoyed political support from the federal executive. When challenged
that the cutoff of Medicaid funds for abortion was unfair to poor women,
President Carter responded with the comforting words that "life is
unfair." President Reagan gives assurance to "right-to-life" organizations that he agrees with them and their campaign. Meanwhile, feminists must continue the struggle in order to maintain the rights the
court has given them.

RECENT DEVELOPMENTS IN REPRODUCTION
POLICIES

When the Ministry of Woman's Rights (MWR) set up its agenda in
1981, reproductive rights was the first priority. Yvette Roudy recruited
Simone Iff, former president of the MFPF (1973–78), to her cabinet
and gave her responsibility for health and sexuality. A feminist, Iff
had participated in a study in 1977 that revealed that the government
was not providing adequate information services on family planning.
For thirteen million women of childbearing age, there were only 377

information centers. Only thirty-two percent of French women aged 15 to 49 were using any modern contraceptive method, the vast majority of them the Pill. The incidence was much lower among the young, farm women, workers, and immigrants. Choisir and other feminists agreed that, although the law had legalized contraceptives, many women remained ignorant, and their lack of effective contraception kept abortion rates high. They criticized the state committee on sex education for emphasizing ineffective methods like rhythm and neglecting the Pill and the IUD. Such practices, said Iff, meant the committee did not want women to decide their own fate.[24]

One month after the Socialist victory in 1981, the Council of Ministers accepted Roudy's proposal for a massive contraceptive campaign. The goal of the MWR was to bring modern contraceptive services to millions of French women. The means was a public relations campaign to provoke interest and discussion and then prod all government agencies to incorporate family planning information and services where possible.

The theme of the campaign was feminist: "Today each woman must be able to choose." Nearly every night for two weeks in late 1981, families saw spot advertisements on television showing a variety of people who needed more knowledge about birth control. Four situations, four inequalities: a farm woman who has enough children; a young couple who live together but aren't ready to marry; a young mother with a small baby who wants to wait before having a second child; adolescents who just want more education about sex and birth control. The intent of these ads was to desensitize the subject, to talk openly about family planning, and to encourage public discussion so it would be more acceptable for women, especially young ones, to bring up the subject with their families and ask for more information.

The MWR called upon twenty ministries, such as the Ministry of Health, Immigrants, Family, Labor, Military, and Agriculture, to aid in providing information. Roudy and Iff enlisted unions and political parties to join in spreading the word. Regional delegates of the ministry were mobilized to make contraception prominent in the new centers of information on women's rights. Feminists and women's organizations also participated, holding special meetings, training counselors, and distributing information pamphlets. In the first year, 1,000 centers for contraception information opened.

By using this program to launch their ministry, Roudy and Iff sent the message that they intended to bring feminist principles to government. Their gamble paid off and the contraceptive campaign was very well received. Many legislators, even in the Center and Right opposition parties, praised the program. They were relieved that since necessary laws were already in place, the campaign meant little political risk for them. By 1981 most politicians accepted the idea that contraception could not only prevent abortion but also provide a safe haven for them from the more controversial abortion issue. Most of the medical profession had also agreed that family planning was necessary and were willing to take an active role in providing services. Whereas in 1965, only four percent of doctors had helped the MFPF, by the 1980s only five percent refused to prescribe modern contraceptive methods to patients. The campaign was popular with the public: In July 1982 a BVA poll showed that seventy-five percent of women and seventy-nine percent of men approved of the ministry's contraceptive information policy. By January 1984, support had increased to more than eighty percent of the French population.[25] There is also some evidence that the policy is working: More availability of information about contraception has coincided with reduced abortion rates among the young. Considering that it was a crime as recently as 1967 to talk about contraception, let alone educate the public and deliver services, these attitudes and practices constitute a major social and political change.

Family planning, as a woman's right and as a means of preventing abortion, is now fully integrated into public policy. The presence of feminists in the executive has been responsible for making contraceptive information and services a regular part of the government's work. In the United States there is neither the official nor the social acceptance of birth control found in France. The importance of contraception in preventing abortion has not yet been incorporated into public discussion or government policy. American television networks still don't allow contraceptive advertisements and public service programs on family planning are rare. High rates of teenage pregnancy have been linked to low levels of information about contraception.[26] The intense abortion conflict seems to threaten those few government services for family planning that have survived. The possibility that family planning policy will be based on the proposition that a woman must have the right to choose, as it is in France, seems remote indeed.

Abortion, as always, presented a much more controversial and intransigent problem to Roudy and the MWR than contraception. Dis-

content with the operation of the 1974 Veil law had been evident when
parliament debated it in 1979. The law had not prevented illegal abortions. The INED reported that 150,000 legal abortions were performed
each year, but that an additional 100,000 were done on French women
in foreign countries. When the law was extended without any changes,
the criticisms intensified. They involved shortcomings in three areas:
the content of the law, the way it was administered, and sabotage by
doctors.

Choisir and the MLAC complained that the ten-week limit was too
severe, and this requirement, coupled with inadequate information, meant
that many women could not come to a decision in time. Restriction on
foreign women and parental consent requirements for minors made
legal abortion impossible for those groups. Critics, charging discrimination against the poor, deplored the refusal of the government to
reimburse women for abortion costs from social security health programs. "The most disfavored financially do not have the right. We
know some women only seek abortion after they have found the
money—then it is often too late."[27]

A study by the MFPF in 1979 revealed barriers in administrative
procedures and sabotage. Services in public hospitals were uneven.
Some refused to perform abortions altogether despite the requirement
in the law that they do so if no other services were available in the
local area. Many doctors delayed the procedure, going far beyond the
legal requirements in order to dissuade women. Some refused to perform abortions after the eighth or even the sixth week. Others required
unnecessary tests, such as ultrasound, before agreeing to terminate the
pregnancy. There were reports of doctors stringing patients along for
several weeks before refusing to do the procedure at all, ignoring the
legal requirement that, if they refused to do abortions, they inform
patients at the beginning.

The Ministry of Health, rather than trying to increase services, emphasized the restrictions to the full extent of the law. The Minister of
Justice was vigilent in prosecuting the doctors who performed abortions after the ten-week deadline. One case involving doctors at the
Pergola clinic in Paris who were charged with aborting a seven-month
fetus produced a sensational headline: "INFANTICIDE!" One of the
doctors was sentenced to five years in jail. Feminist critics used this
case to show that poor women were forced to desparate measures when

handicapped by ignorance, poverty, and an absence of clinics and doctors to help with unwanted pregnancies.

The MWR included the extension of abortion services along with the contraceptive campaign among its first proposals to the Council of Ministers. The government agreed: "The means and instructions necessary will be provided in order that the laws on contraception and abortion be effectively applied in all hospitals in a spirit of understanding and humanity."[28] The success of this policy depended on the cooperation of the Ministry of Health, where Roudy faced formidable administrative blockages. The ministry is large and entrenched, the doctors and hospitals conservative. One high-level civil servant absolutely refused to comply with the proposed directive to expand hospital services on abortion. The stalemate called for a political solution. The Socialist Minister of Woman's Rights persuaded the Socialist Minister of Health to replace the recalcitrant official so that the formal directive could be issued (Décret No. 82–826 7 Sept. 1982). The decree obliged all hospitals with surgical or maternity services to perform abortions, increasing the number offering services from 300 to 500.

The MWR decided not to try to win further liberalization of the content of the 1974–79 law. This decision followed the outcome of the bitter struggle Roudy faced within her own government over the reimbursement of abortion costs. The demand that women be reimbursed for doctors' and hospital fees as part of their health coverage under the Social Security system was a top priority for feminists and many Socialists. They argued that the right of a woman to decide to seek an abortion was of little use unless the poor were relieved of the burden of the costs. The middle- or upper-class woman had little trouble securing an abortion at home and had money to go abroad if necessary. It was the "welfare" case, the poor woman, frequently unemployed or low-paid, who could not afford to have and raise a child and who needed a liberal abortion law. Socialist feminists considered reimbursement of abortion a matter of justice—a test of their party's commitment to equality. The Socialist party included reimbursement in their 1981 election program and Mitterrand agreed, although he showed little conviction: "From the moment we recognize the medical nature of the [abortion] act we must have all the consequences; that's why I consider that Social Security must figure in this business."[29]

During her first year in office, Roudy announced from time to time her intention to keep this campaign promise. Within the government, however, she was having difficulties. In March 1982, while the first official celebration of International Woman's Day was getting underway, the interministerial committee on women's rights met to draw up a definitive list of policy objectives, such as the thirty percent quota in municipal elections and the training of media personnel in contraception education. Roudy proposed reimbursement as well and found herself alone, save for Prime Minister Pierre Mauroy, in defending it. At this point, the financial problems of the government were not a major consideration. The opposition was primarily political—fears that the abortion issue would give the rightist opposition further fuel against the Socialist government already plagued with controversy over its plans to phase out state aid to Catholic schools and private hospitals. Nevertheless, Mauroy and Roudy publicly announced on 8 March that abortions would be reimbursed by September 1982. Mitterrand remained lukewarm to the idea and was content that the proposal be quietly added to the budget of the Ministry for National Solidarity.

In June, a fiscal crisis struck and forced the Socialists to reverse many of their campaign promises and adopt budget restrictions. No new expenditures, including those for abortions, would be allowed for Social Security. Roudy proposed separate funding, but the new Solidarity Minister, Pierre Bérégevoy, refused. After that, the MWR gave up hope of getting reimbursement. In August *Le Monde* published the news that the abortion proposal was dead. Bérégevoy and Roudy blamed the financial imperative; *Le Monde* and *Libération* were skeptical, showing that the proposal had been in trouble long before the budget crisis.

"We are non-aggressive feminists, but sometimes, such as on the issue of abortion in October 1982, it's necessary to go to the street." Thus a moderate feminist member of Mouvement Jeunes Femmes explained her participation in protest demonstrations over reimbursement. Abortion has been the one issue that has united French feminists. When their ministry lost the battle, they willingly and successfully rallied, joined by rank-and-file Socialists. The demonstrations were part-demand, part-festival, and part-nostalgia for the early 1970s, when feminist political muscle had first legalized abortion. This time the president accepted their demands in advance by promising a special reimbursement bill.

When the bill appeared, feminists were disappointed. The money for payment of abortions was to come not from the regular Social Security revenues, but from the government's annual budget. Did this mean that the government had refused to treat abortion as a regular medical procedure? Was it bowing to opponents who fretted about the "banalization" of abortion? Mauroy said no, claiming that since abortion would be included in the list of reimbursable medical acts, the source of the money did not matter. Choisir still considered this funding precarious because it would have to be reappropriated each year. Negotiations were difficult, but with Mitterrand's help the bill passed the Council of Ministers in December 1982.

During the parliamentary debate, the theme of social justice for poor women was prominent in speeches by proponents while the opposition criticized the government for encouraging abortion and ignoring families. Roudy maintained that women and men want "a life freely chosen, a life freely given." Even so, echoing their predecessors under Giscard, government leaders did in fact insist that abortion was a tragedy and not an ordinary medical act, even though it was paid for like one. This attitude separated them from feminists, especially Choisir. Halimi, a member of the National Assembly, feared that as long as abortion was in a special category, its legality was tenuous. Roudy and the MWR walked a fine line, their sentiments clearly with the feminists, but their loyalties with the Socialist government.

The reimbursement bill passed and the issue of abortion faded from prominence at MWR; in mid-1983 Simone Iff faded along with it. While she remained at the ministry for a time as a special advisor to Roudy, her portfolio on health was combined with other areas and given to another cabinet officer. One magazine reported that this was intended to erase the image of the MWR as an abortion ministry and shift priorities to less divisive goals such as employment and education.

The establishment of the MWR contributed to the decision to subsidize abortion through health programs. It has, however, not disturbed the official definition of that policy: Legal abortion is necessary and a woman's choice, but it is an undesirable means of birth control, a special medical act to be avoided through better contraception. In 1985, commemorating the tenth anniversary of legal abortion in France briefly highlighted the current situation. Legal abortions average 180,000 per year (24 per 100 live births), but there has been a drop in foreign abortions. Nearly 800 hospitals, including 368 private clinics, perform the procedure, which is paid for by Social Security. Still, all the administrative restrictions remain, including the requirement that minors obtain parental approval. Estimates of illegal abortions range from 6,000 to 10,000 per year. Choisir persists with its list of unmet demands, including extension of the first trimester abortions to twelve weeks and removal of the conscience clause. Others seek repeal of Article 317 of the penal code that still makes abortion, other than that permitted under the 1970s reforms, a crime. Most feminists want further liberalization and desensitizing of the issue but it has dropped far down on the public agenda. There is little serious opposition to the current laws. Laissez-les-vivre reappeared before the 1986 elections, sponsoring a showing of the American "right-to-life" film "The Silent Scream" to a meeting in Paris. But Chirac's preelection efforts to connect abortion laws to fears of depopulation fell flat, and for the present the abortion conflict has been resolved in France.

In the United States, where public health programs cover only the poor and the elderly, feminists have lost most battles over funding of abortions under Medicaid. A more serious conflict now rages over whether to retain legal abortion at all. By using picketing, boycotts, harassment, and violence the antiabortion groups have expanded the struggle to include the abortion clinics and individual patients and doctors. While courts continue to enforce *Roe v. Wade*, the political controversy rages on, surfacing from time to time in legislatures and election campaigns. French women have had executive leaders sympathetic to liberalization of abortion since 1974, while in the same period American women have heard from their president that life is unfair and abortion murder. President Reagan has repeatedly shown his support for "right-to-life" activists. American feminists, unable to get official support for a woman's right to choose, are in danger of losing control of the issue altogether as the campaign for the rights of the unborn gains momentum.

DEFINITION OF THE ISSUE OF REPRODUCTION

Reproduction had two levels of reality in the history of France. The public reality centered on maternity as a social duty, a responsibility to the fatherland. The private reality found women and men responding to economic and social pressures by cooperating to keep birth rates low. They often competed for control of fertility: Men used methods such as condoms and coitus interruptus, while women refused unwanted pregnancies with the help of the *faiseuses d'anges*. A woman took the greater risk to health and safety by submitting to illegal abortion or bearing and rearing an unwanted child.

Feminists charged that this hypocrisy enslaved women. Only the removal of all restrictions and the guarantee of public services for contraception and abortion could set them free. Reproductive rights issues united moderate and radical feminists. Although they might differ on the relation of sexuality to women's status, they agreed that the capability and resources to decide when to "give life" must be the prerogative of women, unfettered by official nationalist, pronatalist, or moral values.

Policy reforms have greatly reduced the contradiction between public and private realities. In the process of reform, the issue has undergone revisions and official definitions have shifted. With these shifts have come changes in the effectiveness of the policies, the distribution of benefits, and popular support. Only recently has the official stance on reproduction begun to incorporate feminist perspectives.

The first reform was passive, the decriminalization of contraception. In 1967 the Neuwirth law did little more than relieve the government's embarrassment over the blatantly ineffective 1920 law. By 1974, contraception earned a more positive value as a contribution to family and child health. That year abortion too was decriminalized. Administrative barriers and restrictions and the absence of financial assistance, however, made it an impossible choice for many women. The Ministry of Woman's Rights was responsible for a revision in the definition of these policies. As a result of the contraceptive information campaign, the extension of hospital services, and reimbursement of abortion the French reproductive policy provides the means for poor and less educated women to exercise reproductive choice. However, the idea of abortion as an extraordinary backup to failed contraception has remained an important part of the policy.

When reproductive policy was passive, it had limited reality for most women. Commitment to enforcement was weak and there were few government resources to give women access to contraceptives or abortions. As a result, clandestine abortion and traditional contraceptive practices persisted, with women and men still battling for control of fertility. Only the affluent and educated could make use of the law. Not until the feminist idea that reproduction was a woman's decision combined with the socialist goal of equal distribution did the control of fertility officially and effectively come into women's hands. At the same time, the persistence of the official belief that abortion is an extraordinary and undesirable backup to failed contraception for women in distress has kept intact the administrative barriers to abortion. Feminists both inside the government and out have not been able to dislodge this point of view.

The changes in French reproductive policy have benefited women most directly. They have seriously undermined any basis for clinging to the old notion that motherhood is a social duty that women must be forced to perform. Thus women are much less vulnerable than before to the hazards of unwanted pregnancy, criminal prosecution, or botched abortions. The Ministry of Woman's Rights' campaigns have extended these benefits to the poor and less educated as well as the middle and upper classes.

Most moderate and reform feminists recognize that the current policy is a compromise; it's all right for the present but needs further reform. Choisir has an abortion reform bill ready but it is not a priority for them at the moment. Radical feminists are much more dissatisfied with the way abortion is viewed. For them, reproductive choice is basic to sexual freedom—so important to women that the government must permit no barriers to its exercise. As long as abortion is considered to be extraordinary and only as a last resort for women in trouble, they will not be able to freely exercise their choice. Some doctors still refuse to perform abortions. The administrative hurdles remain, and the clock ticking toward the tenth week exerts control over all women.

Although the policy does not enjoy enthusiastic feminist support, the compromises it contains have defused social conflict on a very contentious issue. Since reimbursement began in 1983, the abortion question has not been in the public arena. "Right-to-life" activists are associated only with fringe groups of the Right. The Socialists were reluctant to disturb the arrangement to avoid giving any ammunition to their opponents.

Changes in policy change power relationships. Feminists flexed their muscles on abortion; they forced the government to act. With victory on this issue, the movement gained momentum to carry it through the decade. An important legacy was the creation of Choisir, a major feminist pressure group produced by the struggle over reproductive rights.

The conflict also helped launch the political career of their president, Gisèle Halimi, who was elected to the National Assembly in 1981 and became ambassador to UNESCO in 1985. But the heady experiences of the 1970s caused conflicts and divisions among feminists over goals and tactics. Many refused to take government feminists (the Secretary and the Minister for the Status of Women) seriously. The Ministry of Woman's Rights, representing itself as "institutionalized feminism," has, more recently, helped unify the moderates and Socialists in support of their policy of equal access to contraception and abortion.

This policy of equality changed administrative practice. After the 1967 and 1974 reforms doctors controlled access to contraception and abortion. They claimed sole power to prescribe contraceptives, closely guarded information about birth control, and could, on personal whim, refuse to perform abortions. This domination was equally strong in the private and public sectors. The MWR successfully challenged this monopoly. The contraceptive information campaign trained hundreds of counselors and health aides. Pressure on the Ministry of Health increased the number of hospitals performing abortions. Doctors still are the central actors in the delivery or obstruction of contraceptive and abortion services. At the same time, the MWR's actions have given women a greater role in controlling their reproduction.

The last twenty years have seen a major shift in French policies about reproduction. There has been a convergence of the public and private reality: the government now recognizes that private choice supersedes social duty. More remarkably, feminists have successfully won a share of the control over the conflict about natality. Women must still depend on the cooperation of doctors, but they have some active help from the government. For this, they can thank the Ministry of Woman's Rights.

NOTES

1. Rachel G. Fuchs, *Abandoned Children: Foundlings and Child Care in Nineteenth Century France* (Albany: SUNY Press, 1984), 277.

2. Angus McLaren, "Sex and Socialism: The Opposition of the French Left to Birth Control in the Nineteenth Century," *Journal of the History of Ideas* 27 (1976), 475–92.

3. Quoted by MFPF, *D'une révolte à une lutte* (Paris: Tierce, 1982), 6.

4. Madeleine Pelletier, "Feminism and the Family, the Right to Abor-

tion," trans., Marilyn J. Boxer, *The French-American Review* 6 (Spring 1982), 25.

5. Margaret Sanger, *An Autobiography* (New York: W. W. Norton, 1938; New York: Dover, 1971), 104.

6. Quoted in Angus McLaren, "Abortion in France: Women and the Regulation of Family Size 1800–1914," *French Historical Studies* 10 (Spring 1978), 478.

7. Odile Dhavernas, *Droits des femmes, pouvoir des hommes* (Paris: Seuil, 1978), 147.

8. *Griswold v. Connecticut*, 381 U.S. 479 (1965); *Eisenstadt v. Baird*, 405 U.S. 438 (1972).

9. MFPF, *D'une révolte*, 72–73.

10. Andrée Michel and Genevieve Texier, *La Condition de la française d'aujourd'hui*, 2 vols. (Paris: Gonthier, 1964), 2: 127–53.

11. *Orthogénie* is a neologism to designate all techniques to improve human reproduction.

12. MFPF, *D'une révolte*, 136. Statement by Ordre des Médecins in 1968.

13. Dr. Weill-Hallé recently received the Legion of Honor medal for her work in legalizing abortion.

14. Colin Dyer, *Population and Society in Twentieth Century France* (London: Hodder and Stoughton, 1978).

15. Benoîte Groult, *Les Trois quarts du temps* (Paris: Bernard Grasset, 1983); Gisèle Halimi, *The Right to Choose* (Brisbane: University of Queensland Press, 1973). These feminists give moving descriptions of the suffering.

16. One of their leaders, geneticist Jerome LeJeune, testified at the United States Senate hearings in 1981 on the Human Life Bill that would declare that human life begins at conception.

17. *Contraception et avortement, dix ans de débat dans la presse (1965–1974)* (Paris: CNRS, 1979).

18. Halimi, *The Right to Choose*, 69–70.

19. Dhavernas, *Droits des femmes*, 165.

20. Interview in "Avortement 1975–1985," *Le Monde Aujourd'hui* (10–11 février 1985).

21. *Journal Officiel*, Débats parlementaires (1974).

22. *Roe v. Wade*, 410 U.S. 113, 163. (1972). "For the period of pregnancy prior to this "compelling" point [end of first trimester], the attending physician, in consultation with his patient is free to determine, without regulation by the State, that, in his medical judgment, the patient's pregnancy could be terminated. If that decision is reached, the judgment may be effectuated by an abortion free of interference by the State."

23. Quoted by John Ardagh, *France in the 1980s* (Hammondworth: Penguin, 1982), 367.

24. *F Magazine* (février 1981).

25. Ministère des Droits de la femme, *Citoyennes à part entière* (janvier 1984).

26. Elise F. Jones et al., "Teenage Pregnancy in Developed Countries: Determinants and Policy Implications," *Family Planning Perspectives* 17 (March/April 1985), 53–63.

27. L'Agence femmes information, "Dossier sur l'avortement," (1981).

28. *Le Monde* (19 juin 1981).

29. Choisir, *Quel président pour les femmes?* (Paris: Gallimard, 1981), 112.

4

FAMILY

AN ESSENTIAL PART of feminism is the belief that the status of women in the family determines their status in all other areas of life. Subjection in marriage leads to subordination in work, politics, and social life. Ever since the Catholic church first used canon law to deprive French wives of power and property in the Middle Ages, outspoken women have resisted their bondage. Many were inspired to dream of their own liberty by others who challenged the social order. In the twelfth century Eleanor of Acquitaine "in deciding to change her life, to liberate herself from her husband, who was none other than the king of France, . . . changed the lives of many women."[1] Olympe de Gouges hoped the French Revolution would free women by sweeping society clear of traditional marriage: "the tomb of trust and love."[2] In its place would be a simple social contract between man and woman, with equal rights to children and property. Women inspired by utopians Saint–Simon and Fourier envisioned abolishing family structures to create a new society based on equality in love and child care. To Marxist feminists a classless society promised true freedom for women and men to form unions based on equality and affection. Bourgeois republican feminists put *droit civil*—"equal rights in marriage"—at the top of their reform agenda.

Traditional family law was much more restrictive in France than in the United States. French feminists can point to times, even times of modernization and progress in other areas, when male leaders deliberately used the family law to imprison women under male domination. They can make a fine case for the charge that men, not satisfied with biological limits alone, encased women in a childbearing role for the good of the state. Even moderate feminist demands for simple equality in marriage and divorce law confronted a complex ideology that linked family unity and stability to the stability and survival of the French state itself. The future of France, in other words, depended on the subservience of women to men. Thus no government would respond even to moderate demands for family law reform.

By the time laws were changed in the 1960s and 1970s feminist theories of the family had gone beyond simple legal equality. Moderate feminists had thought legal equality in marriage would relieve women of disabilities in their economic, social, and public life. Now they are skeptical of purely legal reforms in the absence of larger social change. Removal of most disabilities of married women in family law has left untouched the female monopoly on the domestic child-rearing role. Now feminists define family issues in terms larger than legal rules about marriage, divorce, children, and property. While many continue to look out for the economic interests of wives and mothers, they evaluate every government action in terms of its effect on the division of labor in the family. They find that the result of most policy is to elevate the female role of mother to an equal status with the male breadwinner.[3] True equality for women, however, depends on both sexes sharing the responsibilities of breadwinning and child rearing.

NAPOLEONIC CODE OF THE FAMILY

Any difference in French and American family law in the nineteenth century seemed insignificant to the women under their sway. Whether ruled by common-law coverture or the code of Napoleon, society offered women few alternatives to marriage and marriage destroyed all legal economic independence for women. The differences in the legal systems derived from the sources and justification of the law and affected their adaptability. Common-law rules were based on custom and tradition and, in the area of marriage, were partial. In the United States, for example, the law did not prescribe or enforce sex roles and responsibilities in ongoing marriages. Most of what was expected of a husband and wife was contained in the law of separation and divorce. The French code, on the other hand, was an instrument of social engineering. Freedom for the French woman was limited not only by individual laws giving her husband rights to her earnings and property and responsibility for her support and acts. Her status, unlike coverture, was also part of an ideal rational social order, based on abstract principles and carefully crafted into a code of law prescribing the proper behavior of men and women in the family. To change one stone in this social foundation was to bring the entire edifice crashing down.

Opinions differ as to the motive of the drafters of the Napoleonic Code of 1804. It is tempting to focus on the personal life of Bonaparte and read its various provisions as his revenge against uppity women. His enmity for Madame de Staël is well known, and his observation that "a tree which produces fruit is the property of the gardener" left little doubt as to his own views of women's rights. Nevertheless, lawyers, not Napoleon, wrote the code. They were responding to a larger constituency than the emperor's misogyny. The code appeared in the wake of the brutal repression of women's rights during the French Revolution and could be read as the product of bourgeois males determined to remove a threatening political class, women, from public life. While there is little doubt that the code had that effect, it was not a new set of laws. The family code was based on traditional ideals and customs dominant in France since the thirteenth century. What the drafters of the code did that was new was to establish a uniform, rational, and secular law of the family based on clear ideas of the ideal relation between the family, property, and the state. And what of *liberté, egalité, fraternité*? These applied only to the rights of bourgeois men to acquire wealth, status, and respectability.

Social order, property, and authority depended on the maintenance of the blood ties in the nuclear family. This family, not the citizen, was the basic unit of society. The husband/father was charged with the responsibility for preserving the family's interest and integrity. The rights and interests of all individual family members were subordinate to that of the family as a unit ruled by the husband as *chef de famille*. Article 213 provided: La femme doît obéissance à son mari. (The wife owes obedience to her husband.) All property belonged to the family, rather than to individuals. This community of property, including the earnings and possessions of all members, was controlled by the husband as *chef de la communauté*. The property had to be preserved and passed on to the closest blood relatives, ideally the children of the husband. To ensure the rights of these offspring, illegitimate children had no rights, and suits for paternity were prohibited. The penal code also meted out severe penalties for a woman whose behavior threatened the family's integrity: Her single act of adultery could bring three months to two years in prison. The husband was subject to a fine only if he went so far as to embarrass his wife by bringing his mistress into the home.

The code removed women from public life unless their husbands either permitted or required them to be involved. A wife needed her husband's permission to take a job (or he could force her to work); be a witness in a trial; obtain a passport; open a bank or savings account; enroll her child in school; or enroll herself for an examination. She had his nationality, domicile, and name. She owed him sexual and intellectual fidelity as well as her earnings. He made all decisions about property, so she had no right to obtain credit or to make contracts despite her nominal share in the community. In the interests of protecting the integrity of the family, he could open her correspondence and even ask the post office to deliver it directly to him. "In the case of adultery, the murder committed by a husband on his wife, as well as the accomplice, at the moment when he surprises them *en flagrant délit* in the conjugal home, is excusable."[4] There was little recourse or relief, especially after 1816 when divorce was abolished.[5] If the husband died or was incapacitated, the judge took his place in ruling the wife.

Along with this legal inequality of men and women came an ideology of domesticity to place them in separate spheres. After the restoration of the monarchy in 1816, the church was back in good graces of the bourgeoisie. The worthy Fathers extolled the home and woman's place in it, with her purity, fidelity, and passivity. They fabricated the role of motherhood from a biological fact into a religious and patriotic vocation. Wife/mother had the responsibility for the spiritual upbringing of the children, and the reinforcement of family system was enshrined in the code. Mothers were to educate the young in the glories of the bourgeois male-dominated French nation. Thus the "slaves" were formally charged with teaching the virtues of their slavery to the next generation of slaves and masters.

The specific provisions of the code and accompanying ideologies spelled complete subjection of women. To feminists, woman's legal status was "domesticated, raped, rented, exploited, executed when necessary, entirely subordinated, radically deprived of her own destiny."[6] In practice, the personal relations within each family left many women much more freedom and influence than a strict reading of the code would indicate. Women were not answerable to their husbands every day. The doctrine of "tacit consent" assumed that when the wife acted the husband had consented. What the policy did do effectively was severely handicap women for any public role and especially for any protest against the code itself.

Although feminists advocated repeal of the obedience clause as early as 1836, the campaign for family law reform did not get underway until after the establishment of the secular Third Republic. Reform feminists were most active between 1880 and 1914, and key to their program was *droit civil* for married women: divorce, control of property, equal penalties for adultery, suits for paternity. They did not challenge the underlying principles of the family and society but sought adjustments to remove the worst restrictions on women.

French feminists' demands were similar to those made by their American sisters, but reforms were much later in coming. The first American Married Women's Property Acts were passed in the 1830s and legal divorce dates from the eighteenth century. Advocates of women's rights in France faced formidable obstacles. The abstract code-law philosophies and principles resisted the sort of adjustment sometimes made quietly by courts in common-law countries. Cycles of revolution and repression in the nineteenth century stymied political action. Even after the Third Republic permitted democratic interest-group politics, feminists faced opposition from every segment of the male political spectrum. Their cause was "too bourgeois for the socialists, too revolutionary for the bourgeois; too serious for the Parisians and too Parisian for the provinces."[7] So when reforms did come they were late, nonfeminist, and left official views of the family and sex roles intact.

The first amendments to the code allowed married women to open savings accounts in 1881 and retirement accounts in 1886. This official recognition of woman's role as wage earner was intended more to increase the number of contributors to the welfare funds to the benefit of banks and savings institutions than to improve the status of wives. In 1907 married women got the right to manage their own earnings, which were called *biens réservés* (reserved property).[8] However, married woman's civil incapacity and obligatory obedience to her husband remained unchanged, greatly limiting the use of these earnings.

Divorce became legal in 1884. The official justification for permitting divorce was to save the legitimate family: Those who had already left their spouses and set up new households would be able to marry and make their children legitimate. These motives were common to other countries that reformed divorce laws in the nineteenth century—to put the law in line with behavior in order to preserve and protect the institution of the family. Divorce was defined as a safety valve for marriage. Different grounds for husband and wife retained the double standard of morality. A husband could sue for a single act of infidelity by his wife, whereas a wife had to prove that her husband's philandering had invaded the matrimonial home. Until 1897 when married women were permitted to testify in civil cases, a wife needed her husband's permission to appear in court in her own divorce trial.

Gradually the list of adjustments grew: full civil rights to wives who were legally separated (1891) and a law permitting suits for paternity (1912). After World War I laws permitted married women to join labor unions (1920) and to keep their own nationality (1927). All these reforms were extremely limited and contained many detailed and complicated qualifications. For example, the 1912 paternity law appeared to answer the demand by reform feminists to relieve unwed mothers of the entire burden of their children; in reality it was very restricted. Suits could be brought only against single men. The plaintiff had to prove that the pregnancy resulted from rape, abduction, or "notorious concubinage" (regular sexual relations known to the neighborhood); that the man was abusive; or that he had admitted the paternity. A woman seduced and abandoned had difficulty proving her case and opened herself up to a countersuit for blackmail.

Finally in 1938 parliament answered a century-old feminist desire and rewrote Article 213 of the code, removing the requirement of wifely obedience. In practice this meant that a married woman could enroll in school, open a bank account, sign checks, and apply for a passport. But it was demi-civil rights. The family unit retained its privileged position and as *chef de famille* the husband could make decisions that would veto a wife's own choices. He was in charge of the children—paternal authority was undisturbed. He remained head of the community and the domicile. He could still forbid his wife to work, go to school to prepare for a career, or travel abroad if, in his judgment, such actions might jeopardize the family's interest. The law also required her to use her earnings to support the family if necessary. In 1942 the law allowed women to take charge of their families in case their husbands were absent or incapacitated. It was ironic—this status, which women had not enjoyed since the Middle Ages, was restored by the authoritarian Vichy regime, not a democratic one.

All these reforms recognized the social and economic changes that had occurred during industrialization without disturbing the basic principles of the relationship between the family and society. Since 1900 women, including many married women, have made up at least one-third of the labor force. The authorities encouraged women to work as long as it was to help their families; they adjusted the law so that women could better accommodate job and family life and keep having babies (see chapters 3 and 6). Thus women retained their primary role as homemakers and rearers of children.

THE CODE REWRITTEN

Between 1965 and 1975 the Napoleonic family law was almost completely replaced. In a series of statutes passed under three different presidents, married women acquired more marital property rights and achieved equal authority with their husbands in the family. All legal distinction between legitimate and illegitimate children was removed. The state's power to regulate family formation and dissolution declined sharply. The intent of these dramatic reforms was to modernize the law, bringing it into line with changes in social values and behavior. Of secondary importance was the improvement of the status of women. This new family law code swept away nearly all the patriarchal refuse of the Napoleonic Era and replaced it with the principle of equality. But for many feminists it was too little, too late. For them, equality has little meaning without eradication of the sex role division of labor. Although husband and wife have equality in marriage, lawmakers still often assume that women fill the domestic maternal role, a role that has increased in status but that still reinforces sex discrimination in the culture, society, and politics.

That the content of the French reform is similar to those in other Western countries is no accident. A commission for reform of the entire civil code had been in place since 1945, studying laws in other countries and looking for ideas that could be adapted to the French situation. It did not succeed in rewriting the entire code, but it did propose the first reform in matrimonial property rights enacted in 1965. The bill was thirty years in the making. The contradiction between goals for equality and sharing in marriage—that is, the right to manage one's own property versus the concept of shared family assets—had defied resolution for decades. A prewar draft of a bill would have separated the spouses' property during marriage with equal division in divorce. It failed in the Chamber of Deputies in 1932, where opponents clung to the idea that marriage, a community of life, meant a community of property. To have shifting types of property was too confusing for all concerned.

After World War II, the conflict persisted: "Both within the Commission on the Reform of the Civil Code and in the French National Assembly were those who favored a system of deferred community and there were those who favored a more traditional community system."[9] Those supporting traditional community seemed unable or unwilling to reconcile demands for equality between husband and wife. Joint management seemed impossible, so they again fell back on the convenient solution of making the husband and the manager. Finally, a bill for comanagement of property was proposed in 1960, but women's groups objected because it would have eliminated the wife's reserved property.

The 1965 Act struck a compromise by reducing marital property to *la communauté réduite aux acquêts* (community of acquisitions) that would be divided equally at divorce, and by giving couples the option to choose, through a marriage contract, an alternate system of managing their property. The "community of acquisitions" regime, which is chosen by eighty-seven percent of married couples, excludes all assets not acquired during marriage by earnings from "gainful activity." The law deprived the husband of his assignment as *chef de la communauté* and separated the professional activities of both husband and wife from their subordination to the family unit. Practically, this means that a married woman can go to school and prepare for a career, take a job, and start a business and spend the profits without her husband's consent. Under the 1965 reform she retained her reserved property and managed it. The husband kept his responsibility to manage the community, which consisted of jointly owned property and his own earnings. He had to obtain the wife's consent for major transactions involving real property; the wife also had to get his consent for major transactions involving her reserved property.

The government left the husband his status as *chef de famille*; an attempt to change it was defeated. Perhaps it was compensation to the husband for losing the monopoly over the property. In any event it meant that the husband still determined the domicile and retained control over the children. The conflict between shared and equal assets was resolved with the balance tipped in favor of the husband: increased independence for the wife but not full legal equality. The law still gave de jure authority to the man. For most people who have little more than their own earnings, the community of acquisitions in the 1965 law is very similar in practice to "deferred community" and "equal division in divorce" in American states. During the marriage the spouses manage their separate property. On divorce, all assets are divided equally.

The support provisions in Article 214 were also revised in 1965. The original version from 1804 read: "The wife is obliged to live with the husband and follow him to whatever residence he deems appropriate; the husband is obliged to receive her and furnish her with the necessities of life according to his ability and station." Changes in 1938 and 1942 obligated the husband to support his wife but also the wife to pay for some expenses of the household from her reserved property. As a result of these reforms, the article began with the assertion that husband and wife must contribute to the expenses of the family "in proportion to their respective abilities." Then, in 1965, the wife was permitted to count her household work or participation in her husband's business as fulfilling her duties. This was welcomed by some women's groups as long overdue recognition of the economic value of their unpaid work in the home, farm, and shop. But to others it reinforced unequal and separate roles of women. First, this provision only applied to women, not to men. Second, it undermined the value of their work outside the home, reinforcing the idea of the woman's salary as *d'appoint* (incidental) to her primary work as homemaker and mother. This same conflict has surfaced in the United States in response to proposals to give an unemployed wife an interest in the salary and property of her husband based on her work as homemaker.

Patriarchy was dealt a lethal blow in 1970. Arguments in favor of retention of male power in the family that had successfully turned away efforts at repeal of male prerogatives even five years earlier sounded hollow and anachronistic. This was the harvest of May 1968 and the resurgence of the feminist movement. The idea of *chef de famille* was out of date even in the opinion of the nonfeminist Minister of Justice, René Pleven. He reported that women were equal to men as voters, in education, and that young husbands and wives were sharing responsibilities. "The Civil Code can fulfill an educational function by encouraging the spouses to exchange their points of view on all the important questions which arise in connection with the running of the household and the education of the children, as well as to come to agreement, before marriage, concerning a common ethic." [10]

Parental authority replaced paternal authority. Article 213: "Parents together assure the moral and material direction of the family. . . . During marriage, husband and wife exercise their authority in common." The law assumes that each parent acts with the agreement of the other. In 1970, for the first time, a mother could enroll her children in kindergarten or arrange for their medical treatment without getting the father's formal consent. By finally eliminating the hierarchy in the family, this reform was intended to modernize the law and recognize the political equality of women. In all these reforms, however, there is some bone thrown to the conservatives. In 1965 it was keeping the *chef de famille* status until 1970. This time it was allowing the husband to choose the domicile—until 1975, when the divorce law completed the overhaul of the family code.

In his campaign in 1974, Giscard promised a reform of the divorce law as part of his ambitious campaign to speed up modernization of the entire French code. The divorce issue had already been under study during the previous administration and the Minister of Justice had examined the reforms in other countries. Of special interest was the concept of marital breakdown that had become the heart of no-fault divorce laws in the United States, Canada, and Britain. The parties on the Left and many lawyers advocated breakdown, but surveys showed a majority of the public still wanted to keep fault grounds.

Breakdown, consent, and fault divorce all have roots in French history. The first divorce law in 1792, part of an all-out assault on the Catholic church, allowed divorce by consent and for incompatibility of temperament. Consent disappeared in 1804 and divorce itself in 1816. The Naquet law of 1884 brought in fault divorce, nineteenth-century style, for adultery, condemnation to infamous punishment, grave violation of marital duties, excesses, or cruelty and abuse. Fault-divorce laws everywhere soon became inadequate to meet the rising demand for divorce. After 1945 more and more French couples staged divorces, faked evidence, and committed perjury in the same sort of judicial comedy found in the United States and England. [11] The 1975 reform combined the traditions. Fault would remain, redrafted in modern language, and consent would be added. The new language also redefined fault: (1) acts that constitute a serious or repeated violation of marital duties, which are fidelity, assistance, support, and that render intolerable the continuation of conjugal life; or (2) when one spouse is sentenced to prison for a serious crime. By calling for divorce by consent, the French government rejected attempts to monitor marital breakdown and left the decision up to the couple. The French laws were more straightforward than American laws. Most state legislators refused to remove a formal role for the courts in permitting divorce. In practice, American separation and breakdown laws work almost exactly like divorce by consent.

A third way to end marriage provided for the situation in which one spouse wants a divorce but the other refuses and has committed no fault. The government proposed to allow unilateral divorce after long-term disruption of *la vie commune* (conjugal life). The only "disruptions" that will meet the standards of the law are legal separation for six years or severe mental illness for six years. This third type of divorce was very controversial; critics assumed it was for the benefit of middle-aged men grown tired of their frumpy wives. Just as some British women condemned no-fault divorce as a "Casanova's Charter," some French women labeled unilateral divorce "divorce by repudiation," evoking images of Eastern potentates banishing their wives from the harem at will. By contrast, in the United States, many divorce laws permitting unilateral divorce were in place before women expressed concern about their effects on economically dependent wives with little education.

The French government argued that unilateral divorce was necessary to "save marriage." They fell back on the traditional logic that has been used since the eighteenth century to convince conservatives to accept divorce reform.[12] "What can we do about human behavior?" the lawmakers plead. "Men and women find new loves and form new families. Old moral codes may condemn them, but prohibiting divorce won't change it. Allowing divorce will permit the legitimacy of the new unions. We must put legal and moral rules in line with social practice."

The reactions of women to the divorce reform bill illustrate the ambiguity in the relation of divorce to women's rights. Nineteenth-century reform feminists viewed fault divorce as an extension of women's rights because it gave women a means of freeing themselves from abusive husbands and marital property laws. Today, divorce by consent is compatible with feminist ideas of equality and choice in family relationships. By removing regulation by the state it undermines patriarchy and promotes individual freedom. The reaction of conservative women to unilateral divorce, however, shows that some still believe that divorce is something men do to women that drastically lowers their economic and social status.

In practice the divorce law fits the feminist logic. There is little interest in "divorce by repudiation." Only a little more than one percent of divorces are based on disruption of *la vie commune* (1,241 in 1984). About half are by mutual consent (50,529) and slightly fewer by fault (45,300). Women use the procedure more often than men. Sixty percent of the petitions are brought by only one spouse: three of four times it will be the wife (in 1984, 42,493 by women and 16,493 by men).

The government addressed all three types of divorce in the section of the new law pertaining to financial arrangements. If a couple opts for divorce by consent, they must also agree on financial matters and child custody before bringing their petition. For areas of contention, a new paragraph redrew the conditions and eligibility for *pensions alimentaire*, a term for both alimony and child support. Before 1975, alimony was linked to fault; only the plaintiff was due payment. Except in unilateral divorce, alimony has now been replaced by a *prestation compensatoire*. This compensation, preferably paid in lump-sum form, is awarded to a spouse to make up for economic dislocation suffered at the time of divorce. It can be denied to a guilty spouse. The court is to follow certain guidelines in making the award: property of spouses, age, state of health, professional qualification, availability of employment, and time dedicated to the raising of children. If a spouse needs any further assistance afterward she is expected to apply directly to the government, not her ex-husband. Alimony in the old-fashioned sense, a regular payment to an ex-wife until her death or remarriage, is now available only to the unwilling spouse in unilateral divorce—most likely the economically dependent wife. In that case the initiating spouse retains the same duty to support that existed during the marriage. Custody of children used to be awarded only to the innocent spouse. Now the law grants custody based on the best interests of the child. In practice, as in the United States, this means most of the children go to the mother (eighty-five percent in 1984) and the father is ordered to pay the *pension alimentaire*.

Largely through the efforts of Françoise Giroud, the Secretary for the Status of Women, the divorce law contains other provisions that put the next-to-last nail in the coffin carrying Napoleon's patriarchal code. Adultery has lost its status as a crime, and a husband who kills his wife for adultery is no longer excused. Also, husband and wife are equally responsible for choosing their respective domiciles. They may establish separate ones and still meet legal requirements of conjugal life. Husband and wife are also responsible for support of the household. "If the marriage contract does not regulate the contribution of the spouses to the expenses of the marriage, they are to contribute in proportion to their respective abilities." With these changes French family law moved ahead of the American in the direction of equality. Adultery is still nominally a crime in some states. Selecting the domicile and supporting the family, defined entirely in economic terms, remain the primary responsibility of the man.

Giroud and Giscard wanted complete equality in the statute; this meant eliminating the clause that counted the wife's contribution to the home as part of her support obligations. Getting rid of this clause, Giroud announced, would place equal value on the work of both spouses outside the home and undermine the conception of a wife's earnings as incidental to her main "job" as homemaker. Many feminists thought the change itself was incidental. A real move toward equality would have been to extend the provision to husbands. But this could not be expected of conservatives. "They had purely and simply to repeal lines two and three of Article 214; it was not conceivable to extend them to both sexes; can they imagine that a man could contribute to support of the family 'by his activity in the home or his collaboration in the profession of his spouse'?"[13]

Giroud was also interested in enforcing the child support law. The problem of recovery had been around for several years. In 1973 a law permitted a custodial parent to collect child support through the court from the employer or bank of the delinquent parent. Sixty percent of children still received less than the court ordered. Leftist parties suggested that a fund be established by the government to assure poor children adequate income. The government opposed this solution as too costly and believed it would encourage even more parental irresponsibility. Instead, Giroud produced a bill to authorize the tax collectors to collect child support. This law was enacted along with the divorce act in 1975. A mother (or father) who has exhausted private means of collection may apply to the Treasury for help. The underpayment continued, however, and poor single parents turned to government assistance programs. As in the United States, the French government has become increasingly involved in trying to make fathers support their families, a matter that becomes urgent as the number of female-headed families in poverty and on welfare rolls grows in both countries.

FAMILY POLICY

Family policy, as distinguished from laws regulating marriage and divorce, includes programs affecting the economic situation of families. This policy was part of the social legislation enacted after World War II. One program, Social Security, provides for health care and old-age pensions for workers and their families and is funded by contributions from employers and salaried employees. Economically dependent wives are classified as *ayant droit*: they are eligible for assistance only through their husbands. Another program involves state aid to complement wages and help families bear the costs of bringing up children.

From the beginning the lawmakers accepted the model of the single-earner nuclear family by which the husband worked and the wife stayed home and brought up the children. The government offered insurance to cover a man's dependents and paid him cash to help him support his children. Pronatalist motives drove policymakers. Not content simply with family allowances to improve general welfare, they developed crude schemes to encourage women to have more children. In case parents were tempted to stop with one, family allowances began only with the second child. Demographic data showed that the earlier the marriage and the younger the mother, the larger the family. Thus, prenatal and postnatal assistance was given to mothers who had their first child within two years of marriage and for every child born within three years of the last. Nonworking mothers had larger families. The government thus offered to pay a *salaire unique* to mothers who stayed home full-time and who had one child of French nationality under five. If this dissuaded women from returning to work after taking maternity leave for their first or second child, so much the better; it was highly probable they would have more children and never return.

At first the policies seemed successful as birth rates shot up. But the baby boom of the 1940s had more to do with the aftermath of the Occupation and recovery from the grim war years than with payments for babies. Rapid social change soon outdated the single-earner nuclear family. Despite government financial incentives to the contrary, thousands of married women joined the work force, increasing the number of two-earner, if not two-career, families. High divorce rate coincided with more single-parent families. Meanwhile the birth rate began to decline. By the 1960s polls showed fierce antinatalist attitudes in the population. Nevertheless, the government clung to its pronatalist logic. Some said the amount of money from the state was too little to keep women at home. Others blamed the low social status of motherhood. The frequency of reforms increased in the 1970s in response to the changes in reproductive rights. Government ministers promised pronatalists that more attention to families and children would compensate for the legalization of contraception and abortion. In the process, they began to appreciate the complexity of family issues and their relation to the changing status of women.

This new approach was evident in Giscard's campaign for the presidency in 1974. The focus of his policy was to be the entire family, not just women. Giscard said that women should not have to choose between the fulfillment of a family life and personal growth from a profession outside the home. Thus began the shift toward helping both men and women form families together. The authorities suggested that parents would be more likely to have children in an environment where the government helped improve the welfare of all children. Policies became more uniform and egalitarian with regard to parents. In 1977 an overall payment to lower income families replaced five restrictive allocations, including the *salaire unique*. Mothers as well as fathers could receive the basic family allowance, starting with the first child. In 1975 prenatal and postnatal payments became available to all mothers. The plight of single mothers (1970) and fathers (1975) was relieved with the orphan allocation, an extra allowance for widowed and abandoned parents. In 1977 an allotment reimbursed child care expenses for working parents. Unmarried heterosexual couples who live together also became eligible for assistance.

Family policy received even more attention when Pelletier became

Minister for the Status of Women and the Family. Pronatalism was prominent but in a modern form. The government had accepted legal contraception and abortion: no longer could the police be used to punish women for not having babies. Similarly the idea that women could be paid to have children seemed hopelessly outdated. The government began to concentrate on convincing couples to have a third child. Demographic studies showed that most people wanted one and at the most two children. But to keep the population growing the number of births per woman of childbearing age must pass 2.1 (it is currently 1.8). Psychological and economic barriers against that third child must be overcome.

In 1979, Pelletier, pointing out that she had seven children of her own, sponsored a three-day debate in the National Assembly. She presented the facts: women wanted to work outside the home; family planning was a private matter. The state could not regulate birth: therefore it must create a positive environment for families. She proposed special programs for mothers who had more than two children: priority in housing; extra family allowances (10,000 francs tax free); and compensation for their sacrifices in jobs and education. The state's new role would be to make it easier for women to have more children by helping them reconcile their jobs and family responsibilities, not by making them choose between them. The French government hopes that many women will want both and accommodate the demands that result without depopulating the country. Compare this attitude with American political rhetoric in the 1980s. According to what President Reagan told a group of women political activists in 1984, he still sees equality for women as the right to choose between a home and a career. There is little official recognition of the need to help women have both. Of course, the French government may not be that much more feminist than the American in this; rather, its acceptance of some aspects of role sharing stems from pronatalist, not feminist, motives.

Recently, the Mitterrand government enacted an extension of family allocations. Prenatal and postnatal payments have risen. Payments for child care leave have increased beginning with the third child. All parts of the political spectrum agree on the logic of family policy, all, that is, except the feminists. They argue that this policy is just a respectable version of the crude actions of the past that tried to populate the country by keeping women ignorant, dependent, and pregnant. The effect of the policy is to assign women, married or single, to child care responsibilities almost exclusively, widening the separation of sex roles. Feminists recognize the need to help women cope with work and family, but not by doling out inadequate allowances that push women further away from decent-paying jobs. They want child care facilities and shared responsibility by both parents. They want to force men to take child care leave as often as women. They want role change.

RECENT DEVELOPMENTS IN FAMILY LAW

Under Giscard, the government blanketly defined family as a woman's issue. If it concerned children, marriage, or divorce, they gave it to the Minister for the Status of Women. After 1981 that definition changed. Mitterrand separated the family portfolio from the women's ministry. Roudy did not refuse to handle family issues but they were not a high priority to her. What she did was put in place a strict test of relevance: To be of exclusive concern to women, a family issue must have an impact on women's rights and independence. For generations, family law and custom in France kept women dependent and in a separate sphere. The goal of family law and policy must be to further their independence, role sharing, and equality.

Upon becoming minister, Roudy found that most of the necessary reforms of the Napoleonic Code had already been made under the previous administrations. As she admitted, what remained was only some *toilettage* (grooming). Her main goal was to inform women of their rights through the many new centers of information for women. Roudy showed little interest in raising the status of homemaker. Increasing the birth rate had no place in her scheme. She did not even pay lip service to the joys of "bringing children into the world." Instead she made reference to the burdens on women of "producing" a third child and "submitting" to a fourth. She brought up family questions only when they interfered with job training, jeopardized a woman's right to work, or applied to women according to their marital status. "Married or not, mother or not, a woman is at first a person in her own right." To Roudy this meant that all benefits and rights should accrue to women as independent individuals and not be due to their derived status as wife or ex-wife. She insisted that husband and wife must have equal legal status and that the public policy impose no extra burdens or penalties to families in which both spouses are employed.

Although the laws only needed "adjustment," there were some difficulties to resolve. For example, all that was necessary to make husband and wife equal in family law was to establish the joint management of community property. Monique Pelletier had worked on that issue with the Minister of Justice and got a bill all the way through the Senate in 1980. The bill was stalled in the National Assembly in early 1981 and abandoned in the face of the presidential election in May. There was stiff objection from banks and other creditors reluctant to abandon the more simple system of having one manager (male) for family property. Roudy revised the Pelletier bill and finally found enough support to win approval from the Council of Ministers. This reform abolishes the idea of the wife as assistant manager of community property. Spouses may act autonomously with respect to the common property and retain control of their respective salaries. They are not liable for the other's personal debts and they will jointly manage any property of their children. Neither cohabitation nor fidelity is legally required in marriage. Under sponsorship of the Minister of Justice, parliament has hammered in the last nail in the coffin of the Napoleonic patriarchal family code.

An even more difficult issue has to do with taxation. Tax policy is based on a different set of values than social policy or civil law. What concerns tax collectors is revenue and the effectiveness of the laws in raising it. Taxing policy may have an effect on sex equality and legal status but it is rarely viewed that way. Reformers who change civil laws may overlook tax laws. In France in 1970 the civil code established a family of equal adults, with joint authority. However, the tax assessor still based income tax on the unit called a *foyer fiscal* (household). The male head of the nuclear family has continued to be responsible for all taxes due from family members. The feminists in the Giscard administration seemed to accept the explanation from the Minister of Finance that a change to separate taxation of husband and wife might reduce government revenues drastically. All the feminists recommended was that both spouses sign the tax return so at least the wife could find out how much the husband earned.

Roudy decided to confront the inequality in taxation as part of her effort to give married women their own rights and responsibilities as citizens equal to their husbands. Under the law, regardless of how much a married woman earned, she was not considered a taxpayer in her own right although she was equally liable for the taxes of the household. The effect was to undervalue the wife's work, thus lending support to the all-too-prevalent belief that women's jobs were secondary while the really important work was performed by the husband. When two salaries put the family in a higher tax bracket, the husband could always blame the "extra" income of the wife.

The Socialist government assigned a deputy, Ghislaine Toutain, to study the issue and work closely with the MWR in preparing a bill to remedy this inequity. The changes that resulted were largely symbolic: The tax office removed *chef de famille* from the declaration of income form and now requires signatures of both husband and wife. Despite the increased interest by the government, the Mitterrand feminists were not much more successful than their predecessors in changing the tax law. They failed to convince the Treasury to permit separate taxation of husband and wife.

The Ministry of Woman's Rights was not involved in most of the family policy activities of the Mitterrand government. Although family allowances have been increased, they continue to have a pronatalist goal and are not part of the woman's rights portfolio. There is one issue that combines elements of family law and policy that has involved the MWR: the collection of child support payments. The problem of nonpayment or partial payment seems to defy remedy. Nearly 850,000 children of divorce live with their mothers, 57 percent of them with a *mère isolé*, a single mother who usually has very low income. About 600,000 children are due support from their fathers. Less than half receive it.

These statistics convinced Yvette Roudy that the problem of delinquent child support aggravates the feminization of poverty in France. Thus she placed it higher than other family matters on her ministry's agenda. As we have seen, administrations have tried to improve collection by lending the services of the tax office to creditor-parents. An extensive report in 1980, however, showed that the law had no effect on the problem.[14] Enforcement is based on the self-motivation of the creditor-parent. She has to exhaust all remedies through the ponderous state judicial machinery before calling on the slow-moving tax office to bill the errant father. Success in this depends on the mother's knowledge, resources, and tenacity in pursuing the complaint. Many divorced mothers have little education or experience, low incomes, and young children. They are the members of society most in need of special help.

Before being elected in 1981, the Socialists and Communists had wanted a special fund; once in office the Left rejected this welfare-type solution as too costly. The MWR focused on helping women to use the rights available to them. Along with representatives of the family and justice agencies, it sponsored a pilot program in three cities in 1983 to inform women and help them use the existing laws. Based on this program, Roudy recommended using the family allocation system to help single parents care for their children until they received child support payments. A bill passed in late 1984 enlists the staff of the family allowance administration to inform creditor-parents of their rights and help collect the money owed them.

In France the issue of child support has been on the public agenda for several years. All political parties express concern about the plight of single-parent families. Since most of the creditors are low-income women, the government has defined the problem in terms of female poverty, that is, as a women's rights matter. In the United States, too, the government has offered its administrative machinery to track down and extract money from delinquent fathers. The difference is that the issue has rarely been defined in feminist terms, except by feminists. Instead, the American leaders purport to be solving the problem of excessive welfare expenditures. To reduce Aid to Families with Dependent Children costs, the government will help and often require mothers to collect delinquent child support.

Roudy's intention to guarantee women access to health care and pensions *à part entière* (in their own right), regardless of their marital status, yielded only one policy change after 1981. Artisans and small shopkeepers and their wives have traditionally worked side-by-side in family businesses. However, although independent businessmen can enroll in state-sponsored health insurance and pension funds for themselves, the wives had been covered only as their dependents. No recognition had been made of their very real contribution to success of the workshop or business. Rather, their labor had the same legal status as cooking and cleaning. Since a 1982 reform, wives of artisans and small shopkeepers can contribute to the fund in their own names with their husband's permission. Since they are usually without salary, they need to use their husbands' money as well. The reform also made the couple joint managers in their family enterprise, unless agreed to otherwise in a premarital contract.

Another area left unfinished is that of name. A law passed during the French Revolution (6 Fructidor an II) and still in effect guarantees that all citizens, male or female, carry their birth names through life. Unlike in the United States, French public documents identify women primarily by their birth names. There are no legal obstacles to a married woman who chooses not to use her husband's name since the code does not require it. However, as in common-law countries, most women have assumed their husband's name through force of custom. The tradition has been so strong and family name so important in the patriarchal culture that the woman's use of her husband's surname was seen as a privilege she gained through marriage. If divorced she lost that right and had to use her birth name. The divorce reform in 1975 permits only the wife rejected by her husband through unilateral divorce to keep his name (this caused some controversy because of the fear that a vindictive wife might disgrace her ex-husband's family).

The code law required that the children take their father's name. Several feminist groups, however, have wanted more flexibility in the assignment of surnames to children. In practice more and more couples combine their names and enroll their children in school under the new names. Finally, in December 1985, a Socialist deputy successfully amended the bill for joint management of community property to permit a child to use the names of both parents, or just the father's. The mother still does not have the legal right to pass only her name to her children.

DEFINITION OF FAMILY LAW AND POLICY

It seems almost too tame to call the changes in family law between 1965 and 1975 *reforms*. The French statutes were stunning revisions bearing little resemblance to the incremental decisions that dismantled coverture in the United States. French politics had rendered few changes between 1804 and 1965, and these had done little to dislodge the many disabilities of married women. Then, in one decade, married women regained legal rights they had not enjoyed for 700 years. The changes in the logic underlying the code were even more dramatic. When adopted in 1804 the family law was the triumph of bourgeois social engineering. When finally rewritten, the code had to respond to society, not design it. It now must fit the behavior of women and men who work, learn, and make decisions as equal human beings. The result—a modernized family law code—changed the place of the family in relation to the state. Before, the male-dominated nuclear family was the stronghold of the nation's authority and property. Today, the government accepts a variety of family forms and permits more open, egalitarian relationships between men and women.

Although the result was a drastic improvement in women's legal rights, the changes were not intended to achieve feminist goals. Feminist groups were not very active in promoting the reforms and many found them anticlimactic. Women could vote and were in the labor force; removal of marriage disabilities was long overdue. The government only acted as part of an overall modernization of the code and brought the law in line with changes in the position of women that had already taken place. Only in 1975 did the Secretary for the Status of Women inject a feminist note by helping to put finishing touches on some egalitarian measures.

There remains a tension, maybe even a conflict, in the logic of French family law and policy. The law is based on equality and permits sharing of roles by men and women while the state, through its social policy, assumes or assigns separate roles and responsibilities in the family—the traditional ones. This is most evident in the parental role. The family policy is intended for a society in which women are responsible for bringing up children and men for supporting them. Its goal is to relieve some of those burdens. At first, family allowances were paid to men because it was the husband's income that supported the family. Then, the *salaire unique* aimed to keep women at home caring for small children. Later, there was an effort to overcome inequalities inherent in the division of labor by trying to raise the economic and social status of motherhood and women's work in the home.

As long as the state showed an interest in helping families and defined family policy as a woman's issue, however, the official view persisted that no matter what else they do, women raise children and men support them. The inevitable consequence of this logic was to reinforce the economic dependency of women. The tension between goals of role sharing and role separation became acute during the discussion of divorce reform. Women simply needed protection because equal marriage and divorce laws rendered them vulnerable. When the law made unilateral divorce possible, the state had to step in with special provisions to guarantee women economic support. Now, more and more women are raising children by themselves. The state has tried to compensate with a wide range of assistance programs to make women self-supporting and help them collect child support payments.

But, at the same time, by not questioning the separation of sex roles, the work of all women outside the home has been undervalued. In turn this led to great disadvantages in employment opportunity.

The increased role of the state in family assistance in France underscores the rather unusual alliance between pronatalists and reform feminists. Any statute that is defined as helping women could also be defined as helping women have more children. For example, feminists sought legal divorce in 1884 as a means of freeing women from abusive husbands. That reform was also preceded by arguments that divorce would allow couples who truly loved each other to marry, and such couples would be more likely to have children. Feminists demanded paternity suits to force men to share responsibility for their children. Pronatalists thought such suits would also make it easier for single women to have children. Feminists and pronatalists both supported programs of maternal and child health and family allowances. In evaluating policy proposals, feminists wanted to help women with real-life burdens of motherhood while pronatalists counted the babies.

There has always been a theme in women's politics that eschewed utopian or radical theories and concentrated on the problems of motherhood, especially among the poor. Today Center Right feminist Monique Pelletier offers what she calls "calm" feminism. It is pronatalist, not by expanding state regulations regarding childbirth, but by making the environment welcoming to children. At the same time Pelletier is a strong advocate of equality in the work force and in the family. She often finds herself at odds with others who demand role change. Yvette Roudy argues that Pelletier's approach risks reinforcing dependency and inequality without appreciably lifting the burden on women.

The Mitterrand government changed the way family law, social policy, pronatalism, and feminism relate to each other. There were not many additions or revisions in the policy or law code. What changed was the definition of the issues. First of all, pronatalism and family policy were separated from women's rights. Roudy did not talk about the family as a woman's issue or about improving the environment for having children. For her, children are the concern of the family, that is, of both men and women. Georgina Dufoix, the Minister of Social Affairs, launched a campaign for helping families have more children by "taking account of the child by society, of thinking of children in all acts of daily life and permitting parents to be accompanied by their children everywhere.'' She did not discuss the problems of women alone having to manage motherhood and careers.[15] To the Mitterrand feminists, family issues are general social issues. Family law pertains to women only to the extent it affects them differently than men in terms of inequalities in marriage, divorce, and taxes, and to the extent that policy reinforces economic dependency and undervalues women's work. Role separation and role inequality in the family must both be eliminated before women can enjoy equal opportunity in politics, society, and the economy. This view of family law and policy coincided with a shift toward a leadership role for the government in promoting a goal, women's rights, rather than responding to social change and pronatalism.

NOTES

1. Michèle Sarde, *Regard sur les françaises* (Paris: Stock, 1983), 249.

2. Olympe de Gouges, ''The Declaration of the Rights of Woman,'' reprinted in Darlene Gay Levy, Harriet Branson Applewhite, and Mary Durham Johnson, eds. *Women in Revolutionary Paris, 1789–1795* (Urbana: University of Illinois Press, 1979), 87–96.

3. Odile Dhavernas, *Droits des femmes, pouvoir des hommes* (Paris: Seuil, 1978).

4. Article 324, *Code pénal* (1810).

5. This was the only part of the Napoleonic Code of the family to change when the monarchy was restored.

6. Dhavernas, *Droits des femmes*, 42.

7. Maïtâé Albister and Daniel Armogathe, *Histoire du féminisme français, du moyen age à nos jours* (Paris: Des Femmes, 1977), 372. Quote attributed to Marguerite Durand when her paper *La Fronde* went out of business in the early 1900s.

8. A wife's special reserved property was similar in function to a married woman's separate property created by many of the Married Women's Property Acts in America and England. See Dorothy M. Stetson, *A Woman's Issue: The Politics of Family Law Reform in England* (Westport, CT: Greenwood Press, 1982).

9. Mary Ann Glendon, *State, Law, and Family* (Amsterdam, New York, and Oxford: North Holland Publishing Company, 1977), 144.

10. Quoted in ibid., 118.

11. Max Rheinstein, *Marriage Stability, Divorce and the Law* (Chicago: University of Chicago Press, 1972).

12. The 1792 law was the exception; enacted during the Revolution, it was intended to increase individual liberty and natural rights.

13. Dhavernas, *Droits des femmes*, 115.

14. By Colette Même, conseiller d'Etat, 1980.

15. *Le Monde* (24 mai 1985). ''Le Gouvernement lance une campagne pour l'accueil des enfants.''

5

EDUCATION

To FEMINISTS, public education has been both a good and a bad. As a good, the right to education enabled women to read, write, and understand their world. "To express oneself, is power."[1] To read, write, and understand are political rights, tools whereby women can fight oppression, make demands, change lives. Feminists also demand education as an economic right, a means of improving women's lives materially. Proper guidance and job training can prepare women for well-paid jobs either as first-time workers or when returning to work after raising a family. Only coeducational schools and curricula will satisfy feminist demands for equal opportunity: women must have access to the same knowledge and training that men have through completely integrated (*mixte*) schools and classes.

Equal access alone is not enough; feminists also want to change the bad aspects of the system that perpetuate the subordination and marginality of women. "We live in the illusion of equality as it concerns the education of children, boys and girls. . . . Education is not neutral, it is sexist as much in the family as in the school."[2] The inferiority of women, their economic, cultural, and political inequality, is due not to biology but to the way they are taught. As Simone de Beauvoir put it, "One is not born, but rather becomes, a woman." The schools reinforce the patriarchal system by transmitting sex role stereotypes to each new generation. Despite the decline of separate schools, education has failed to give girls the means to achieve much beyond their traditional roles. Feminists demand that all attitudes and practices that perpetuate separate education tracks for boys and girls be eliminated. To do that involves a full-scale remodeling of the program of public instruction from the selection of textbooks to the training of teachers.

The problem is that sexism runs much deeper than state-prescribed curricula and texts. To feminists, knowledge itself is sexist. Scholarly neglect of women has deprived each new generation of girls of any vision of themselves in the world: "It is only since women have begun to feel themselves at home on the earth that we have seen a Rosa Luxembourg, a Madame Curie appear. They brilliantly demonstrate that it is not the inferiority of women that has caused their historical insignificance; it is rather their historical insignificance that has doomed them to inferiority."[3] Stereotypes will not disappear from the school system in the absence of more research on women by scholars with feminist rather than patriarchal biases. Real education rights for women will not be possible until this new knowledge replaces the old. "Feminist research and research on women cannot constitute a separate domain reserved to a few specialists. Its existence, its vitality, its expansion are intimately tied to the collective battles of women: the struggle for legal and civic equality, for the control of their fertility and their bodies, the struggle for participation and representation in political and syndical organizations, the battle for the right to education and for equality of rights at work."[4] Thus, as feminists define the issue, improving women's status through education means expanding women's studies in the universities, supporting feminist research, and finding creative opportunities for female scholars and artists.

EXPANSION OF WOMEN'S EDUCATION

The nineteenth century began with the elimination of all public education for women; it ended with a state education system that offered girls the chance to study from primary school through university. Despite the political turmoil and changes of government that characterized the 1800s, educational opportunities were gradually extended to both females and males. Monarchies, empires, and republics alike dealt with education reforms for both sexes. What remained unchanged throughout the period, however, were several unshakable themes. First, education for girls was almost completely separate from education for boys: separate schools, different curricula, and distinct goals. There was an obsession with the moral danger arising from any mixing of the sexes. An early objective of primary school was to stamp out the base instincts of the pupils. The first primary school regulations under the restored monarchy in 1816 were clear: "boys and girls can never be united to receive instruction because of propriety and morality."[5] An edict in 1861 required communes that could only afford one school to erect a barrier in the classroom to separate the sexes completely.

Second, education was to suit pupils to their proper social roles and serve state needs. Since the roles of men and women were absolutely divided, so their education must be different. For a girl it meant preparation for her role in the family as homemaker, as companion to her husband, and as educator of her children. During the nineteenth century that role became more important to the state; thus the government paid more attention to the education of girls to fill it.

Finally, education was not extended to females to improve their opportunities in society beyond finding a proper husband. There was only the weakest link to preparation for any paid occupation outside the home, despite the increase in the number of women in the work force during the period. The opposite was the case for males; education had to prepare them to be workers and leaders of society. The purpose of women's education was to prepare them to be the wives and mothers of those workers and bourgeoisie.

Before the French Revolution formal education of women had always lagged behind that of men. Yet demands for improvement were long-standing. Periodic treatises on the woman question had linked woman's status to the sort of education she received rather than her nature. In the 1400s Christine de Pisan made an eloquent case through her life and her poetry for instructing women. Two hundred years later the great feminist Poulain de la Barre devoted an entire book to the proposition that women were not inherently inferior; in fact, they were really not much different from men.[6] Their brains, spirits, and minds were human: "L'esprit n'a point de Sexe" (The mind has no sex).[7] Poulain even discounted biological differences, contending that the sexes were equivalent in the sense that their bodies were equally adapted to reproductive functions. Sex differences, he argued, were due to differences in education. "Whatever temperament women have, they are not less capable than we of truth (vérité) and study. And if we find at present some fault in them, or even that all do not see things as seriously as men do . . . it must be blamed on factors exterior to their sex and on the education that we give them."[8] He went on to describe

what men taught women: timidity, avarice, credulity, prattling, super-
stition, inconstancy, and artifice . . . when they are capable of learning math, physics, medicine, logic, and astronomy.

Some of the Enlightenment *philosophes*, who dealt with ideas of
individualism and reason, even thought women capable of reason. In
the 1780s Condorcet offered proposals to extend education to both
girls and boys. Up to that point in French history, what education was
allowed for either sex was for the upper class, either in the family
with tutors or at religious schools. The French Revolution introduced
the idea of state schools—free public education. A law in 1791 required a state primary school for every 1,000 inhabitants. The law was
never enforced and it was formally repealed in 1802.

Instead, Napoleon installed the beginning of a nationwide state school
system for boys only, dispatching girls to whatever the Catholic church
offered in the way of instruction. A few brave souls protested the
reconstruction of the barrier to knowledge that kept women walled in
by ignorance: "Why speak so much of the beauty [of women] and neglect the qualities of the soul? Are they not saying that women are classified among these domestic animals which are used only for the advantages of their bodies and some pleasures, results of instinct . . . ?"[9]
The emperor argued that a woman didn't need any formal education
outside the church. The priests and nuns were perfectly able to provide
the moral direction needed to be a wife and mother.

Thus began, in concrete terms, the reaction to the upheavals of the
French Revolution and the return of virtues of family, home, and religion as expressed through the separation of the sexes. During the
Restoration (1816–1830) the state remained content with religious
schools. When in 1833 the *loi* Guizot established public primary schools
for boys, girls who were able to go to school at all remained the
charges of the priests and nuns. A few women were able to escape
their state-approved destiny and become writers. They moved in intellectual circles where they learned about the utopian ideologies of Saint-
Simon, Fourier, and Enfantin. They complained about the notoriously
bad education in religious schools. There was some reading and cal-
culation, but the emphasis even in secondary school was on religious
instruction and moral training. Most schools were more interested in
retaining students and saving money than imparting knowledge.
Teachers, products of these same schools, often knew little more than
the students. During periods of social upheaval, such as in 1830 and

1848, feminists joined others in agitating for change. Their first demand was for equal education. Finally, in 1850, the *loi* Falloux established the girls' primary school, the *école des filles*. In 1867, Victor Duruy increased the number of girls' schools to one per commune of 500 inhabitants or more, making primary education available to all.

From the first, the state viewed its new schools as instruments for molding the culture to suit government needs. In 1833 *loi* Guizot, for example, brought moral and religious teaching to the public school. The policy was to instill in young French people traditional ideals of family, church, and obedience and make them less susceptible to revolutionary ideas and organizations. The establishment of the *école des filles* was perfectly consistent with that goal. If anyone needed a moral and religious education, it was a future mother. The purpose of public education for a girl was to prepare her for her role. In expanding the number of *écoles des filles*, Duruy argued that learning would increase the value of motherhood: "She will be consulted, she will be treated like an equal. Her authority will grow and will be more assured; her ennobled position will become what it should be, and her children will respect her more." [10]

The leaders of the Third Republic continued the pattern of direct socialization and took charge of women's education. The result was a dramatic improvement of the entire state education system, benefiting girls as well as boys. In 1880 Camille Sée's law created state *lycées* for girls, and, a year later, the *loi* Ferry made primary education free, mandatory, and secular for all children aged six to thirteen. There was no feminist intent behind this policy. Rather, republicans saw the church as the enemy of democracy. Their goal was a political culture devoid of religious influence, unified and congruent with democracy. Although women would not be voters in the new republic, it was extremely important that they receive a secular education to complement that of men. They would educate the young and also could affect the ways their husbands voted. An indirect way of weakening the political influence of the church was to limit the power the priests held over women. To do that meant changing the education of future mothers. Girls must not be left in the clutches of the nuns and priests while the boys moved on to modern lay education. Duruy said, "Woman will belong either to science or to the church." [11] She must be won from mysticism to science.

The fathers of the Third Republic, however, did agree with their predecessors about one thing: Social unity depended on segregation of the sexes. Different lives demanded different preparation. Boys who would be workers and voters would not study the same subjects as future homemakers and mothers. As they said in the Senate in 1880: "It is not a question of giving them [women] all the knowledge they are capable of acquiring; it is necessary to choose what can be most useful to them, to insist on what best fits their nature of mind and their future status as mothers, and to give them certain studies for the work and occupations of their sex." [12]

A study by Linda Clark of sex role socialization in primary education in the Third Republic shows the diligence with which the Ministry of Education sought to carry out education for separate roles. [13] Little boys and girls in public school, mostly from working-class families, received moral instruction and prepared for lives of work. Vocational education was segregated—boys sent to work with "wood and iron" in traditional shop courses—and girls to sewing classes where what they learned suited their primary vocation in the family. (A fine sewing hand was particularly useful because it could bring paid work a wife could do at home, always preferable to deserting the hearth and going out to work.) By educating mothers, the state was also preparing teachers because every mother was *éducatrice* for her children and her husband. As the moral force she would teach men social virtues of peace, patience, and respect, especially respect for the law and love of the *patrie*. By keeping a clean and comfortable home she might dissuade her husband from drink and misbehavior. Investment in the education of girls was truly an investment in social harmony.

The obsession with segregation continued well into the Third Republic. The problem of providing two separate schools in small rural communities had, before 1870, led to the decree requiring the erection of barriers in classrooms. Jules Ferry abolished the barriers and tried to resolve the problem by building more schools. Despite such efforts, *mixité* (coeducation) in primary education persisted in some of the small villages and towns. But in the cities and in the *lycées* there was a carefully preserved two-track education system.

Sex segregation meant segregated curricula and teaching staffs. Even science had a sex: physics and biology for boys and domestic and applied science for girls. Since secondary education was for educating the wives and mothers of the bourgeoisie, the girls' *lycée* did not award the *baccalauréat*, or "bac," the coveted prize of secondary education in France, but a less worthy diploma. When universities began enrolling women during the last decades of the nineteenth century, the separate *lycée* curriculum made it difficult for many to qualify. Latin was required for admission and Latin was not taught in the girls' *lycée*. No wonder Marie Sklodowska (later Curie) from Poland found herself the only woman in her classes at the Sorbonne in the 1880s. In 1900, 621 French women were enrolled in university, although many failed to complete the course. Not until 1912–13 did French women outnumber foreign women in French universities.

Separation of the pupils meant separation of the faculty as well as courses. The state established normal schools or courses in each department to train *institutrices* (female primary school teachers). This gave some women a chance to enter a profession that would no doubt have been closed if schools had been coeducational from the start. To educate instructors for the girls' *lycée* meant advanced postsecondary education for women and the establishment of the Ecole Nationale de Sèvres in 1881. The *agrégation* in letters and science was opened to women in 1884.

Apart from this exception, which bears a striking resemblance to the long practice of the Catholic church of allowing women into segregated religious orders as teachers and nurses, sex segregation meant retardation of women's opportunity for education. Table 4 compares the dates of milestones in progress toward public education for males and females in France.

In 1830, fifty percent of the boys could sign their names, while only thirty-three percent of the girls could do so. In 1875, 6,000 boys per

Table 4
Educational Progress, by Sex

Milestone	Males	Females
1st state lycée	1802	1881
State primary school system	1833	1850, 1867
2 million in school	1830	1870
agrégation	1821	1884

year were receiving the *bac*. Even forty-five years later only 1,000 girls per year were reaching the same goal. "Having constituted a brake on the scholarization of girls, this segregation has contributed to maintaining woman in an inferior situation, confining her to household tasks and making her a servant of her husband." [14]

Throughout the Third Republic, feminists demanded coeducation in schools and more vocational training for girls. Several of the feminist congresses passed resolutions for *mixité* at all levels of education. [15] After World War I feminists allied with education reform groups and won a law (1924) making curricula at boys' and girls' *lycées* essentially the same. The most significant result was the addition of Latin and Greek to the girls' program, better preparing them for university entrance exams. At the same time, the alternative of a special girls' diploma remained for those who wanted "to develop the habits which a woman must employ in her home." [16]

Despite these reforms, the state, if anything, increased its emphasis on separate sex role socialization that had so long characterized the public schools. Added to the familiar themes of morals, home, and fatherland were the fruits of the radical pronatalism of the 1920s and 1930s. School texts admonished girls that their first duty as adults would be to bear children. "Work outside the home was labeled as undesirable because it led to child neglect, bad housekeeping, the flight of husbands to cafes, and the overtiring of women who combined outside employment with housework." [17] So thoroughly had the traditional message permeated the textbooks that the Vichy administrators had only to bring back the church; otherwise *kirche, kinde*, and *küchen* were complete. [18]

The subsequent decades saw the gradual mixing of the schools, but separate teaching staffs, *agrégations*, and single-sex state schools survived into the 1970s. As in most countries, letting down the barriers was a matter of evolution rather than conscious policy in pursuit of principle. "The rule of integration progressively extended to public instruction was the concrete expression of official recognition of equality of the sexes in secondary school." [19] Girls gained equal opportunity in education as a consequence of a series of reforms begun by the fathers of the Fifth Republic that is still under way. In 1959 the school-leaving age, which had been fourteen since 1936, was raised to sixteen. New postprimary schools were required. In 1963 a reform established a new middle school curriculum and the CES diploma. [20] These schools were fully coeducational and gave added push to the general mixing of the sexes in the secondary schools. Integration of the *lycées* occurred gradually, the most prestigious Paris schools being the last to accept girls on equal terms with boys. Although women could join in the competition before male juries for the *agrégation*, separate degrees continued until 1975. Finally, single-sex schools were phased out at the primary levels. "The imperatives of the economy, together with those of pedagogy, made attitudes change in this area. Liberalization of morals did the rest and the primary school, the last bastion of separation of the sexes at school, passed in the last fifteen years, without a shot fired, to the area of coeducation."[21] One thing is clear: Final removal of sex discrimination in admission in public schools in France was not a prize won by feminists. It was a response to the extension of the vote in 1946, the gradual expansion of education, and the demands of modernization.

There are many parallels between France and the United States in the pioneering efforts toward women's education. In both countries girls first received learning in church schools. When the public got involved, education was still expected to suit females to their special roles as wives and mothers. Secondary education, although slow to develop, was thought necessary to make girls even better companions to their husbands and rearers of the young. Expansion of education meant professional opportunities in both countries for women to become teachers. Otherwise, special courses in "domestic science" were the most vocational training girls could expect.

There were some differences due in part to the cultural and political environments. Religious education has remained a political issue for a longer time in France. The school system, like the state, is more centralized; it is more responsive to national ideas about the uses of education and the conflicts regarding clericalism and republicanism. In the United States, the many state-level public school systems have produced more variation. Opposition to the mixing of the sexes in primary and secondary school was not as strong, nor were there such direct efforts as the French used to maintain separate sex-specific curricula. Elementary skills of reading, arithmetic, and morality were considered useful to both sexes, even in their separate roles. With math, language, and science, more women would learn mental discipline and live happier and more fulfilling lives as wives and mothers.

The critical teacher shortage in the United States toward the end of the nineteenth century was met by opening special normal schools to train women as elementary teachers. Primary school faculty became and have remained nearly entirely female in both the United States and France. Since most American high schools were coeducational, however, there was no special need to provide women teachers; men were predominant in the secondary school teaching posts. While the American girl had less trouble than her French counterpart in attending integrated schools, she was also less successful in getting into the best colleges and universities. Postsecondary education in the United States was segregated in many public as well as private schools. Female colleges gave women their only opportunity to become professors, deans, and administrators. Nevertheless, in both France and the United States, both the expectation and the reality were that most girls would stop formal education early and work or play until they married.

CONTEMPORARY ISSUES AND PROGRAMS

Education policy appears to be the object of constant study and reform in France. The Ministry of National Education has the resources, traditions, and bureaucracy to claim a monopoly over the initiation of change. After World War II the ministry's goal was to make the school system more egalitarian and relevant to the needs of the expanding economy. The state education system, which had been a vast but tightly controlled hierarchy, has become more diverse and decentralized. Tremendous growth has occurred in secondary, vocational, and higher education. Whereas at one time all had agreed that the great mission of the education system was to transmit French culture and republicanism to future generations, since the war there has been frequent disagreement on the content and purpose of instruction.

Despite large increases in the number of girls (they now outnumber boys in the *lycées*), feminists charge that the education system continues to perpetuate patriarchy and sex discrimination. All the expansion, innovation, and integration has not dislodged the belief that education serves a different purpose for girls; it prepares them to be wives and mothers and assume occupations "appropriate" to their sex. The feminists' problem is to convince the huge Ministry of Education to take steps to provide real equality and cease perpetuating sexist stereotypes and images of women. Until the establishment of the Ministry of Woman's Rights, little was accomplished, however.

Mixité (coeducation) alone does not guarantee equality of education for women. In both France and the United States, the mechanisms of tracking, through counseling, curriculum, and stereotyping, assure that girls have a more limited choice of alternatives than boys. All policies that attempt to expand and improve the quality of education without destroying the tracking mechanisms will be of little benefit to females. For example, in France, educational reforms in the late 1960s and early 1970s focused more attention on *orientation*, or preparation, of young people for jobs. During the three or four years after primary school, school officials guide students into vocational schools where they may earn a variety of certificates and diplomas in skills, trades, and occupations. In the middle school curricula, among teachers, counselors, and students, there is the widely held view that jobs have a sex. There are female jobs and male jobs. Vocational centers label 390 skills for males, 171 for females. In state-run job training programs girls are offered a choice of only 30 occupations while boys select among over 300. Not only are there fewer choices for girls but the female skills are low-paid and in little demand. Feminists maintain that vocational education in school prepares girls only for unemployment. They are not encouraged to plan for a working life, although a majority will be in the work force. Rather, they seek an appropriate "female" occupation that will occupy them only for a few years or on a part-time basis. Girls are counseled to prepare for dead-end jobs as garment and textile workers, as secretaries and hairdressers. Parents do little to challenge these biases. A recent survey of parents showed that many thought their daughters should have a vocation to "fall back on" in case they are forced through some emergency to support their children. And the images they had of such handy occupations were the stereotyped professions of teacher, secretary, stewardess, receptionist, nurse, midwife, beautician.

Tracking also affects students preparing for higher education and advanced technical training. The *bac* curriculum has become flexible (some would say watered down). Students are able to specialize and earn a variety of different *bacs* in literature, social science, technologies, math/physics, or natural sciences. The most highly prized are in science, math, and technical fields. With them, students can compete for entry to the prestigious *Grandes Ecoles* whose graduates compose the elite of business, industry, and government. Math has replaced Latin as the key to success. But girls overwhelmingly major in literary and social science fields. Few study math; few can quality for top degrees. In 1984, thirty-seven percent of students graduating in the math/physics curriculum were female. Over half of them did not go on to jobs or advanced degrees in the science field. Females make up only twenty-four percent of the preparatory classes for the *Grandes Ecoles* and only ten percent of their student body.

Thus, although the expansion of universities has greatly increased the number of women in higher education, the tracking system prevents them from being able to share equally in the benefits. More girls earn the *bac* than boys, but they are prepared for less prestigious jobs. Feminists agree that immense sex biases throughout secondary and higher education must be overcome, not the least of which is the limited vision the girls have about their own lives. A major source of the problem of tracking and inequality is the attitudes and beliefs of the students about sex roles reinforced by what they learn in the classroom. Feminists are united in demanding that sexism be eliminated from the content of education. Since 1970, groups have urged the purging of stereotyped images of females and males from textbooks and class materials, especially those used by impressionable primary pupils.

Images of males and females presented to French schoolchildren are similar to those traditionally facing their American counterparts. Father reads, goes to work, and pursues an active life. Mother and her daughters quietly sew, iron, and watch the boys play. Women in work roles are laundresses, dressmakers, nurses, and secretaries. Women are not portrayed as firefighters, astronauts, intellectuals, or doctors. Female farmers are always throwing grain to chickens, never driving tractors as they do in real life. In sum, the texts keep to a social configuration dating back to the nineteenth century in which marriage is presented as the only choice for a girl: "the art of ironing, the taste for sparkling dishes, and the tranquil joys of sewing as the female counterpart of male virtues: dynamism, courage, and imagination. This is without doubt the reason for which leisure activities are never brought up, that sports entertainment and traveling are reserved for papa, as well as the right to smoke 'his' pipe and read 'his' newspaper as soon as he returns home. Mama never smokes, rarely reads and when she goes out on Sunday, led by her husband, she drinks lemonade like the children."[22]

Not enough attention in the curriculum has been placed on the history of women. When women are treated it is never from a perspective of women's rights. Feminists would like to see an analysis of history presented in which the mechanisms of sexism are examined in every historic period. They want to reveal the lives and works of the great crusaders for women's rights, but also to take a fresh look at old heroines.

Since 1974, the feminists inside the government and out have identified the educational issues important to women's rights. Françoise Giroud commissioned a study of sexism in school texts and encouraged her representatives in the regions to work for changes. Giroud and Pelletier both recognized that government programs for vocations, guidance, and technical training gave little real opportunity to women because of occupational segregation. Roudy made the improvement of vocational guidance for girls an important goal of her ministry. She worked with the Minister of Education in developing a new policy to overcome inequality in preparation, focusing on eliminating job segregation and giving girls a chance at training in the new high-technology fields. The policy included preparing nonsexist counseling materials and training teachers to diversify the guidance given to girls and increase their representation in science and technical studies.

The Minister of Education presented the three-part plan in a circular to the middle school administrators: (1) the same information about a wide range of careers and training programs will be given to mixed classes of boys and girls; (2) "effective integration of all technological training will be put into effect with the least delay" and girls will be accepted and welcomed into these programs; (3) all means will be sought to create an open and positive attitude toward women in all firms hiring young workers. The ministry's goal is to "contribute to a more equitable sharing of qualifications and professional responsibilities between the sexes and greater diversification of female employment."[23]

The MWR initiated some of its own policies in this area. It has subsidized pilot training programs in new technologies. In 1984 it launched a public relations campaign: "In school we look in all directions: a career does not have a sex."[24] In the style of other MWR campaigns for contraception and employment, the spot ads appeared on television, posters, and in schools. They emphasized that the selection of a vocation was just as important to a girl as to a boy. In 1985, the MWR offered women a scholarship program in science and technology. Each four-year *bourse* allows a woman to pursue advanced study in fields in which females are most underrepresented.

In addition to the pilot training programs and the information campaign, the regional offices of the ministry have held special workshops and seminars for teachers and counselors to inform them of ways of expanding the horizons of girls. In Franche-Comté, the regional delegate sponsored a contest for students to develop audiovisual programs on the subject "My career, it's my freedom." It is clear that the ministry envisioned a major shift, not only in preparation for employment but in the attitudes of girls toward the importance of a career to their lives. The goal was to promote role change and equity.

There was also a keen interest among government feminists in addressing the problem of sexism in the classroom. Roudy helped the Minister of Education promulgate an ambitious policy to fight sex bias in the public school:

Educators have an essential role to play in the battle against sexist prejudice . . . in order to change attitudes and make all discrimination against women disappear . . . ;

They must bring out and criticize in all educational materials (texts, slides, films, tapes, etc.) the persistence of sexist stereotypes . . . ;

The opportunity must be taken in all activities to show how the opposition . . . of images and roles of woman and man is illegitimate . . . ;

They will lead students in reflecting on the participation of women in economic and social life and on the guarantees of equality that must be theirs in all political, economic, social, cultural and legal domains as well as on the problem of the division of domestic tasks and roles.[25]

The MWR took direct action to change stereotyped images of women in textbooks and teacher education. Roudy, along with representatives from the Ministry of Education, parent organizations, teachers, unions, and the school inspectors, offered a plan to local school districts. Since textbooks are the responsibility of local authorities, the MWR offered to help a community review its texts to eliminate the stereotypes. Under contracts signed with several large communes (Nantes was the first in 1982) local committees agreed to analyze the texts and replace offending ones. This contract program was enhanced by a series of local regional expositions showing the range of stereotypes found in school materials and their effects.[26]

Roudy consulted with editors and undertook a project to educate student teachers about sexism. The MWR in cooperation with the Centre Audiovisuel Simone de Beauvoir has produced a video documentary entitled "Les Enfants du sexisme." This program is regularly shown to student teachers at eighty-six normal schools. The film presents conversations with children and shows how the system reinforces sex role stereotypes that limit opportunity for women.

Policy promoting women's rights in education in France is different in form from United States policy. There is no comprehensive law equivalent to Title IX. Most equal opportunity programs consist of internal directives from the Minister of Education. Still there are similarities in content. For the most part public education is coeducational in both countries. Special provisions in Title IX prohibit sex discrimination in vocational and guidance programs, although they don't receive quite the emphasis they have under Roudy's campaign to convince girls of the need to have a career. In both countries authorities face sensitive problems of censorship when trying to change the content of books. In the United States the Department of Education refuses to prohibit sexist texts under Title IX. It urges that action be taken at the state and local level, preferably by authors, editors, and teachers. Even in France, with much more centralized control over the school system, educators must be taught to recognize sexism and persuaded to eliminate biased classroom materials; they cannot be ordered to do so.

American law goes further than the French to include many nonacademic concerns such as athletics and student organizations in the equal education policy. There is less participation and interest in sports among women than men in France but athletics has not been linked with policies developed to eliminate sexism and inequality in schools. There has also been no official recognition of discrimination in student organizations; this may reflect the lower number and importance of such organizations for French students. No policies have been proposed in these areas.

WOMEN'S STUDIES AND FRENCH CULTURE

From the conventional point of view, women seem to have more prestige in the culture in France than they do in the United States.

Whereas the American society values masculine traits of strength, competitiveness, and violence, French society praises the feminine: love, light, softness, finesse, tenderness. There is a seemingly boundless obsession with the female form in art and advertisements. The official view is that women share in creating the French culture. Even the national symbols are female: the virgin martyr Joan of Arc and the valiant freedom fighter Marianne.

However, a closer examination shows that there is a limited domain where women can create and make their contribution: the home. The French concept of homemaking has little to do with keeping a spotless kitchen and serving nutritious meals. In the model bourgois family these chores are to be done by servants (although in fact they are scarce). Homemaking is the art of dressing, of conversation, of entertaining. The French woman is in charge of the culture and elegance of the home where the refinement and beauty of society reside. In this she inherits the tradition of charm, beauty and *savoir reçevoir* (knowing how to entertain) that has surrounded French women, so the myth goes, since the Middle Ages. "All is permitted of women, even talent, even intelligence or creativity on condition that she does not leave her female preserve where man joins her with delight."[27] The fact is that both the study of women and the use of female creative talent are underdeveloped in France. Bridging the cultural gap between men and women requires more research by and about women. American academic women in various social science and humanities disciplines have argued in favor of incorporating the study of women into the mainstream of scholarship in universities. They have developed courses, degrees, journals, caucuses, and conferences. American feminists have persuaded public schools to include the new knowledge of women into the public school curriculum. French feminist intellectuals, on the other hand, at first separated themselves from the universities and research institutes and sought to develop a different culture based exclusively on women's bodies, experience, and values. Feminists started their own publishing houses (the most prominent were Des Femmes and Editions Tierce) but they remained aloof from the state education system. They produced little that could be used in school texts. Of course, some academics in France have also studied women and several important works have been included in the women's studies lists of major publishers. In 1977 a group of feminist teachers and researchers established a journal of theory, research, and debate on women's issues called *Questions féministes*.[28] What was different from the American situation was that women's studies were not inserted in any systematic way into the universities in France. For many years only one state campus had a post in research on women—the University of Paris VII. There has been little financial support for women's studies per se in literature, social science, or history.[29]

Yvette Roudy recognized the need for research about and by women. She claimed that the permanent examination of women's position in society provides the capital for development of a struggle to improve women's rights. She had an ally in the director of the government's Centre National de la Recherche Scientifique (CNRS), who has himself published some work on women. The two agencies sponsored the first conference on women's studies at Toulouse in December, 1982. The three-day meeting attracted women from feminist organizations and research collectives as well as universities. Their papers showed the breadth of inquiry about women, but also the controversy about ideology and methods. They agreed that France was behind other countries in women's studies and blamed it on the lack of institutional support. But they criticized United States women's studies for failing to achieve their goal of integration. Beatrice Slama of the University at Vincennes agreed: "It is for us a matter of principle. Marginality can be subversive. We say NO to marginalization. We don't want to create a new place of containment, a new scientific ghetto with the derisory benefit of a quasi-monopoly in a branch of knowledge which reproduces the sexual division without combatting the effects. . . . Teaching about women is not an exclusivity nor a speciality, it is a new way of looking at the world."[30]

To help the feminist scholars catch up, the Ministry of Woman's Rights took a number of initiatives. With the CNRS they cosponsored the first series of grants for women's studies and feminist research in 1983. The program sought projects in three broad areas: (1) feminist critique; (2) women, state, law, and society; and (3) the women's movement and the image of women. The CNRS now includes the subject of women in its other grant programs on the Third World, technology and work, health, society, and the family. The MWR also proposed new posts in women's studies at the state universities. The Minister of Education recently established four: political science at Nantes, *droit social* at Rennes, biology at Paris III, and contemporary world history at Toulouse. Finally, the ministry used its subsidies to encourage organizations such as the Centre Audiovisuel Simone de Beauvoir to pursue projects promoting feminist culture. It also awarded two literary prizes: the George Sand prize for the best novel by a woman and the Alice prize for the best children's story by a woman.

The French are very proud of their culture and its contribution to world civilization: after all, France has given the world law, philosophy, and art. Today, scholars encounter the newest ideas in Paris, the crucible of international as well as French intellectual life. Part of the struggle for equality in education for French women will involve a claim to participate in the evolution of the national culture. It's a formidable goal that must start with the exploration of women's true cultural tradition.

DEFINITION OF THE ISSUE OF EDUCATION

As a policy issue, education is rarely an end in itself; it has importance only in relation to some other goal. Policymakers ask: What is the purpose of education? They must match the program of study with the students to achieve some social end, such as citizenship, patriotism, culture, or employment. Historically that goal in France has been to mold a culture congruent with the interests of those in power, often in opposition to social trends. Republican educators have promoted images of class harmony in the midst of labor strife, pronatalism in the face of declining birth rates, and the joys of domesticity while hundreds of thousands of women went to jobs outside the home. The task of feminists is to convince policymakers that education should be a means of achieving women's rights and changing patriarchal society. In the past, feminists agreed among themselves on the relationship between education and women's rights: They sought both equality and integration. Contemporary feminists believe that these goals are not enough. They want to eliminate tracking and make the state education system as helpful to girls in preparing for careers as it is to boys. Schools must no longer be mechanisms for role separation and sexism; rather, they must promote role sharing both through the content of course work and the system of career guidance.

For all their agreement on the education issue over the years, feminists have had little success. The government policies that gradually provided public education for females in the form of schools, teachers, curricula, and materials were not defined as a way of giving women

equal rights to use that education. The logic of all the education reforms from 1850 to 1924 was to help women prepare to assume their
"proper" social role in the family and through that role to sustain the
family in the service of state goals. At first it was the conservatives
who wanted to discourage social change. Then liberals under the Third
Republic used women's public education as a means of reducing the
influence of the Catholic church. After World War II it was modern-
ism, not feminism, that broke down the formal sex barriers and eliminated the single-sex schools.

The effect of this policy logic was to build the French public education system on a foundation bifurcated by sex. Single-sex schools
permitted separate sex role socialization, watered down curricula, and
established a narrow track for girls to follow from school to family
and certain suitable, but limited, occupations. Two unintended effects
of the separation led to improvement of rights. The elimination of the
church's monopoly on women's education and the establishment of
state schools gave women more chances to learn and removed the
stifling restrictions of convent schools. The single-sex *lycées* produced
a demand for female teachers, which in turn required the state to open
higher education to women.

All subsequent reforms have smoothed over the separation of the
sexes but have not eliminated it. The issue of coeducation as a vehicle
for improving women's rights has rarely surfaced in the public arena.
The gradual disappearance of single-sex schools over the last thirty
years has done little to challenge or dislodge the habits of the previous
century. Traditional attitudes among parents, teachers, and the girls
themselves keep their experiences narrow and their choices few. Despite equal curricula, admissions, and *mixité*, tracking persists. Girls
are found overwhelmingly on a female track that would not have em-
barrassed republicans 100 years ago.

Today, the primary issues in education policy in France do not pertain to women's rights, despite feminist action. The government and
interest groups quarrel about questions of state aid to religious schools,
modernization of the system, and equal opportunity for all economic
classes. Although these may affect women's education (a majority of
pupils in religious schools are girls) they are not proposed as such.
Feminists in and out of government have begun to outline the major
education issues that pertain to women, namely sexism in texts and
guidance. These must compete, however, with other issues for atten-

tion. The MWR sponsored some pilot projects and persuaded the Ministry of Education to take some steps to reduce tracking and sexual stereotyping. Roudy argued that without cultural change legal equality will have little effect on women's lives. She envisioned a shift in sex roles of the most basic kind, from role separation and equity to role change and integration. A means to this would be the orientation of girls to lifetime careers on the same basis as boys.

The feminists' greatest hope of success is to prod the education bureaucracy toward a massive overhaul that will bridge the double foundation and rid public education of all sex segregation. It is a monumental goal. Bacause of the MWR, for the first time there was a feminist response inside the government to the question of the purpose of education for women: so they can get the best jobs; so that the young will see a brand-new image of women sharing in all sorts of activities with men; and so that the research resources of French universities will be spent on feminist scholars who dare to rewrite history and redesign culture.

NOTES

1. Yvette Roudy, *La Femme en marge* (Paris: Flammarion, 1975; 1982), 66–7. In developing this point, Yvette Roudy cites Balzac: "You must be horrified at the education for this reason, so well-known in Spain, that it is easier to govern a nation of idiots than a nation of educated." She goes on to say: "From the moment the marginal achieve the means of expression, they emerge. They exist."

2. Gisèle Halimi, *Le Programme commun des femmes* (Paris: Grasset, 1978), 271-2.

3. Simone de Beauvoir, *The Second Sex* (New York: Vintage, 1952; 1974), 148.

4. Michèle Kail, "Histoire du colloque," *Femmes, féminisme et recherches* (Toulouse, 1982), 17.

5. Cited by Pierre Giolotto, "Côté fille, côté garçon," *L'Education* (17 décembre 1981), 10.

6. François Poulain de la Barre, *De l'égalité des deux sexes* (Corpus des oeuvres de Philosophie, 1673; Fayard, 1984).

7. Ibid., 59.

8. Ibid., 97.

9. Maïté Albistur and Daniel Armogathe, *Histoire du féminisme français, du moyen age à nos jours* (Paris: Des Femmes, 1977) 249. Quoted from the first issue of *L'Anthenée* (1808).

10. Odile Dhavernas, *Droits des femmes, pouvoir des hommes* (Paris: Seuil, 1978), 240. Quoted from *Rapport Cauchard* (16 juin 1866).

11. Quoted in "L'Ecole des filles," *Le Monde de l'Education* (juin 1975), 7.

12. Quoted in Dhavernas, *Droits des femmes*, 247.

13. Linda L. Clark, "Socialization of Girls in the Primary Schools of the Third Republic," *Journal of Social History* 15 (Summer 1982), 685–97.

14. Giolotto, "Côté fille," 13.

15. Albistur and Armogathe, *Histoires du féminisme*, 353. Congrès international du droit des femmes (1878); Congrès général de sociétés féministes (1892); Deuxième congrès international des oeuvres et institutions féminines (juin 1900), Congrès international de la condition du droit des femmes (septembre 1900).

16. James F. McMillan, *Housewife or Harlot* (New York: St. Martins, 1981), 124. Quoted from Decree of 15 March 1928.

17. Linda L. Clark, *Schooling the Daughters of Marianne* (Albany: SUNY Press, 1984), 102.

18. Ibid., chap. 6.

19. "L'Ecole des filles," 6.

20. Collège d'Enseignement Secondaire.

21. Giolotto, "Côté fille," 9.

22. Ministère des Droits de la femme, *Les Femmes dans une société d' inégalités* (Paris: Documentation française, 1982), 136.

23. Ministère de l'Education nationale, "Orientation des jeunes filles," Circulaire no. 82–182 du 29 avril 1982.

24. Ministère des Droits de la femme, "L'Orientation des filles," *Citoyennes à part entière* (avril 1984).

25. Ministère de l'Education nationale, "Action éducative contre les préjuges sexistes," Arrêté du 12 juillet 1982.

26. At least two publishers of textbooks have admonished authors to eliminate sexism. Prodded by the Association "pour une école non-sexiste," Magnard and Nathan have distributed translations of nonsexist guidelines developed by McGraw-Hill to their authors.

27. Michèle Sarde, *Regard sur les françaises* (Paris: Stock, 1983), 31.

28. The journal was renamed *Nouvelles Questions féministes* in 1981 and remains an outlet for feminist scholarship. Commenting on its role in the new attention to women's studies in France, Christine Delphy writes: "At the heart of this intellectual progress are the feminist teachers and researchers who for the past several years have been coming together in discussion groups or around publications, and notably around *Nouvelles Questions féministes*"; "French Feminist Forum," *The Women's Review of Books* 3 (March 1986), 17.

29. *Regard sur les françaises*, the major scholarly work on the history of

French women, was written by a French woman who has a permanent position at a university in the United States.

30. Beatrice Slama, "Etudes féminines, études féministes," *Femmes, féminisme, et recherches*, 926.

6

WORK

No FRENCH WORKERS have been more exploited, or more ignored, than women. Since the beginning of industrialization, they have been the least trained, lowest paid and first fired. For many years their plight was not a priority on any reformist or revolutionary agenda. Labor unions tended to ignore women and overlook their needs; some actively opposed their right to work. Socialists treated their condition as one of many symptoms of capitalism that would disappear in a socialist society. Feminists also tended to dismiss the concrete problems of female workers as token of a larger evil: patriarchy. When parties and governments have extended aid to women workers, it was not to improve their status as workers but to help them as mothers and home-makers. Therefore, despite the steady and substantial participation of French women in the work force for 100 years, their relative employment status has not much improved.

Until the 1960s a standard statistic prevailed: "Women are one-third of the work force and one-third of women work." But no longer. Since 1962 the proportion and number of women workers has increased steadily and dramatically, paralleling changes in the United States labor force (See Table 5). In 1984 women were 42.4 percent of the work force in France and 43.4 percent in the United States. The growth, primarily in the tertiary, or service, sector, is due in large part to married women with children entering the labor market (80 percent of the increase between 1968 and 1975). Although 43.4 percent of all women over 16 are employed (compared with 54 percent in the United States), 64 percent of those aged 25 to 55 are in jobs (62 percent in

Table 5
Females as a Percentage of Labor Force, France and the United States,
1962–1984

Year	France	United States
1962	34.3	33.8
1968	36.2	39.2
1975	38.2	39.9
1980	39.2	42.6
1982	41.0	43.0
1984	42.4	43.4

Sources: INSEE, Données sociales, 4e edition, 1981.
           Citoyennes à part entière, 1985.
           Department of Labor, Handbook on Women Workers, 1983.
           Bureau of Labor Statistics, Monthly Labor Review, 1986.

the United States). In both countries, these unprecedented changes in women's employment have coincided with more attention in the public arena to their problems.

WHO WILL SPEAK FOR WOMEN WORKERS?

After centuries of neglect, working women now have several would-be champions who claim to understand their problems and know how best to solve them. Many feminists recognize that paid work is one of the keys to liberation. Jeanne Deroin had said as much in the 1840s when Proudhonian socialists tried to take jobs away from women: "The right to life is based on the right to work."[1] But for a long time moderate and reform feminists showed more interest in *droit civil* than economic and social questions. Most feminists of the Left accepted the socialist premise that all work in the capitalist economy is alienating and oppressive and could liberate no one, man or woman. The task was to change that capitalist system and thus free all workers.

• Simone de Beauvoir helped reconcile feminism and socialism by focusing on the different roles of men and women.[2] While paid labor in the capitalist economy limited the cultural development of men, women were oppressed far more by another institution—the family. Work might alienate man but marriage enslaved woman. Her only hope for standing on her own in society was to have a *métier*.[3] First she must overcome patriarchy; then she would be in a position to rebel against capitalism. Socialism alone would do little to change the oppression of women. Men control both the family and the factory. Whether capitalist or socialist, management or union, conservative or revolutionary about their own work relationships, they are all reactionary about the employment rights of women. De Beauvoir argued that the special demands of women for training, opportunity, and pay must be a top priority of feminists.

Yvette Roudy traces women's oppression in the work force to dependency in marriage and the sex role division of labor. Equality in work and family requires role change. The role of man as a father must be just as important as a woman's role as mother. Both need to work and care for children. Roudy's commitment to role sharing means that she opposes several apparently pro-woman ideas, including salaries for housework and special accommodations for mothers to demands of work and family that perpetuate the division of labor. Roudy insists that homemaking is not a career. A woman's salary should not be considered *salaire d'appoint* (secondary income). As long as it is, women will be treated as a reserve labor force: undertrained, underemployed, underpaid, underpromoted. The only way to fight reactionaries of both the Left and the Right is to insist on a woman's right to work *à part entière* (in her own right).

One of the major unions, the Confédération Française Démocratique du Travail (CFDT), has also recognized the relationship between work, dependency, and family sex roles. In 1976 the national leadership adopted the following resolution:

Each woman must have the possibility to work and assure an economic base for her independence without any discrimination in law or fact. In order for this right to work to be fully recognized, it is necessary to fight against all those who try to keep the predetermined roles and division of labor between men and women. Cantonized in their traditional roles they cannot really participate in social, cultural, union, and political life.[4]

There is still no widespread agreement on a conception of women's work. The problem of reconciling equality with role differences that has plagued the women's work issues since the nineteenth century continues to divide feminists, unions, and political parties. There are contradictions among the demands of working women themselves as well as controversies over the significance of women in paid employment. Some people still believe that women have special problems and should get special treatment. These defenders of *la différence* are found even among feminists. From the radicals—who want a separate female economy—to the reformers—who want extra services for women— equality is not enough. Many women demand special programs to ease the burden of their working lives even if such special protections undermine equal opportunity in a more general sense. The largest union, the Confédération Générale du Travail (CGT), seeks ways of easing tensions between home and work responsibilities for women. Their most urgent demands for women concern maternity leave and crèches (day care). Their verbal support of equality and the right of women to work does not directly challenge the sex role division of labor.[5]

The political parties are even more divided than the unions on the definition of the issue of women's work. Some conservative Gaullists have been especially outspoken about their beliefs that women should not work outside the home. They admit that women may be occasionally called upon to take a job because of economic need, either their own or the country's, but this should be temporary. Woman's primary duty and fulfillment is in the home. According to Jean Foyer, former Minister of Justice: "Man gets his dignity and security from employment; woman gets both from marriage."[6] Probably the most famous statement of the conservative Gaullist view is that of M. Beuillac, former Minister of Labor, in his declaration of 28 September 1976:

On her [woman] rests the equilibrium of the family; in a world increasingly hard, she represents softness and ease; in a world where ambition and competition are unleashed, in a world where everything is for sale, the homemaker maintains other values: love, generosity, charity . . . if women, the mother, can remain in the home it is a good thing. As much as man has a fundamental vocation to work in the factory and office, so a part of woman's life can take place elsewhere.[7]

It was a short step from this romantic vision to the practical suggestion made in the Senate to deal with rising unemployment: "The work of women, of which no one questions the legitimacy nor the legality, and enriching as it may be for the country, is not a small factor in unemployment and denatality. Rather than sending women to work, better send them to bed."[8] Serious public debate on this suggestion was encouraged by the timely appearance of a book by a popular journalist entitled *I Returned to the Home*, extolling the virtues of homemaking and unpaid domestic work.

Feminists, frightened that such attitudes would perpetuate sex discrimination in the work force, have looked to the parties of the Left for support. There, mixed with the rhetoric of equal opportunity, they encounter deeply held paternalistic ideas about women workers. Although the Socialists and Communists have accepted women's right to work, they have, until recently, continued to embrace the logic of separate sex roles and have accepted protective laws and proposals to help working mothers. In the last decade, however, both parties have taken steps toward egalitarian thinking by recognizing that family responsibilities are not the exclusive concern of women workers.

This shift can be demonstrated by comparing two of the massive bills the Communist party brought before parliament in the 1970s. A 1974 bill sought to improve women's lot without challenging their special domestic assignment. Hélène Constans argued that this bill was based on "the reality of women's lives" in which they must mix maternity with work. "The status of woman is not in fact separable from her function in maternity and reproduction."[9]

In 1977 the party's omnibus proposal emphasized woman's right to work and moved toward the idea of men and women sharing family responsibilities. Deputies asserted that although the family was important to women, it was not their exclusive concern. "It is not good— and this practice is more and more contested—to burden the woman with the task of rearing the child. The child needs his father, as the father needs to fulfill his role with him."[10] The bill linked the right to work with measures of equality in the family.

The Socialist party, under the influence of Yvette Roudy and other feminists, has gone even further toward challenging traditional roles. In 1978 the party affirmed women's right to work and denounced the sexual division of labor, that is, "the opposing of roles, women at home, men in production; the opposing of jobs, male and female (the latter always undervalued)."[11] They advocated a series of measures to involve men more equally in the activities of the family as a complement to women's equality on the job. Both Socialists and Communists suggest similar policies: crèches and other state-funded child care facilities; more collective services for housework; concordance of work and school schedules; a reduced work week of thirty-five hours to increase time available for families; as well as integration of the job market; effective equal pay laws; job training and promotion for women. Despite all that, neither party challenges the principle of protective labor laws for women.

PROTECTIVE LEGISLATION

Special protective legislation for women workers has a long history in France, reflecting social acceptance of women's employment outside the home. Despite official rhetoric about the virtues of *la mère de famille* and *la femme au foyer*, women have long made up a substantial portion of the work force. The proportion of women to men has rarely dropped below one-third since the 1870s. Several factors explain this.[12] First, the family wage economy was widespread and persisted into the industrial period. Under this system all family members were expected to contribute income and the family's prosperity was measured by the proportion of earners to consumers. It was well into the twentieth century before the idea of investing in the education of children took hold among the workers and they accepted the contribution made by mothers staying at home. Second, small family businesses and farms where wives worked alongside husbands persisted. Finally, job segregation by sex required a supply of women workers for domestic labor, in textile and garment industries, and teaching. Later, the growth in the tertiary sector increased demand for women in white-collar jobs, social service, and health care fields.

For more than 100 years the official stance of the French government was to accept, even encourage, women's active participation in the work force. It was permissible for women occasionally to take paid employment, not for themselves but to make an economic contribution to their families. The state's role was to help both employers and husbands share the labor of women. This meant special rules to accommodate *la double journée* of working wives and mothers. The first proposals came from bourgeois feminists with the founding of the Third Republic. They wanted some egalitarian reforms, including the right to work, union rights, and equal pay. But the majority by far were for special protections, including an eight-hour workday, prohibition on heavy weight lifting, and a full range of support for pregnancy: leave, pay, and child care.

These demands, because they were defined as helping mothers, found a receptive audience among republican and Catholic leaders. The legislators, far from opposing work for women, recognized it as an important part of the economy and the family. Yet they saw the need to shield wives from overwork so that they could adequately perform their family responsibilities. "It is fitting that the government protect women, in the interest of the husband and the family, against abusive exploitation by 'bosses.' "[13] Only the Socialists and their unions remained doggedly opposed to the employment of women, because of various motives, including Proudhonian misogyny, fears of competition, and outrage at working conditions.

The French parliament set about adopting a series of statutes that reduced the hours and duress of work and gave women some help with childbearing and care. Many of these restricted women's work: no women in the mines (1874); no night work and the eleven-hour day (1892); chairs for women employees (1900); regulation of women working in display windows (1913). In the same period that most of this protective legislation was being passed in France, similar laws were enacted in the United States. The motives were comparable—to ease the burdens of motherhood on women and protect the weaker sex. In neither country were male workers envious of these protections; either they believed that there were immense differences between the sexes and their jobs or they were relieved to find restrictions on a rival group of workers.

The logic of these protective laws, intended to support motherhood and the family, led to provisions for maternity leave in France. A statute in 1909 required an eight-week leave, but it was unpaid, and pregnant workers could be fired before giving birth. Soon after, public employees got paid leave: teachers in 1910, postal workers in 1911, and the entire civil service in 1928. In 1936, the *Accords Matignon*, an important national agreement among labor, management, and government, formally recognized the social function of motherhood.[14] In

1966 layoff for pregnancy was prohibited and paid maternity leave for all workers increased to fourteen weeks, six before birth and eight after.

Another motivation that accounts for acceptance of a maternity leave policy was the profound pronatalism among male leaders of both the Left and Right. Some may have entertained fantasies that married women could be prevented from working (also tried at various times in the United States), but most accepted the necessity of their income to many families. Maternity leave was a means of encouraging women to continue to bear children while working. The formal recognition of the social function of motherhood paved the way for specific legislation to help women in many ways to reconcile the demand and responsibilities of both work and family.

Paid maternity leave remains a central part of French labor policy today, while in the United States equal employment laws have displaced maternity leave as such. Labor legislation has historically been the responsibility of the various states and many adopted a range of protective regulations. The federal equal opportunity laws superseded state protective legislation and any maternity leave policies came to be considered as favoring one sex. The Pregnancy Discrimination Act of 1978 defines pregnancy as one of a class of temporary disabilities that must be covered by any disability leave and pay plan an employer offers. Disability plans rarely allow employees to stay away from the job for more than six weeks. While American feminists want to relieve women of bearing the burden of having children alone, they agree that such aid must be guaranteed within a logic of equality—not protection. They fear protective laws will always have a discriminatory effect on women. In the United States equal opportunity laws are considered incompatible with special protections for working mothers.

Current Status of Protective Legislation

While United States protective laws have faded away as incompatible with equal opportunity, many remain in force in France where they still enjoy support by all political parties and labor unions. During the Giscard presidency the definition of labor issues began to change as ideas of improving the employment status of women took hold. Nevertheless, Françoise Giroud and Monique Pelletier not only did not seek to repeal the nineteenth-century protections, they added to them. Giroud carefully avoided the difficult question of identity by calling for the social equivalence of men and women. She pointed out that many people used to agree with Leon Blum that the good society was one where a man earned enough money so that his wife didn't have to work. "The 'good' society of the future is seen today as one where each one, man and woman, will be able to manage his/her own life." [15] But Giroud did not consider women and men to be the same kind of workers. Most women will be in the work force at some time in their lives, but intermittently; therefore, there must be special services for them. In 1974 the government was explicit about the special needs of women workers: "Security finally for women in permitting them to reconcile their responsibilities as mothers, their occupations and their legitimate desire to play, in the same way as men, an active role in society." [16]

The major employment legislation for women in the Giscard presidency was the law of 11 July 1975. The intent of the government was to strengthen protections for pregnancy and maternity. The act threatens prison or fines for any employer who uses the reason of "pregnancy to hire or refuse to hire, cancel a job contract or transfer employment." Employers are constrained from asking about pregnancy in hiring or reducing salary because of it and must find alternate temporary employment if a pregnant woman is not able to perform her job. Support for this law in the National Assembly came from all parties for familiar reasons: to ease the burdens of motherhood and encourage women to have more children.

After 1978 Monique Pelletier continued the theme of reconciling home and family for the woman worker but she cast her position in vaguely egalitarian terms: "Woman, like man, must be able to assume her role in public life, in the enterprise and at home. Professional life and family life must be able to be reconciled or alternated. It is this contradiction that must be dealt with without denying the differences between women and men." [17] Pelletier proposed creative use of part-time work, flexible time, *alternance*, and early retirement to permit mothers to drop out of work for a while without losing their permanent status or rights. She also wanted to give mothers who did not work but raised several children pension credits for retirement. The government did shave off some of the restrictions from the old legislation, repealing sections of the labor code requiring an employer to assume the moral guardianship of his female employees and eliminating the ban on night work for women in management positions. The prohibition on work in the mines and shift work remains in effect.

Many feminists have opposed the continued proliferation of special protections for women workers because they believe special protections perpetuate the female monopoly over family responsibilities and housework. "Labor law basically only recognizes the family through the special status it confers on women. It thus reproduces a sexual distribution of roles in which a woman is equated with the family." [18] Gisèle Halimi of Choisir argues that special provisions for women, such as part-time work, have the effect of limiting job opportunities. "Who has made a career, who has made decisions, who has assumed responsibilities while working part-time?" [19] Feminists fear that beliefs in the separation of the sexes have become so deeply engrained that even laws drawn in sex-neutral terms will have a discriminatory effect on women.

The controversy over family responsibilities and women's employment status has led to a reevaluation of three policies: maternity leave, child care, and part-time work. In the case of leave, the redefinition occurred on the floor of the National Assembly. In 1977 the government introduced a bill for *congé de mère*—"mother's leave." Mothers would be entitled to up to two-years leave for child care, in six-month segments. The Minister of Labor saw this as an extension of guarantees already in place and no doubt hoped for pronatalist consequences: "This new right constitutes a supplementary step in the definition of protective measures which surround maternity of salaried workers— dispositions which I recall were conceived in the double interest of mother and child." [20]

The chairman of the National Assembly Committee on Social, Cultural, and Family Affairs proposed an amendment extending this leave to fathers. He argued that such protective measures handicap women but if extended to men could increase their involvement with their children. Although the government disagreed, it did not oppose this redefinition and the bill was renamed "parental leave." By the time it reached the Senate it was presented not as a women's issue but as a family issue intended to benefit children. Despite this change in language, feminists warned that because of cultural role expectations, the leave would still be used primarily by women. They advocated increased child care facilities to enable both parents to work full-time.

State-supported child care for working mothers has long been a proposal of both feminists and leftist parties. In 1964, Michel and Texier charged that the state's recognition of the social function of motherhood did not extend to any interest in helping raise children and permitting women to work.[21] Rather, it offered part-time work and, worse yet, mother's salaries and family allowances. Studies of child care facilities document the scarcity of places. The education system takes charge of children at age three; for younger children the state offers crèches, *pouponnières*, and *garderies*. Most child care is funded at the municipal level, the state being reluctant to add much to the effort. Regina Fodor's study in Paris showed less than sixteen available places per 100 working mothers.[22] Evelyn Sullerot found that many women must enlist family members or hire child minders.[23] Many have to leave the work force either temporarily or permanently after their second or third child. The Socialist and Communist bills and manifestos in the 1970s picked up on the theme and advocated more social services (*équipments socials*) to solve problems posed by women's employment. But even after the Socialists won the majority, they were able to increase services only slightly. Instead they have installed paid parental leave despite the objection of the Ministry of Woman's Rights. The government feminists feared that since the pay for child care leave is so low (1,000 francs per month in 1983), fathers will rarely take it because the loss of their usually higher salaries would be a drastic cut in family income. Once a mother is on leave, quitting work altogether becomes more likely. When women take maternity and parental leave they lose ground in developing careers and earning power; they become increasingly less attractive to employers. This reinforces their underpaid, undertrained, underemployed, and underpromoted status as workers.

Feminists advocate child care—the government offers part-time work. While more opportunities for part-time work may appear to make it easier for parents to combine work and family responsibilities, in practice it is a barrier to equal opportunity. First, women occupy the majority of these jobs. Second, they continue to work full-time in the home. Further, with part-time work, there is less status, training, and fewer social rights and work benefits. This is convenient for government and business; they get cheap labor from women without any investment in training or social services for child care. But as long as there is a two-tier system between part-time and full-time work, the policy reinforces existing sex discrimination.

The feminists joined with the parties of the Left in advocating a reduced work week or all workers from forty to thirty-five and eventually thirty hours, with no reduction in pay. Since the goal is to provide more free time for all workers, it shifts the perspective about the relation between work and family. It ceases to be a woman's problem and becomes the concern of all workers and of employers and the government, too. Not only will both parents have more time to devote to their families, but they will be able to participate in associations, political activities, and have more leisure time. Less fatigue will make them better workers.

When the Socialists assumed power in 1981, they reduced the work week to thirty-nine hours. But the economic realities of *la crise* prevented any further reduction. Women workers continue to seek part-time jobs and unions demand that the government upgrade their status. While employers and the government expect that women want part-time work as a substitute for full-time careers, a recent study shows that part-time employment may have a wide variety of uses in women's lives.[24] Much depends on the type of job and the family situation. The demand for flexible time is neither seasonal nor weekly, nor an intermediate step toward leaving the work force altogether; rather, it is "biographical"—individual to each woman. Roudy was able to defend part-time work, but not as a way of helping women have more time for child care. She said that part-time work helps both women and men when it is used in connection with programs of training and retraining. "I remain convinced, however, that to allow the principle of part-time work for women in a permanent way will end up enclosing them in an occupational ghetto."[25]

The assumptions behind policies addressing the problems of work and family focus less and less on women and cast solutions more and more in sex-neutral terms, as social, parental, or human concerns. The term *parent* has been substituted for *mother* in many labor laws. Since cultural norms lag behind policy, this forces attention on putting fathers to work caring for their children. The MWR was vigilant to make sure that any concessions made to families did not become the exclusive concern of women and undermine their status and rights as workers. But government feminists confronted a society in which women usually retain primary responsibilities for their children. This sexual division of labor had until very recently been enshrined in a pronatalist labor and family law code.

The feminist group Choisir has a plan to speed up the integration of men into active parenting of small children. The proposal, called "joint education leave," consists of half-time leave for both mother and father taken simultaneously. They would take turns at home and working: one week full-time work, one week full-time leave. They would each receive full salary at work and eighty percent while at home, but only if both parents participated. The benefits would be considerable, according to Choisir. The child would be cared for by both parents and have the full experience of close contact with an adult male as well as an adult female. Both parents would be at home and able to continue their careers. Their interdependence and cooperation would promote marital harmony. The employer would be helped; he could hire two half-time employees to replace the couple and thus reduce the unemployment lists. The cost to the government would be less than building enough crèches to care for the children of working parents. There would also be some relief for the unemployed. Choisir is especially enthusiastic about the long-term effects of joint child rearing on reducing the sexism perpetuated by the rigid sexual division of labor.

Feminists in both America and France complain about the failure of men, employers, and government to share responsibilities for child care and permit women to have an equal chance at careers and salaries. United States policy tends to separate family issues entirely from employment, leaving family burdens in the private sector for women to bear alone. In France, the government has for a long time connected the worlds of family and work but has carefully defined the result as a women's issue. Thus in both societies the sex role division of labor in the home has continued to prevent women from achieving equal rights in employment.

French policy promises more opportunity for women in the future. The gradual redefinition of the family-work question from a woman's issue to a sex-neutral social issue reinforces and encourages the changes toward role sharing in the home. In the United States, however, as policy is presently defined, it will do little to encourage men to adjust their work in order to have more time rearing their children. Although Congress has debated a bill requiring unpaid disability and parental leave, a policy requiring employers to allow for paid parental leave, such as that passed in France in 1977, is a long way off.

EQUAL OPPORTUNITY LEGISLATION

The idea of equality for women in employment is not new in France. Demands for equal pay date from the nineteenth century. What is new is serious implementation of an equal opportunity policy. There has been no lack of symbolic policy gestures by the French government. The *Accords Matignon* in 1936 included provisions to bring female workers' wages within fifteen percent of those of men. A 1946 decree repealed the concept of a female salary altogether. The constitutions of 1946 and 1958 guaranteed legal equality of the sexes. France signed the ILO Convention 100 for equal remuneration of manual workers in 1952 and Article 119 of the Treaty of Rome for equal remuneration of male and female workers in 1957. Government decrees of 1946, 1951, and 1971 admonished employers and labor unions to remove barriers to equal pay for women. One problem with all these agreements and admonitions: there were no sanctions for paying women less than men for the same work.

In 1965 the government established a Committee on Women's Employment (CWE) (*Comité du Travail féminin*) in the Ministry of Labor. For several years, Marcelle Devaud, a senator and member of the French United Nations delegation, had recommended that the government establish such a committee. She envisioned an agency similar to the Women's Bureau of the United States Department of Labor whose main goal would be to promote women's employment rights from within the government. The Women's Bureau, established in 1920, had spent forty years promoting protective legislation. It only gradually and reluctantly accepted the contemporary American feminist demand for complete equality. The CWE, on the other hand, made equality and the right to work its basic goal from the start.

The committee, composed of representatives from labor, management, and women's organizations, was primarily an advisory group. In its report of 1971 it recommended that the government enact a new statute for equal pay with sanctions. Private bills had already begun to appear in the parliament. The committee described its proposal as a necessary "supplementary legal instrument" and followed with recommendations for new policies for training and job integration. But the Pompidou-Messmer government made the equal pay bill its only policy for women workers. It was narrowly drawn and had limited enforcement: "All employers are required to assure, for the same work or for work of equal value, equality of remuneration between men and women; The different elements composing remuneration must be established according to identical norms for men and women."[26] Inspectors of Labor were charged with responding to complaints from workers and small fines could be levied for infractions.

Critics in the opposition parties charged that the bill was limited and ineffective. The provisions were based on a narrow definition of the women's work issue in the same spirit of symbolism that motivated all the previous decrees and treaties. The problem of women's salaries was a symptom of the basic structural inequalities in the employment of men and women. Only with attention to these inequalities would equal pay laws be more than simply words. Prominent Socialist Michel Rocard, in a long speech during the debate on the bill, analyzed the causes of the low–work status of women and outlined the policies necessary to achieve equality: job training, extension of collective bargaining, social services, as well as strengthened enforcement and serious penalties against offending employers.

The Minister of Social Affairs, Joseph Fontanet, realized the weakness of his bill: "I admit, like the speakers, that its efficacy is not certain, that it is risky in some respects, that we do not know exactly what will be its weight because it is difficult to put such a general rule in practice." But in response to the demand for more penalties he went on to say: "I am in this regard very reticent. Long experience has cautioned me against the tendency of increasing infractions. A famous historian of Greek civilization said that the excess of repressive legislation was either one of the causes or one of the signs of Hellenic decadence."[27] This is an astonishing comment in a country where the state has traditionally fine-tuned society through an intricate web of rules and infractions covering all aspects of life. Suddenly, when it involved women's rights, ministers were converted to the virtues of limited government. The equal pay bill passed intact. It served the feminist cause only as a symbol of the government's ineffectiveness and inattention to women's rights.

When Françoise Giroud joined the government in 1974, she made employment one of her projects. She appointed a work group to study the question while assuring the CWE that she would cooperate with them. Her own group reported that legal solutions were of limited use in improving the work status of women: what was needed was a change in attitudes. Giroud recommended only a few changes in the work code. Among her 100 measures for women were 2 or 3 recommendations for making the equal pay act more effective. In January 1975, however, she proposed that the government extend the existing policy against race discrimination in employment to include sex discrimination. She presented her proposal to the National Assembly in the form of amendments to the bill banning discrimination against pregnant women: "Any person in the capacity of employer who, without legitimate motive, hires, refuses to hire, or fires a person because of sex or family situation will be liable for fines, 3,000–30,000 francs and/or prison sentence of 2 months–2 years." [28] On the floor of the National Assembly, Giroud briefly explained that her amendments would add sex and family situation to a list of prohibited categories (origin, race, nationality, and religion) already part of the 1972 antiracist act. There was no further explanation, no debate, and the amendments passed.

With the 1975 law, the official definition of the issue of women's work took on features of more general antidiscrimination policy, not unlike the United States law on civil rights. In both cases, sex discrimination was prohibited as an afterthought; in France the thought came three years after the original law, whereas in the United States sex was added to Title VII of the 1964 Civil Rights Act on the floor of the House of Representatives. The effect in both cases was to stall the implementation of the anti-sex-discrimination provision. In France, the antiracist law carried a tremendous potential loophole: the exception of "legitimate motive." When sex was included in the act there was no discussion in the legislature as to what motives might legally permit an employer to refuse to hire a woman for a certain job. In the absence of such discussion, any reason was accepted as legitimate. The 1975 law had not been brought through regular policy channels and there had been little consultation with interest groups. Giroud maintains that this was usual procedure when the government wished to reduce controversy on a proposal. It would often bring a surprise amendment to the floor of the assembly, preferably when attendance was small, and sneak it through. Maybe so, but in the area of labor policy, employers and unions do not feel bound by laws unless they have participated in their development. [29] In effect, the 1975 antidiscrimination law was just one more symbol of the government's lack of commitment to rights for women workers.

The *Loi* Roudy: Equal Opportunity

Finally in 1983 the French government enacted a comprehensive statute seriously intended to abolish sex discrimination and promote equal opportunity for women and men in employment. It represented a major shift in the logic of public policy relating to women workers, concentrating on them apart from their domestic roles. In dramatic contrast to the 1972 and 1975 laws, this statute was carefully crafted, and was the work of two administrations involving widespread participation of groups and individuals of all political parties and ideologies. Although it bears the name of the Minister of Woman's Rights, its enactment owes much to her predecessors as well.

In 1976 a directive from the European Economic Community (EEC) prompted a new and complete study of employment discrimination policy. At the time, the only alternatives to the government's symbolic action were the Communist bill for working mothers and a Socialist proposal to improve enforcement of the equal pay act. At the EEC, however, there was a growing awareness of the need to go beyond the limited language of Article 119 of the Treaty of Rome and take a series of concrete steps to narrow the gap between male and female workers. The EEC directive required member states to put into effect "the principle of equal treatment for men and women as regards access to employment including promotion, and to vocational training."[30] At the least, member states were expected to remove both direct and indirect discrimination and provide legal remedies to individual workers.

The French government, prodded by the EEC directive, returned to the women's employment issue in 1978 when Giscard d'Estaing appointed Nicole Pasquier to be Secretary of State for Female Labor in the Ministry of Labor. She in turn appointed a work group to study sex discrimination in all aspects of employment. After widespread consultations and testimony from unions, management, and many feminist and women's organizations, the chair, Robert Beaudoin, presented a report in 1980 outlining major changes in the law. Based on the Beaudoin report, Pasquier and Monique Pelletier, Minister for the

Status of Women, drafted a bill for equal employment opportunity that was adopted by the Council of Ministers. The Giscard government feminists were on their way toward a major reform when the presidential elections of 1981 intervened, unhappily for them and their boss as it turned out.

The new minister Yvette Roudy made employment her number-one priority. The Ministry of Woman's Rights drafted a new proposal incorporating several aspects of the Pasquier bill: The repeal of the "legitimate motive" loophole; a ban on unequal or protective laws in labor agreements; giving unions authority to bring cases on behalf of aggrieved workers; and requiring an annual report from large employers on the status of participation of male and female workers. They strengthened the bill by including criteria for evaluation of men's and women's jobs and encouraging individual programs of *rattrapage* (catch up).

The ministry consulted the social partners (i.e. labor unions and employers' organizations), women's associations, and the feminists; they painstakingly worked over every article with the Ministries of Labor, Training, Justice, and Treasury. In this process they learned that feminists wanted the right to intervene in cases on behalf of women workers but the unions would not allow it. They found that it would be less controversial to leave existing protective laws in place and settle for prohibiting any new protections directed only at women. These consultations took a year and a half, but finally an acceptable bill, one that had the support, knowledge, and participation of both labor and management, was presented to parliament.

The Center Right parties objected, but not to equality of opportunity or even the provisions of the bill. After all, their government had originally drafted it. Rather, they opposed the change it represented in the definition of the women's work issue. Here was a policy on women's work that made no mention of their family roles. Conservative Hélène Missoffe warned that the government must recognize that women have different lives. Basing laws on assumptions of equality would be dangerous and end up hurting women in the long run. With the Socialist majority in the National Assembly the Roudy bill passed easily but faced crippling amendments in the Senate, which was controlled by the opposition. The government invoked its constitutional power and invited the National Assembly to "rule effectively." The bill became law 13 July 1983. The next year was spent putting various aspects of the law into effect and issuing the necessary decrees.

Let's examine the equal employment policy in France and compare it with that of the federal government in the United States. There are many similarities. In both there is a general prohibition of sex discrimination in employment in the private sector including hiring, promotion, firing, pay, and working conditions. Discrimination in training is also prohibited. The policy applies to the large nationalized sector in France while it extends to local and state employees in the United States. Both allow sex as a bona fide occupational qualification in very few circumstances. In France the Council of State has approved a list of occupations that can be reserved for males or females: artist model, actor/actress, and fashion model. The United States regulations list justifications such as privacy or business necessity instead of types of jobs; specific jobs are to be decided on a case-by-case basis. In neither country may contracts with labor unions benefit one sex, except that protections for pregnancy and child birth are still permitted in France.

The 1983 law provides a definition of equal work, or work of equal value, for use in enforcing the equal pay statute: "work is considered to have equal value that requires comparable (1) occupational knowledge evidenced by qualifications, a diploma or degrees, or professional experience; (2) abilities based on acquired experience on the job; (3) responsibilities; and (4) physical or mental burdens." The United States equal-pay-for-equal-work laws apply to jobs of similar skills, effort, responsibility, and working conditions. The French approach to equal pay seems to be in the direction of comparable worth, although this concept has not yet surfaced in policy discussions. There is emphasis on the knowledge, experience, and preparation for the job as well as the actual work. The French policy allows pay to be compared throughout all the branches of a particular enterprise and requires that employers carefully examine their entire job-classification scheme to make sure that the different elements that make up the salary are based on the same criteria for men and women.

The French policy, like the American, encourages employers to take affirmative action; it is called *rattrapage* (catch up) or positive discrimination. An employer charged with discrimination can avoid penalties by adopting a plan for equality that may include special efforts to overcome past discrimination in hiring, training, promotion, and working conditions. The state has a small fund to subsidize such programs, an incentive not available in the United States. The 1983 law prohibits the adoption of new protective employment policies although it leaves existing statutes intact. This is different from the United States, where federal equal-employment policy takes precedence over state protective laws.

Enforcement differs in the two countries because of differences in their constitutions and overall labor policy. For one thing, the equal employment law in France was devised especially for women, whereas in the United States sex is one of a number of prohibited classifications (along with race, color, religion, national origin) to be enforced. The United States established a special agency, the Equal Employment Opportunity Commission, (EEOC), to answer specific grievances, while the French rely on existing administrative structures. The French have a special committee but it does not answer individual complaints. The Conseil Superieur de l'Egalité Professionnel replaced the old Committee on Women's Employment. It is composed of thirty-six members including experts and representatives from all employment organizations. The council works with ministers responsible for women's rights, labor employment, and training. Its job is to oversee the administration of the equal employment policy. Its main responsibility is to work with employers and unions, providing information, receiving annual reports, and assisting in developing plans of positive discrimination.

The Inspectorate of Labor is charged with the enforcement of all aspects of the French labor code. If an employee believes she has been the victim of discrimination she sends her complaint to the labor inspectorate. An inspector then visits the work site and investigates. He or she need not inform the employer of any specific charges; since he or she has a wide range of authority it could be a routine visit. In this way he or she protects the anonymity of the employee making the complaint. The Inspector may conciliate or hold a hearing. If conciliation fails, the Office of Judgment hears the case and can levy penalties. If the employee does not want to act on her own, she can ask a union to intercede: they are specifically empowered by the law to bring enforcement actions. The employee can also bring her case to the Prud'hommes council, which has the authority to levy penalties against an employer for violating the law. Rarely would the case go to a regular law court. In the United States, on the other hand, the EEOC has the function of investigation and conciliation but cannot penalize or issue injunctions. For that, one must be prepared and have the resources to sue in regular court. Most of the procedure in France is low-cost and legal aid is available. Potential penalties include fines and/or jail terms, whereas the most an American employer can lose, other than legal fees, is employees' back pay.

The French policy has been in effect only since 1983, while equal opportunity has been United States policy since the mid-1960s. The MWR executive made a strong start in enforcing the *loi* Roudy. All the necessary implementing decrees were in force within one year of passage compared with the United States, where women had to wait four years for administrative guidelines on sex discrimination on Title VII and until the mid-1970s for full coverage of the law. In France much of the necessary consultation was completed before the statute was passed so that important actors, such as the unions, management, and labor inspectors, had already accepted the provisions. The French do not have to wait years to find out what the law means through tedious processes of judicial interpretation; these rulings come quickly from the Council of State and many were included ahead of time in the code itself. On the other hand, it was through the courts that the subtleties of sex-neutral discrimination became illegal in the United States. Unnecessary employment policies that are facially neutral and have a disparate effect on one sex, such as height and weight requirements, are not prohibited by the 1983 *loi* Roudy. The legislature must pass another amendment to the law code in order to outlaw these practices in France.

In the United States and France the problem of sexual harassment arose as an employment issue after the passage of equal opportunity laws, but they have been extended to cover it. The EEOC issued guidelines that defined sexual harassment as prohibited sex discrimination and outlined employer responsibility. In France, the issue came to public attention in late 1985 as the result of a conference sponsored by the Ligue du Droit des femmes with a subsidy from the MWR. These early discussions have focused on the nature and extent of the problem. One of the main goals is to overcome the widespread view that the so-called *droit de cuissage* is merely the remnant of medieval patrimony, not a concern in the era of sexual liberation. Roudy advocated immediate attention to language: "I prefer to speak of sexual blackmail. In effect, a man tries it because he is in a situation of power (or believes he is) to obtain favors."[31] Roudy classified sexual harassment as sex discrimination and urged women to use the mechanisms in the new equal opportunity law to fight it.

The feminists at the Ministry of Woman's Rights were very optimistic about the *loi* Roudy. They realized that much must be done to enforce the provisions and even more to make sure that working women are aware of and use their rights. They placed a great deal of hope on the annual reports required of employers (those with 300 + employees immediately after the act passed, 50 + employees by 1986). For the first time there will be data available on salaries, hiring, promotion, and training, by gender. From these reports they hoped to know and then change the extent of participation by women in training and retraining programs.

The MWR made much noise about job training. It was a popular policy: Regardless of political persuasion, everyone agrees that poor training is one of the causes of women's lower work status. The MWR sponsored pilot programs in new technologies and mobilized the regional delegates to encourage better training everywhere. Roudy secured guaranteed places for girls in the youth programs offered by the special Ministry of Vocational Training. Despite all this, the majority of French workers continue to receive their job training from the enterprises themselves. These training programs are now covered by the equal employment law and employers are responsible for eliminating sex discrimination. Equality plans may include measures of positive discrimination to improve the occupational training of women.

The MWR was also interested in watching the unions in their enforcement role. Feminist groups who were consulted about the *loi* Roudy had demanded legal status to represent women workers in cases of discrimination. Then the unions objected vigorously and successfully to any outside intervention on their monopoly over worker advocacy. In 1985, the new antisexist law (fully discussed in the next chapter) gave some legal powers to women's rights organizations to intervene in cases of discrimination in hiring and firing; the union, however, still has a monopoly inside the enterprise over such questions as pay, training, and promotion. The feminists fear that unions will not be responsive to women's interests. Decades of opposition to women working, fear of competition, and acceptance of the primary role of women as homemakers and mothers cast suspicion on the unions as advocates of sex equality. Union feminists disagree and think that only with the involvement of labor organizations will employers be induced to cooperate. The MWR employment specialists were aware that it was the unions who wanted to retain protective laws. They wait to see if any cases arise in which women are denied jobs because of bans on night work or other protective regulations. If such occurs, there will be a basis for prodding the unions to accept repeal of all remaining protection except that relating to pregnancy, child birth, and lactation.

THE PUBLIC SECTOR

Public employment has been an important source of jobs for women workers and a model for the private sector in eliminating sex discrimination. Welfare state policies sharply increased employment in female professions such as teaching, social services, and health care. The French government needs people in service occupations, vocations in which women have received most of their training since the nineteenth century. The state is also reputed to be the least sexist employer in France. Less burdened by motives of profit and the market, the public employer is freer to adopt democratic values. Civil service practices of recruitment through open, competitive examinations and job classification by grades seem more egalitarian and less vulnerable to sex discrimination than the old-boy network in the private sector. At the same time, since equal opportunity is a general norm of public service employment, whatever discrimination does exist seems more serious than similar practices by private enterprise. Feminists interpret sex inequality in the civil service as a gauge of the true intent of the male political elite.[32]

One woman worker in four works for the government. Forty-eight percent of the public employees are women, while they are thirty-seven percent of the private sector workers. (In the United States, women make up less than thirty-five percent of the federal civil service). However, a breakdown of the job patterns in France shows that their participation mirrors private sector employment. Women cluster in certain "women's jobs" found in the service and education ministries; women are also found disproportionately at the lower grades of the civil service, while very few are in the *Grand Corps*—the policy-making elite.

This pattern reflects social influences and the historical growth of female labor in the civil service itself. From the time when women were deprived of citizenship during the French Revolution until they received the vote in 1944, they had no claim to public employment. The various administrative departments had complete control over their own recruitment. Men could always apply to any ministerial corps; women had to be specially admitted. Women were reserve labor, hired at the discretion of the government. Although there is now a statute covering all civil service employment, a patchwork of rules and practices survive to this day. The professional corps within each ministry, be it education, the post office, or bridges and roads, are zealous in retaining a monopoly on recruitment. In effect, this situation produces a wide variation of participation and opportunity for women in public sector employment.

A few women were employed by the state as early as the 1790s. But it was not until the end of the 1800s that the first corps, the teachers and postal workers, officially admitted women. As the typewriter took over the offices, women took over the government office jobs. After World War I, more and more bourgeois women had professional opportunities in the state bureaucracy as nurses and teachers. These female corps were the first to receive maternity leave.

Feminists had demanded equal access to government jobs since 1892 (Congrès générale de sociétés féministes). Finally, in 1936, the Popular Front government officially decreed the principle of equality in civil service. Nevertheless, recruitment of women remained at departmental discretion. There was nothing to prevent the war ministry from declaring it would hire no women or the Minister of the Interior from setting up strict quotas. Discriminatory civil service practices lingered much longer in France than in the United States, where women gained legal access to almost all civil service exams in 1919 and equal pay for equal work in 1923. The right to vote, won in 1920, prompted these reforms. Even so, discrimination against married women was legal in the United States civil service until 1936. The low status, job segregation, and distribution of women in the lower grades were similar in both countries.

When women finally were permitted to vote in France, the government began to pay more attention to removing barriers to public employment. Gradual inroads were made in corps and departmental autonomy. In 1946 the government enacted a General Statute on the Civil Service. Article VII declared the principle of equal access, but allowed exceptions for "physical inaptitude" or "psychological difficulties that a female presence could provoke." The result was that entire corps remained closed to women while others had quotas or token females. Some changes were more effective. The Ecole Nationale d'Administration, a new *Grande Ecole* established in 1945 to train the administrative elite, was equally open to both sexes. The Magistrature also let down sex barriers and became a stepping stone for prominent political women such as Simone Veil.

Although Article VII has been modified several times to close loopholes and exceptions, some corps have been successful in finding new ones to avoid hiring women. A 1959 amendment removed the reference to psychological difficulties: "For application of the present ordinance no distinction is made between the two sexes under reservation of exceptions in particular statutes [pertaining to a corps or ministry] and as required by the nature of the job." This allowed fixing of physical and psychological job qualifications that women could not meet. Again in 1975 a new article sought to tighten the regulation by naming those jobs which could be restricted: "No distinction is made between the sexes. . . . However, when the nature of the functions or the conditions of their exercise justify it, certain corps on a list established by the Council of State, after consultation with the Civil Service Council and the advisory committees, may have exclusive recruitment of men or women or distinct conditions of access for men and women." The loophole was narrowed, but still permitted unequal access to over twenty corps and single-sex recruitment in five (three for men and two for women).

Civil service recruitment became a tool in Monique Pelletier's efforts to give special help to single mothers. A law in 1979 raised the upper age limit of eligibility for examination of women who had reared children and for single women (divorced, widowed, not married) with children in their care. This did little to overcome the penchant of some agencies for restricting or eliminating women, let alone the persistence of sex discrimination in promotion and pay.

The United States government seems to remain ahead of the French in using public employment to promote equality. In 1962 the Attorney General ruled that recruiters could not specify the sex of applicants they desired for a position, a practice dating back to 1870, and the Civil Service Commission issued regulations banning sex discrimination in federal personnel practices. This was reinforced by President Lyndon Johnson's executive order banning discrimination against women in the federal bureaucracy. Then, in the 1970's, the government adopted affirmative action policies to increase the representation of women at the higher grades.

Under the Socialist regime, inequalities in French civil service persisted. The government, the major employer of women, is riddled with clustering and job segregation, with great variation in participation of women from one ministry to the next. Education is the most feminine, followed by Health and Labor. With less than twenty percent of their work force female, Interior, Environment, and Transport have very low participation. Salary and job classifications encourage equal pay but the practice of giving different *primes* (bonuses) leads to unequal income. The higher bonuses are usually found at the ministries with fewer women, such as Finance. Women are underrepresented in management and technical positions. Although they constitute forty-eight percent of the total public work force, there is often much lower representation in Category A, the highest management grade. It ranges from seven percent at Transport and Industry to thirty-nine percent at Culture, forty percent at Youth, forty-five percent at Labor, and fifty-three percent at Education. The low representation is more dramatically illustrated at the very top civil service elite, the grand corps. In 1982 only 3 of the 152 ambassadors were female, three of twenty-eight university rectors, six directors of ministries, and no prefects. On the other hand, 99 percent of the secretaries and 82.4 percent of office workers in government were women.

This pattern did not happen by accident and barriers limiting access to various departments have been long-lasting. By 1981 there were still female quotas in more than twenty corps. Promotions, subject entirely to the discretion of ministries, permitted further discrimination at higher ranks. Feminists charged that throughout the civil service, women with similar educational qualifications as men held lower status positions. Finally, in 1981, Roudy offered another version of Article VII to close the loopholes and eliminate once and for all separate recruitment criteria and procedures for the corps. Her bill passed with little opposition. In January 1983, Roudy and the Minister of Civil Service issued regulations urging ministries to eliminate all language that implies positions are restricted to one sex. They also gave priority to training of female employees to help them qualify for promotion within the ministry and cautioned supervisors "to seize every opportunity to increase the number of women to be promoted." Another loophole permitting discrimination against lesbians was also closed in

1983. The law that was abolished had allowed the government to refuse to hire anyone not considered of "good morality."

Despite the reforms, a report in late 1985 showed that fifteen corps, including the police, *instituteurs*, and physical education instructors, still place limits on the recruitment of women. Feminist critics don't expect much to change inside the civil service because reforms rely for compliance on the good will of each administrative agency. The MWR tried to prod the other ministries to equalize the bonuses and encountered the usual resistance of civil service corps and Grand Corps to any external influence, especially if it is regarded as political or partisan. Progress in feminizing the top grades of the public sector will be as painfully slow in France as it has proved to be in the United States.

DEFINITION OF THE ISSUE OF WORK

The conflict over the issue of women's work has long been characterized by the contradictions between the goals of equality and the acceptance of the differences in sex roles. Even feminists have been affected, at times demanding both equal rights and special treatment for working mothers. For most of the time since the French Revolution conceptions focusing on the special nature of women have prevailed, resulting in protective and restrictive laws. Related issues of pronatalism and antiracism have also affected policymaking on the subject. Since World War II, however, advocates of equality have gained ground. Reform feminists have increasingly argued for equal rights to training, hiring, promotion, and pay, while refusing to accept that family roles are of exclusively feminine interest. They took advantage of the EEC directive on equal opportunity to gain control of the women's work issue. Since 1978 and into the Mitterrand years, the logic of policies promoting women in employment asserted that equality is unrelated to family status. In embracing equality, the government has not dropped protection entirely. Policies for mothers remain, as do certain prohibitions on heavy work. Other special policies, such as child care leave and part-time work, have been recast as general family issues not restricted to women.

The history of the controversy on the work issue has had important results that are especially striking in comparison with the United States. Widespread rights and generous benefits for maternity are in place and remain compatible with equal employment opportunity laws. The problem of reconciling the demands of family and work is a public, not a private, responsibility, redefined as a concern of both men and women. Symbolic equal pay and antidiscrimination gestures have been replaced by the full incorporation of women's right to work and right to equal opportunity into the labor code. This brings the existing extensive enforcement mechanisms for worker rights to bear on the problems of women, especially access to jobs, training, promotions, and pay. The social partners, labor and management, have a stake in the policy and work directly with government in administration of the law.

The cost of integrating women's rights into general labor policy has been the reduction of participation by feminist groups. Before the new laws, feminists had direct representation on the Committee on Women's Employment. The new equal opportunity council has no membership from feminist organizations, although individual feminists may represent other groups. The participation of unions in enforcing the law me it denial of feminist involvement, except for a small part under the new antisexist law. Acceptance of the unions' monopoly over worker rights has been a part of social policy in France for many years. A tradeoff was necessary; women would gain access to the regular state enforcement mechanisms of the labor code while feminists would lose the chance of direct advocacy on behalf of individual workers. Now feminists are consulted only by government feminists whose tenure is determined by the fortunes and attitudes of the president, his ministers, and their political parties.

The equal opportunity laws enjoy widespread popularity. In a poll taken in December 1983, ninety-three percent of those who had heard of the policies on equality found them important for improving women's rights.[33] Feminist groups too are pleased with the equal opportunity legislation and the efforts of the Ministry of Woman's Rights. Some want a tougher law and others give credit to Roudy's predecessors, but all support it. Finally women have a chance to improve their condition as workers, to get training for real jobs with good pay, and to compete for promotion. Much depends on mobilizing women, especially young ones, to acquire a métier, to learn and use their rights, and to take responsibility for their lives.

Some worry about the gap between policy logic and actual behavior. Current policy is directed toward an image of the family in which both parents are employed and both share homemaking, child care, and child-rearing responsibilities. For the many real-life families who don't fit this image, however, equal opportunity laws fall short. The burden of child care continues to fall disproportionately on mothers and limits their chances to make use of the new laws. Even in cases in which husbands perform household tasks, their participation does not alter basic sex role patterns. The husband tends to assume the outside jobs (*bricolage*), drives the car, and cares for the children on Saturday morning while the wife cleans the house, cooks, and does the laundry.[34]

Policies based on the concept of role sharing have a disparate effect on families in which roles are still separate. When paid parental leave was instituted by the Socialist government, for example, the MWR feared it would encourage women to leave the work force permanently. Measures to develop more part-time jobs have met feminist opposition. In February 1985, several feminist associations denounced the Socialist policy as "contrary to the spirit and the law of equal opportunity because it is aimed at women who constitute eighty-seven percent of part-time workers."[35] Only in a few families in which earning power is equal between husband and wife would it make little difference which parent stayed home or took a part-time job to care for children.

Public opinion may soon catch up with the law. Already in 1983 ninety percent of French women thought that work and motherhood were equally important. Fifty-nine percent agreed that work is indispensable and desirable for women. Young women aged 18 to 24 believed a career leads to increased independence, social relationships, and personal development for women. A majority ranked their métier as more important to their future happiness than either marriage or children.[36]

NOTES

1. Quoted by Yvette Roudy, *La Femme en marge* (Paris: Flammarion, 1975; 1982), 86.

2. Jacques J. Zephir, *Le Néo-Féminisme de Simone Beauvoir* (Paris: Denoël/Gonthier, 1982) 120–43.

3. Although *métier* translates imprecisely as "career" or "occupation" there is really no satisfactory English equivalent. It means knowing how to do something for which one can earn a living. The word has become part of

English usage and Webster's offers another useful definition: ''an area of activity in which one is expert or successful.''

4. Quoted by Jeanette Laôt, *Stratégie pour les femmes* (Paris: Stock, 1977), 215–6.

5. L'Agence femmes information, *Bulletin*, 174 (21–27 octobre 1985), 3. In late 1985, the CGT women's conference agreed that their top priority is ''the right to work.'' Women will be pushed into flexible time as an alternative to full-time employment, said women's section head Jacqueline Leonard.

6. Quoted by Benoîte Groult, *Ainsi soit-elle* (Paris: Grasset, 1975), 37.

7. Quoted in Laôt, *Stratégie pour les femmes*, 115–6.

8. Senator Henriet, *Le Monde* (11 décembre 1979). Report of declaration.

9. ''Femmes,'' *La Nouvelle Critique* (mars 1975), 22. Quoted by C. Gilles.

10. *Journal Officiel*, Débats parlementaires (16 juin 1977), 3861.

11. Parti socialiste, ''Féminisme—Socialisme—Autogestion'' (février 1979), 23.

12. Louise Tilly and Joan Scott, *Women, Work, and Family* (New York: Holt, Rinehart and Winston, 1978).

13. Quoted by Odile Dhavernas, *Droits des femmes, pouvoir des hommes* (Paris: Seuil, 1978), 254.

14. Catherine Bodard Silver, ''A Sociological Interpretation of the Position of Women in French Society,'' Mimeo. (New York: Center for the Social Sciences at Columbia University, 1980), 40. Silver points out that the *Accords* placed motherhood ''as a social function, similar to the military service for men, which had to be financially supported by the whole community.''

15. Françoise Giroud, *Cents mesures pour les femmes* (Paris: Documentation française, 1976), 17.

16. *Journal Officiel*, Débats parlementaires (juin 1974), 2495.

17. *Journal Officiel*, Débats parlementaires (octobre 1978), 5760.

18. Marcelle Devaud and Martine Levy, ''Women's Employment in France,'' *International Labour Review* 119 (November/December 1980), 746–7.

19. *Journal Officiel*, Débats parlementaires (novembre 1981), 3898.

20. *Journal Officiel*, Débats parlementaires (16 juin 1977), 3854.

21. Andrée Michel and Genevieve Texier, *La Condition de la française d'aujourd'hui* (Paris: Gonthier, 1964), 129–174.

22. Regina Fodor, ''Day-Care Policy in France and Its Consequences for Women,'' *International Journal of Urban and Regional Research* 2 (October 1978), 463–481.

23. Evelyne Sullerot, *Les Françaises au travail* (Paris: Hachette, 1973).

24. Danièle Kergoat, *Les Femmes et le travail à temps partiel* (Paris: Documentation française, 1984), 202.

25. Ministère des Droits de la femme, *Citoyennes à part entière* (mars 1985), 10.

26. Loi du 22 décembre 1972 sur l'égalité de rémunération entre les hommes et les femmes.

27. *Journal Officiel*, Débats parlementaires (21 novembre 1972), 5562.

28. Ibid. (22 avril 1975), 1941.

29. Douglas E. Ashford, *Policy and Politics in France* (Philadelphia: Temple University Press, 1982), 195.

30. Council Directive of 9 February 1976, *Official Journal of the European Communities* No. L, 39/40, 147.

31. Ministère des Droits de la femme, ''Oser dénoncer,'' *Citoyennes à part entière*, 47 (novembre 1985), 8.

32. Dhavernas, *Droits des femmes* (Paris: Seuil, 1978), 299.

33. Ministère des Droits de la femme, *Citoyennes à part entière* (janvier 1984).

34. Anne-Marie Daune-Richard, *Travail professionel et travail domestique* (Paris: Ministère du Travail, 1984).

35. L'Agence femmes information, *Bulletin* 145 (4 mars 1985), 4.

36. Ministère des Droits de la femme, *Citoyennes à part entière* 28 (février 1984), 12. Report of Sondage Figaro Sofres—décembre 83.

7

SEXUALITY

CENTRAL TO THE ideology of French radical feminists is the belief that the control of sexuality is the key to all the powers men have enjoyed over women. The radical feminists claim women's right to define their bodies, to set them free from patriarchal restraint, and to use them to create culture. In the early 1970s this subject electrified hundreds of consciousness-raising groups and mobilized thousands of feminists to confront the phallocracy—the power of the penis. Moderate feminists joined them in demanding changes in the content and definition of policies affecting rape and battery, prostitution, pornography, and sexism. At the heart of the these policies is a deeply entrenched myth about female sexuality. Altering policy means destroying the myth.

The French sexual myth is so strong that it finds believers throughout the world. France, the land of love, produces a woman unfettered by American Puritan guilt or English Victorian reticence. "Whatever different forms the stereotypes and commonplaces related to the image of French women at home and abroad take, the dominant trait is unchanging: kitten, child-woman, femme fatale, prostitute, mistress, seductive, elegant, experienced, sensual, sexy, amoral, submissive, the French woman is seen as a creature often charming, but also a little contemptible."[1] According to feminists, God did not create the French woman, man and his culture did. Man constructed the female starting with her sexual feelings; this dominance over her personal identity is the keystone of patriarchy. The myth pervades art, science, religion, and law. Deeply entrenched as it is, feminists have resolved to wrest control of female sexuality from men even if it means attacking their fantasies.

Man plays God by decreeing that the natural sex act is coitus. This definition has several important effects. Women cannot engage in natural and normal sex without men. Sexual pleasure is defined as man's pleasure: erection, penetration, ejaculation. Woman's role is to attract a man, receive his penis, and satisfy his desires. Seduction is expected. Men are urged to "take" women with strength and power. Woman, whose role is to attract and please man, nearly always consents to be "taken"; it's part of her nature. All things are acceptable, even desirable, as long as they conform to the male view of sexuality. Rape, therefore, is an extension of "natural" sex. Men are allowed to buy sex or live off prostitutes. Pornography liberates fantasies by portraying normal elements of the sex act—domination and subservience—in extreme forms. On the other hand, all attempts by women to pursue sexual pleasure autonomously from men are forbidden. Masturbation and homosexuality are threatening, unless these acts are performed to excite a male audience. Lesbians are made to feel at best, guilty and unnatural, and at worst, worthless, even nonexistent.

The so-called sexual revolution has not changed sex for women; it has only made sex less private. At one time the moral code protected most women from exploitation by denying them sexual pleasure. Now there are no protections but pleasure is still centered on the male. From posters to magazines to film, female sexuality is marketed; everything is permitted as long as man is the consumer and the salesman. No better example of the one-sided sexual liberation can be found than the *petits annonces* for sex partners in weekend editions of *Libération*. Despite the unfettered language and enticing suggestions, the framework fits very conventional male/female roles. When a heterosexual couple advertises for a bisexual to form a threesome, for example, it is rarely for a male, usually for a female. Even female homosexuality must fit into a male-centered model.

Feminists conclude that while men speak love they hate women and fear female sexuality. Misogyny fuels the engine of patriarchy and unites men to preserve it. This is evident in their acceptance of the abuse of women by rape and exploitation through pornography and prostitution. More dramatic evidence of misogyny is the official tolerance of female circumcision among the ethnic minorities in France. Direct mutilation through clitorectomy and infibulation is popular in some Arab and African cultures. The parents of mutilated daughters explain that the practice is necessary to correct nature's error in giving girls a male organ, the clitoris. The effect of circumcision is to deny women sexual pleasure, independence, and control over reproduction. African political leaders have defended the practice as a vital custom that sets them apart from the culturally imperialistic West. Just how alien is the practice to French culture?

Clitorectomy was practiced in both Europe and America in the nineteenth century. Its purpose then as now was to "normalize" female sexuality, that is, to give it the exclusive function of reproduction. The surgery was an extreme application of conventional sexual morality. Today, clitorectomy is rare among the French, but the zeal for regulating female sexuality has not weakened. Feminists argue that the patriarchy achieves its goals through cultural mutilation and oppression. The authorities tolerate the cutting of the daughters of African immigrants in France because the values it represents are not that much different from their own. It seems doubly cruel that women are the tools for perpetuating this sexual slavery, but this too is not without parallel in French culture. Both French and African mothers fear that unless their daughters' sexuality is regulated, they will have difficulty attracting husbands.

Feminists struggle to gain control of the definition of female sexuality. As usual they disagree on the means to achieve their goal. The Psych et Po school of *néo-fémininité* advocates the complete separation of women's bodies from men. Undisturbed by heterosexual contact, woman can explore the meaning of her own sexuality, know her body's "unheard-of songs."[2] Women will use their bodies to create a new culture with a women's art, politics, and literature. Other radical and moderate feminists want to redefine female sexuality by separating it from both coitus and procreation. Their goal is to free women from patriarchal oppression and permit them to develop on their own, explore their bodies, and choose their pleasures, with or without men.[3] In this way, women will have autonomy, dignity, and control over their own bodies without the intermediation of men but need not separate themselves entirely from men.

The new definitions could affect the way the government responds to matters relating to women's sexuality. Both radicals and moderates have worked to change laws that have reinforced the sexual abuse of women. They have addressed for the first time the need for a new perspective on rape, prostitution, and pornography and argued that laws in these areas must be concerned with eliminating sex discrimination and exploitation of women. As in other policy areas, they want to redefine these issues to promote women's rights. With respect to sexuality, the effort goes beyond the regulation of practices to an assault on cultural sexism, the exploited image of women, and the sexual fantasies of men.

RAPE

Until 1980 the French penal code did not mention the word rape (*viol*). Prosecutions for sexual assault could be brought under Article 332, which punished any assault on morals (*attentats aux moeurs*), defined as a violent act against another person that was contrary to morality. Over time the courts developed a legal definition of rape that was found only in the annotations to the penal code: "Illicit coitus with a woman who one knows does not consent." Some formal aspects of this definition were clear: it was solely vaginal penetration by a penis, eliminating anal, oral, or other forms of sexual assault; it could only be committed by a man on a woman; and it could not be committed in marriage which was, presumably, licit coitus. The prosecution had to prove the assailant knew the victim did not consent, a fact as difficult to prove as lack of consent. A defendant had only to say, "I believed she agreed." An assault on morals, including rape, was a felony carrying a penalty of ten to twenty years in prison. Prosecutions were brought before the criminal court (*cour d'assises*) in front of a jury. In practice, however, the formal charge of rape was rare. Most sexual assaults were treated as lesser crimes (*délits*), such as assault and battery (*coups et blessures*) or public indecency (*outrage public à la pudeur*). These were tried before a magistrate in a lower court (*cour correctionel*) and carried minimal penalties.

Until the 1970s rape was neither officially nor unofficially a woman's issue. First of all, as a crime, the attack was legally against society and its standards of morality. Second, the injured party was the family (father or husband) of the victim. A man's honor was at stake and prosecution by the state was the redress for the attack. Finally, the public held various definitions of the crime. In the absence of a statutory definition, society's views had a tremendous impact on the behavior of police and the courts. For many the only incontestable rape was the assault on a virgin or a chaste wife. In the first case the hymen was destroyed along with its value as evidence of the purity of a young marriageable woman. In the other, the rapist could force an "odious" bastard on a man. The assault robbed middle- and upper-class men of their property.

A popular conception, especially on the Right, was that true rape is a rare and private act, committed only by psychopathic men. According to this view, most acts of violent sex are therefore not rape but a natural extension of male and female sexual relations. Man is supposed to be the pursuer, woman the prey. Men have chased women from the beginning of time and do so in every culture. Women accept their passive role and most are somewhat masochistic. Those involved in violent sex are usually sexually experienced. They want to be desired and they will often pretend to say no, when they really want the man to overpower them, to "take" them. Some people believe that it is impossible to rape a woman, that a man can have sexual relations with a woman only if she consents. They credit a Frenchman, Balzac, with the favorite motto oï defense lawyers in rape cases: "You can't thread a needle that moves."

Men on the Left believed that rape did exist but tended to view the rapist as the real victim. The existence of the crime itself was a way to persecute the poor. In a capitalist system the poor rape out of frustration; they are not really responsible because the system drives them to it. Like Eldridge Cleaver (*Soul on Ice*), they are fighting back against their oppressors by raping women of the dominant class. Leftists save their special sympathy for the African and Arab immigrants who are sexually deprived and often tricked by white women. Although men of every class engage in violent sex, only the poor are prosecuted.

Rape was a critical issue for the feminist movement from the beginning and along with abortion was considered to be crucial to liberation. Like abortion, it united the radicals and the moderates. Unlike abortion there was no official definition of the issues to overcome; *violeur*, "rapist," was rarely found even in standard French dictionaries before 1976. Feminists did not have to overturn ancient laws or combat an entrenched bureaucracy. Rather they had to shatter the popular conception of rape as a natural extension of the sex act that women desire and expose it as an attack on women per se, regardless of their age, sexual experience, or their relations with men. Feminists found that their view of rape as a crime against women placed them in opposition to men, even their allies on the Left, in a way that they had not faced on the abortion issue. "In attacking rape and rapists we had fused, without knowing it or wanting to, men without distinction of age, nationality, or sexual practice, into a patriarchal bloc."[4]

In their effort to break the silence and complicity with sexual violence against women, feminists used severe language to frame their issue. Rape is murder—a rape victim is a "murdered woman." It is an act of fascism, war. Rape signifies permanent violence or the threat of violence against women as a means of control. The fact that rapists go unpunished reveals the participation of legal institutions in this oppression. Both the act and the official tolerance of it represent patriarchy in its worst form with all its misogyny, oppression, and exploitation. Rape is punishment meted out to women who dare to free themselves from men and to move autonomously on the streets or in bars. If a woman is not in the care of one man, the assumption is that she belongs to any man. It is the fate of women who travel alone and almost certain treatment for hitchhikers. Yet for all this repression, violence, and fear, it is taboo for women to speak of it. If they complain, it is they who are guilty, they who by their behavior invited the attack (unless they are sequestered virgins). There is always an explanation for violence against a woman that makes it anyone's fault but the male rapist's.[5]

The campaign against rape began in 1972 at a big meeting in Paris, "Journée de dénonciation des crimes contre la femme," and continued with more meetings, discussions, demonstrations, and pressure on the government. Feminists broadcast the shocking news: when a woman says no, it's not yes, it's no! (Quand une femme dit non, c'est pas oui, c'est non!). To gain access to public opinion, Gisèle Halimi and Choisir used a tactic that had been successful in making abortion a public women's issue: a symbolic trial. This one was at Aix-en-Provence and involved the brutal gang rape of two Belgian women who had been camping in the Provence region. The case gave the feminists the chance to demonstrate a number of things that were wrong with the rape law and its administration. Despite the fact that three men had repeatedly and violently attacked the women for four hours, the attack had not even been charged as a rape. The case was to be prosecuted as a simple assault and to be tried before a magistrate. The women were lesbians and Halimi accused the government of not considering them "real" victims. She fought for nearly two years to have the case moved to criminal court and tried as a felony. In 1978 the case finally came to the Aix criminal court, where the three men were convicted of rape. Choisir published the transcript of the trial.[6] All the elements were there: the harassment of the victims, the rapists' claim that the women consented, and the details of the violent attack.

Meanwhile, a small group of MLF activists made a direct appeal to Françoise Giroud, the new Secretary for the Status of Women.[7] This was prompted by the publication of a translation of Erin Pizzey's book on wife abuse in England and her subsequent visit to Paris in the summer of 1975.[8] Feminists were eager to expose the special victimization of women in France and linked the issues of wife battery and rape. Neither rape laws nor simple assault laws under which most cases were tried applied to women attacked by their husbands. These feminists prepared a proposal that would change the criminal rape statute and provide shelters for battered women and sought a meeting with the new secretary for women.

There was little reason to expect much help from Françoise Giroud. In one of her first interviews after her appointment she said "I am not a feminist, because I am not a sexist." What Giroud meant as a testimony of her scrupulous adherence to equality, some feminists read as criticism of their efforts. This declaration "communicates her desire to separate herself from any feminist label; she puts herself with those who find us ridiculous."[9] Later, on meeting Erin Pizzey, Giroud said she doubted that wife battery was a problem in France and that, even if it were, it did not belong in her portfolio.

At best, the meeting between Giroud and the MLF group was an education for the secretary. After listening to the case and examining the dossiers on rape and battered women, Giroud agreed that the victims of these crimes might need some assistance, through shelters and specially trained female police officers. She denied that any of these areas pertained to her special responsibilities and recommended action by local governments. Finally, she did not agree that the rape law needed change. Giroud may have learned something about violence against women in France but nothing concrete emerged from the meeting.

The next year the public discussion on the rape issue was well-launched. A great day of debate and demonstration organized by MLF at the Mutualité, 25 June 1976, attracted many of the prominent feminists: Simone de Beauvoir, Benoîte Groult, Delphine Seyrig, Simone

Iff, and Yvette Roudy. Active groups included Choisir, the Ligue du Droit des femmes, and the Mouvement Jeunes Femmes. The day produced a feminist manifesto on rape:

1. Rape is not a fable, it is the daily reality for women.
2. Rape is not by chance—it is the expression of permanent violence against women.
3. Rape is not punished as a crime against women.
4. Rape is not a law of nature; that is the myth of patriarchy.
5. Rape is neither the desire nor the pleasure of women.
6. Rape is not destiny.

At first glance, feminist campaigns for changes in rape laws in France differed from those in the United States. Here, reform involved fifty state statutes. Common law had for centuries labeled rape a crime with serious penalties. American feminists often found powerful allies among lawyers and the police who wanted more effective prosecution of the crime. Nevertheless, the problems of defining the issue in the two countries were similar. Under the common law administered in the United States, rape was narrowly defined as illicit carnal knowledge without consent by a man of a woman. Trials and convictions for the crime were rare. Women were often blamed for the assault and concern for the defendant's rights condoned the unlimited attack on a victim's character, sexual history, and testimony in court. This followed often callous treatment by male police officers who believed women either couldn't be raped or enjoyed being overpowered. Feminists in the United States and France struggled to change public opinion to see sexual assault not as an extension of normal sexual activity, but as a crime of sexual power used to punish and control women.

During the 1970s, French feminists and women activists had prepared public opinion for a new policy. In 1978, the year of the trial at Aix, one of several private bills filed in the legislature by feminists, Socialists, and Communists passed the Senate. It was sponsored by Senator Brigitte Gros, a feminist and independent who had testified at Aix:

From now on, the law must intervene to protect woman from all violent attacks against the integrity of her body, and of her mind and the peace of her soul. A woman raped is a woman tortured. A woman raped is a woman wounded, battered, degraded, humiliated sometimes for her entire life. Rape is an intolerable crime. Its repression but also its prevention have become a new exigency of our civilization.[10]

That the French parliament finally adopted a rape statute in 1980 owed a great deal to Monique Pelletier, Minister for the Status of Women. It was Pelletier who, on behalf of the government, accepted the basic concept that rape was a crime against women that for the most part went unpunished. Pelletier took charge of the Gros bill. During the National Assembly debates she continued the feminist theme that rape is a criminal attack on the dignity of women. "This is why, as minister responsible for the status of women, I take the floor today before your assembly, moved to speak in the name of all women."[11] With government support the reform was enacted quickly, but not without some disagreements between the National Assembly and the Senate. The lower house successfully enlarged the definition of the crime to include oral and anal sexual assault as well as the use of foreign objects. They wanted a penalty of ten to twenty years in prison, but the Senate won a lower penalty for "simple rape."

The new law, adopted 23 December 1980, defines rape: "Any act of sexual penetration of whatever sort it be, committed on a person other than oneself, by violence, force, or surprise, constitutes a rape." This improves on the old definition by expanding the nature of the assault to include oral and anal penetration, removing the marital exclusion, and eliminating the requirement that the defendant admit he knew the victim did not consent. Proof of force, surprise, or violence is enough to establish that the crime occurred. Rape, per se, is now a crime, punishable by five to ten years in prison. A heavier penalty can be ordered in cases of rape aggravated by several conditions: "where the victim is particularly vulnerable, by reason of pregnancy, sickness, infirmity, or physical or mental deficiency, or a minor of less than fifteen years; where there are two or more accomplices or rapists; where the assailant is a relative or has a position of authority over the victim."

The statute contains several important reforms in the administration of the law. Any association that has had the goal of fighting against sexual violence for at least five years can file a suit for private damages during the criminal trial, if the victim agrees. Thus, feminist organizations and others can use their resources to help victims in prosecuting and punishing rapists. This was an important victory for the feminists that Pelletier had supported: "the role which women's associations have played in rape cases is important in all regards: reception of victims of sexual aggression, giving aid and counsel, and denunciation of traditional attitudes about the crime, in order that they be tried in all cases in higher courts."[12] Second, the rape victim has the option to waive the requirement of a closed trial, but the trial cannot be opened without her consent. Similarly, the media may only publish her name or any information about her that would allow people to identify her if she gives permission.

To Americans who are so accustomed to the anonymity of rape victims despite public trials it may seem odd to expect that a victim would give consent to publicity about a sexual assault when she has the chance not to. Removing the anonymity of the victim is a step toward removing her shame, according to French feminists. The belief that a woman has been ruined by an assault sustains the public image of rape as a moral or sexual crime. That image, they argue, has resulted in women's unwillingness to report sexual assaults to the police or go through with the prosecution. Anonymity may reduce embarrassment for a single victim but in a larger sense, as does privacy in any sexual matter, it perpetuates the ignorance and disgrace of women as a whole. Feminists wish to reserve all the shame and humiliation for the rapist, not the victim. They hope the victim will one day be seen as a heroine, proud to do what she can to punish men who prey on women. The option for open trials and publicity remains a feature of the law awaiting changes in public opinion.

In other ways the reforms in France are familiar to Americans. Most United States laws have expanded the definition of the crime to include all forms of sexual assault regardless of the sex or marital status of the victim. They focus not on the consent or resistance of the victim but on the degrees of force or violence used by the assailant. Many relate different levels of punishment to degrees of severity of the crime. Florida's sexual battery statute, for example, makes simple rape a second-degree felony.[13] Aggravated battery, including an assailant in a position of authority, a handicapped victim, or the use of drugs, is a first-degree felony. The most serious crime, a life felony, involves the threat or use of deadly force, such as a knife or a gun. The American reforms have erected rules of evidence to shield the victim from excessive public inquiry into her previous sexual experiences. There is no counterpart for this in the French reform. On the other hand, the presence of women's rights associations in court may help the victim fend off attacks on her morality by the defense attorney or the judge.

In the United States only the victim, not support groups, can bring suit for damages through a separate case in civil court.[14] Feminist associations have concentrated on helping the victims of assault by lobbying local government to establish support services. Many police departments have personnel specially trained to assist victims from the moment they report a crime and to be sure all evidence is preserved. Counselors and paralegals at sexual assault crisis centers help victims through the procedure of presecution and trial.

Government feminists in France have been pleased with recent improvements in the prosecution of rape. In its first report on the status of women in France, the Ministry of Woman's Rights applauded the impact feminists have had in changing the definition and administration of rape laws. Since the Aix trial, most rape cases have been tried in criminal court, where penalties are heavier. "The feminists have thus succeeded in designing rape as a crime against the integrity and dignity of women; justice has decided for its part some means of punishing it."[15] Women seem to be more willing to report rapes to the police; the number of cases has increased from 1,695 in 1979 to 2,859 in 1984.[16]

The Ministry of Woman's Rights declared its interest in raising awareness about the real consequences of crimes against women. They sponsored regional meetings on women and violence and sensitivity sessions for the police. The ministry adopted three general goals for helping rape victims: to improve the initial treatment they receive at police stations immediately after the assault, to discourage harassment and make the victim feel secure; to ease the trauma of the medical examination; and to offer financial assistance to women's organizations who provide information to victims. The MWR sponsored pilot training programs for police officers with feminist organizations SOS-Femmes battues and Mouvement Jeunes Femmes. The Ministry of the Interior has pledged to place specially trained personnel in every police station to provide assistance to all victims.

Feminists, however, find fault with the treatment of women in court. Since the victim is usually the only witness in a rape case, the judge and the defense often spend an inordinate amount of energy examining her. This is not limited to court testimony and cross-examination. The judge can order an inquiry of the psychological, moral, and health status of the victim as part of the preliminary investigation. While these are not required and the victim may refuse, they are conducted with no set guidelines. Feminists argue that these inquiries have little relation to the question of consent and do nothing more than harass the victim if she submits to them and cast doubt on her word if she declines. "Evaluation of credibility is not a scientific notion. It belongs to no branch of medicine, even psychiatry . . . nothing permits one to derive from a simple discourse the existence of a material fact (sexual relations) or a psychological attitude at a moment in the past (consent)." [17] In 1982 an advisory committee of the justice ministry, including representatives from the MWR, recommended that these investigations be kept to a minimum and not be considered as substitutes for the absence of material proof: "It is not the victim that we judge and her private life . . . should not become an excuse to put her on trial." [18]

After 1980 the rape issue received little public attention. In 1985 three public assaults on young women, two on trains and one on a Paris boulevard, in which witnesses refused to help the victims, revealed that rape is still *banalisé* (considered ordinary). A trend toward "open air" violence was spotted by the media. Feminists organized to bring their views about rape once again to public attention. A Collectif d'associations contre le viol, including MFPF, Choisir, and Maison des femmes, announced a campaign against the silence ("Ne laissons pas le viol se banaliser") with a demonstration followed by a manifesto against rape. The manifesto echoed the demands of the 1970s: rape is a crime, an attack on the integrity, dignity, liberty, on the rights of all women. It represents daily institutionalized oppression. [19]

The Collectif included a call for aid to victims of rape. Efforts in this area by the MWR have not had much impact. Training of police has not gone beyond the pilot stage. Less than six percent of the police officers are women. The MWR subsidized some brochures for rape victims, such as the one published by Mouvement Jeunes Femmes, entitled "Un Viol Quoi Faire?" It counsels a woman first to go to a doctor, if possible, in a hospital. Then the victim should immediately give the facts of the assault to the police, when she may make a complaint directly or through an attorney. There are no shelters specifically for rape victims but some may be helped at several centers for battered women. SOS-femmes viol received small grants to help with shelters and counseling. One of the first shelters near Paris, the Centre Flora Tristan, was established by the Ligue du Droit des femmes in 1978. The first in central Paris, the Foyer Louise Labé, was opened in 1985. Both received subsidies from the MWR. Another, Solidarité femmes in Grenoble, is one of the most active. There are now more than twenty-five shelters in France for women in distress.

PROSTITUTION

Prostitution prompts ambivalence, more so than any other issue of sexuality, even among feminists. The idea of selling sex, although unpleasant to many people, presents no clear picture of oppressors and victims. Anyone in society may be involved, from the powerful to the social outcasts. Often the people most committed to the practice are the prostitutes themselves.

France was not the first country to nurture prostitution but it is famous for making it a public service. The "French system" of state regulation was fully developed after 1800 using laws, administrative regulations, and police practices dating back to the 1300s. No single national law on prostitution existed; "Instead the system was based on the imaginative interpretation of the provisions of a variety of laws, some of them fundamental to the French government and none concerned specifically with prostitution."[20] The police in Paris were the architects of a policy of *tolérance* that was copied in other municipalities. Prostitution was neither legal nor illegal. *Tolérance* meant that any practice used to fight venereal disease, pimping, or soliciting was also tolerated, no matter what its effect on women.

By the 1830s the French regulations were fully in place. Dr. Parent-Duchâtelet in his 1836 report found prostitution to be endemic to society. He recognized a permanent demand for a class of "morally defective" women. "Prostitutes are as inevitable, in a mass of human beings, as sewers, roads and garbage dumps. They contribute to the maintenance of order and tranquility of society."[21] Yet they were an evil, especially by spreading that "most dangerous disease, syphilis." The duty of the state was to control this unsavory practice and prevent the spread of disease. Sir William Acton reported to the English from Paris: "The great object of the system adopted in France is to repress the private and secret, and to encourage public or avowed prostitution."[22]

The government required prostitutes to register through one of the licensed brothels (*maisons de tolérance*) or obtain a personal license (*carte*) if, and only if, they had enough money for their lodging. All were to submit to medical exams every fifteen days and if found to have venereal disease were sent to St. Lazare Hospital, which doubled as a prison. The morals police (*bureau des moeurs*) enforced the policy. Their goal was to identify and regulate all prostitutes and prevent clandestine, that is, unregistered prostitution, which was considered most likely to spread disease. When a woman registered, the police were supposed to dissuade her from the life, sending her home to her parents if necessary. However, once registered, prostitutes were public property. There were strict regulations on dress and behavior, prohibitions against soliciting, and restrictions on the location and design of the brothels. Any woman suspected of prostitution could be picked up for a medical exam. The police were suspicious of those who wished to leave the profession and would remove a name from the public rolls only if there were parents or a husband to assume responsibility. Anyone who became ill, broke a regulation, or was found to practice clandestinely spent time in St. Lazare.

During the more than 140 years that the French system was in place the logic behind the regulation of prostitution varied. At first, the intent was to control disease, then to accommodate the unsavory social demand for morally defective women by setting them visibly apart from society. At times the police became obsessed with clandestineness, reacting to rumors that vast numbers of women were *insoumises*—unregistered, unregulated, and infecting the male population. Any woman in a public place was subject to arrest and a brutal medical examination. As the middle class grew in wealth and status the double moral standard spread as well. Young men of the propertied classes were initiated into sex by prostitutes, thus sparing the protected daughters of the bourgeoisie from this responsibility. The romantic cult of virginal femininity and the religious virtues of motherhood left most ''honest'' women inaccessible to the pleasure and desires of men and required the services of the morals police. A system of prostitution both forbidden and tolerated, both a horror and a necessity, both clandestine and open, was the result.

There were periodic protests against the French system. Inspired by

Josephine Butler's campaign against the Contagious Diseases Acts in England, French feminists in the 1880s opposed the state's exploitation of women and the restriction on their movements and liberties. The feminist press demanded the repeal of state regulation. Unlike in England, however, there was no clear target of abolition, no one law to overturn, but rather a scattering of rules and practices subject to arbitrary enforcement and abuse. Abolitionists denounced the threat of arrest faced by innocent women rather than the plight of prostitutes under the system. Some showed that despite the often brutal tactics of the morals police, the policy of *tolérance* was ineffective. Clandestine prostitution increased as venereal disease spread from the morally defective to the respectable middle class. Still, the argument that the system was a protection for men prevailed, and state regulation survived until after World War II.

In 1946 the government closed the registered brothels. Many madams had been suspected of collaborating with the Nazis during the Occupation and there was widespread desire for reform. Nevertheless, registration and health inspection of prostitutes continued until the beginning of the Fifth Republic. In 1949 the French government signed the United Nations convention on the suppression of traffic in persons. This declaration was based on the view that while the system of prostitution was morally bad, the prostitute herself was a victim. The real crime was the exploitation of women by *proxénétisme*, that is, procuring and pimping. Signing the convention meant agreeing to eliminate practices, such as mandatory registration, which tended to keep women in prostitution by giving them a permanent public identity. The convention was formally incorporated into French law in 1960 when prostitution, the exchange of money for sexual favors, was decriminalized by statute. The government issued an ordinance creating a service in each department for the prevention and rehabilitation of prostitutes. The goal was to help prostitutes get the education, counseling, and job training that would allow them to leave the "life" and also to help persons in danger of becoming prostitutes.[23] These laws spelled the end to health inspections and the remnants of the morals police, but replaced them with laws against pimping and soliciting. The state's new goal was to destroy the network surrounding prostitution without interfering with the act directly. In practice, police have periodically cracked down on soliciting, engaged in massive arrests of women under the guise of social assistance, and charged men who had personal relationships with prostitutes with pimping, thus maintaining the regulation of a nominally legal practice.

In 1973 police intensified their campaign in several major cities, fining prostitutes for "passive" soliciting and arresting their pimps. The prostitutes complained of harassment. By closing hotels, police upset their regular work patterns although what they were doing, selling sex, was not illegal. The crackdown on pimping put all personal associates of the women at risk. They charged that by repeated fines the state itself turned into a pimp, receiving income from prostitution. Finally in 1975 when the national government tried to limit the sale of apartments to prostitutes and increase the penalties for pimping, 150 prostitutes staged a demonstration and occupied the Church of St. Nizier in Lyon. They sent a letter to President Giscard: "French law does not prohibit prostitution and in theory we are citizens like everybody else. But because society is ashamed of 'wanting us' they treat us like delinquents, as beings upon whom the police can use all their repressive power." The protest was met by stony silence from the government. Even Françoise Giroud was reluctant to respond: "I thought that prostitution was for a minister for the status of women a 'poisoned' gift. It risked associating the status of women with prostitution in people's minds."[24]

In November, 1975, the hookers held a national congress at the Mutualité hall in Paris. They argued that since a demand for prostitution exists and the practice is accepted by the public, prostitutes had a right to work in good conditions. They asked for an end to police harassment and fines, for access to housing in hotels and apartments, and for eligibility for Social Security, family allocations, and retirement benefits. There was a discussion of the antipimping laws, but there was disagreement on that question. Some said the state should repeal these laws, while others wanted protection from brutality and exploitation by pimps.

The "hooker interlude" passed with no official recognition from Giroud or her successors at the Ministry of the Status of Women. Minister of Health Simone Veil, however, did commission a study of prostitution that recommended the granting of prostitutes' demands for reduction or elimination of police repression, extending social benefits, and changing pimping laws to allow private relationships with men. These proposals died from lack of interest by the government and opposition from the Left.

The 1975 strike confronted feminists with their own ignorance and ambivalence about prostitution. In 1970 the MLF had glibly declared a common bond: "We are all hysterical, crazy, and prostituted."[25] All suffered in common from the effects of male dominance. When the sit-in began in Lyon in May 1975, feminists quickly avowed solidarity with their oppressed sisters and joined the strike. They found that it was not so easy to say "we're all prostitutes" after they finally met some. Days of talking and listening revealed that prostitutes considered themselves neither avant-garde feminists nor hopeless victims of patriarchy. They were in fact quite committed to traditional sex roles and merely wanted their own occupation accepted as legitimate. They didn't want to rebel against their lives or against men, but for their lives to be considered normal. Some feminists suspected the 1975 strike was in fact organized by pimps who had been more threatened than prostitutes by the government crackdown. In any case, feminists learned that in order to fight prostitution it would be necessary to fight prostitutes.

The relation between prostitution and women's rights remains problematic for feminists. Most moderates and socialists include prostitution in their general indictment of sexual inequality and classify the prostitute as a victim of male dominance despite the demands of the hookers themselves to the contrary. In *The Second Sex*, Simone de Beauvoir contends that the prostitute embodies all forms of exploitation of women: emotional, economic, physical. "Common prostitution is a miserable occupation in which woman, exploited sexually and economically, subjected arbitrarily to the police, to a humiliating medical supervision, to the caprices of the customers and doomed to bacteria and disease, to misery, is truly debased to the level of a thing."[26] In 1975 Yvette Roudy offered prostitution as the natural product of the patriarchal system.[27] Benoîte Groult deplored the situation as "virility pushed to horror," defining prostitution not as a sexual outlet but as another manifestation of sexist power over women.[28] Gisèle Halimi and Choisir argued in their 1978 common program that the "prostituted woman" is a victim of sexuality without love, alienated from her children, controlled by her pimp, and harassed by the police. They advocated public policies to help women get out of that life and into "real" jobs.[29]

Other feminists, including many of the radicals and proponents of *la différence*, argue that for all the problems, prostitution is preferable to marriage, the showcase of patriarchy. At least the professional limits her relations with the virile sex to business. She, unlike the poor wife, is not required to love her oppressor or praise the institution of oppression. And she has control of her own money and property. In fact, the sex-for-money relationship could be one of the rare opportunities women have to take charge in heterosexual relationships. Some see in prostitution the potential for sexual pleasure defined and controlled by females. Therefore, prostitution is considered by feminists to be either the most oppressive or the most liberating sexual relationship available to women. None of the feminist associations have made the issue a high priority. This ambivalence impedes change in public policy.

There are some parallels in the status of the issue of prostitution between the United States and France. The law is technically different: the act of prostitution is a misdemeanor in forty-nine states and most of Nevada, where there are regulated brothels in four counties. The United States is one of the few nations that has not signed the 1949 United Nations declaration against illegal prostitution and traffic in persons. In practice, policies in the two countries have similar priorities: controlling soliciting and pimping. American police, trying to reduce business for streetwalkers, resort to decoy operations to arrest clients as well as hookers, while the French police, hoping to discourage soliciting, pick up and fine the prostitutes. The American public, especially in the big cities, shares French ambivalence toward prostitution, accepting its inevitability, but agreeing that is should be controlled to reduce on-street soliciting or restricted to certain neighborhoods. American feminists are as divided as French feminists, some also seeing the prostitute as the most oppressed of women and others the most liberated. Margo St. James, organizer of COYOTE, attended national conventions of NOW in the 1970s.[30] But many moderate American feminists agreed with Françoise Giroud that the issue was a "poisoned gift" and would hurt other less morally sensitive goals such as the ERA and comparable worth. Many American and French feminists include prostitution as part of a general indictment of sexism, but it is not a priority on either policy agenda.

Unlike Giroud and Pelletier, Yvette Roudy recognized prostitution as a women's issue. Feminists in the Mitterrand government found little to praise about the situation. Their initial report on the status of women in France defined prostitution as the "extreme symbol of domination by man of women." The "life," far from being liberating, costs a woman "degradation, isolation, shame, separation from society and entry into another *milieu*" (a term also used to refer to the gangs of pimps controlling the trade).[31] The causes of prostitution are found in ignorance and poverty, compounded by economic dependency and exploitation by pimps. Often, women in the business are single mothers, many abandoned by their families and vulnerable due to the sexual and psychological abuse they have suffered. They are frequently recruited by their love for a pimp. Seeing prostitutes as victims points the way toward a social policy: to help prostitutes leave the degrading life and come into the mainstream of society. "For our ministry, and others agree with us, revision of measures which discriminate against prostitutes, while reducing their marginalization, could contribute to limiting their dependence on a pimp and encourage them to take responsibility for their own rehabilitation."[32]

Roudy assembled an interministerial committee composed of representatives of Woman's Rights, Interior, Justice, National Solidarity, Budget, and Foreign Affairs. Their primary goal was to revitalize and extend the 1960 ordinance requiring *services publics de réinsertion sociale* (SPRS) in each department. In twenty years only seven departments had established such services, although they did include many of the major cities—Strasbourg, Marseilles, Bordeaux, Montpellier, Lille, Paris, and Lyon. To help promote SPRS, Roudy's interministerial task force recommended training sessions for social workers to better understand government policy and the problem of prostitution. "We are looking for ways to help women who are victims to liberate themselves from their chains and quit prostitution," said Roudy.[33]

There are a few advocacy groups for prostitutes. One of them, Le Nid, submitted a list of demands to President Mitterrand in 1985. It shows that their concerns have changed little in ten years. They reject both regulation and prohibition and instead want the right to a private personal life, to raise children, to rent or buy lodging. Le Nid supports reinsertion but cautions that it will be a long and difficult process. As long as police continue their arrests and fines for soliciting and for pimping, women will be labeled for life, unable to get other jobs. There will be no freedom of choice in sexuality until prostitutes can leave their occupation as easily as they enter it.

A 1975 law gives associations the right to sue pimps for private damages during criminal trials. In 1980, for example, some prostitutes at Grenoble went to court and accused their pimps of using violence to keep them in the "life." Although there have been a few such cases, in general, the government retains the responsibility for prosecuting pimps. In 1978 the Minister of Interior produced a study claiming that procuring women for prostitution amounted to a multibillion dollar business, the third largest in France, run by networks of gangs with international connections. "I can't battle it alone," said Roudy, arguing it was a matter for police and international agencies. Apart from statements deploring the exploitation, there were no direct policies coming from the MWR or the interministerial committee. Since 1978, arrests for *proxénétisme* have actually declined.

PORNOGRAPHY

Feminists confronted the subject of pornography for the first time in the early 1970s when the press ridiculed one of their articles on female sexual pleasure in the MLF paper *Le Torchon brûle* as being pronographic. The Ligue du Droit des femmes was appalled that an article "written by women to explain how our body is made in order to know it better and cease being sex objects" would be condemned while all sorts of films, advertisements, and sexual assaults were accepted as "natural" or "inevitable." [34] They pointed out that it has always been acceptable for men to portray women's bodies any way they pleased. Standards of bourgeois morality used to keep the most explicit images private, the style varying according to the class and education of the consumers. The atmosphere of sexual liberation has made the pornography once reserved for the elites and the purveyors of dirty postcards available to everyone. The so-called sexual revolution has not meant liberation for women but only the democratization of their oppressed image.

Sex exploitation has been incorporated into the modern consumer society. The barriers of modesty lowered, advertisers may freely use the bodies of women to sell products. Women see themselves on posters all over town in attitudes once hidden behind the brown paper wrapper. One such advertisement in 1974 was for Dim, a brand of women's hosiery. It showed a woman on all fours, presenting her rear like an animal. The Ligue drafted a manifesto:

I am the dog-woman Dim who is displayed on the posters. I am the pivot of advertising. I make the consumer society go. I am the body which is sold and which makes things sell. I am the consumed consumer. I am the turkey that they stuff incessantly with ads . . . I refuse to be defined through the desires or needs of men.[35]

They envisioned an attention-getting manifesto against pornography like that on abortion. In contrast to that issue, however, few stars were willing to protest the advertisements.

In France as well as the United States, the pornography issue reveals a long-standing controversy among the defenders of conservative bourgeois morality, sexual liberation, and free speech. The conservative view insists that community standards prohibit the public display of lewd or indecent behavior. Their object is to protect respectable women and impressionable children. They have come to a truce with the sexual liberals who insist on the right of adults to partake in private of a wide variety of sexual activities. In public, women must not be exposed to sexuality; in private, men are denied nothing.

Feminists do not fit comfortably into this controversy. They have protested that women's ignorance of sexuality has increased their suffering. They consider the public discussion of sexuality a help to women because they can gain the information to make them independent of men. This would seem to make feminists the natural allies of sexual liberals who are always chipping away at the standards of the moralists. On the other hand pornography disgusts many feminists. Further, they cannot condone an array of images of women in degrading positions at every bus stop, newsstand, movie theater, and billboard. Yet if they complain they are labeled prudes (one of the few nouns that is feminine in both English and French) who favor censorship. Often they find themselves the reluctant allies of the most reactionary elements in society. In seeking to define the issue of pornography as a threat to women's rights, French feminists occasionally have taken direct action. Several years before American feminists confronted the sex shops of Times Square, a memorable battle was fought in Paris over *The Story of O*. Written by a woman in the 1950s, the book, because of its poetic style, has been called high-class porn or "quality erotica."[36] It is the well-written tale of a young woman who through love willingly submits to sexual bondage. She is degraded, brutalized, and totally enslaved, first by her young lover and then by his "uncle." The book begins with her initiation into bondage. She must be available to her masters at all times and must wear clothing permitting access to her body, all the while she continues her career as a high fashion photographer. Her body bears the scars of whippings; later she is chained and branded. Throughout her degradation, though she cries from the pain, she is proud and happy. At the depth of her enslavement she is envied by a fifteen-year-old girl who wants to be just like O. The story praises the concept of slavery by consent; for love, O goes to total openness. One of the two endings portrays her ultimate liberation through death at the hand of her lover.

Old obscenity/free speech battles about publishing such works have been played out long ago. In the 1970s, however, a film of the book appeared in the regular movie houses. Advertising for the newly released film blanketed Paris, at bus stops, on billboards, in magazines. Even the quasi-feminist magazine *Elle* ran the advertisements for the film of O. They showed the heroine naked and in chains. The copy addressed what "all women" know about sex, love, and submission. "Every woman will agree that the chains we don't want to break are those that a woman puts on her own wrists when total love renders her consenting to everything." The message of the film and the ads: "O, the submissive one, is in reality the real victor. She triumphs with the absolute weapon of women: pleasure given, pleasure shared, pleasure taken."[37]

Would this portrayal of female sexuality stand unchallenged? None of the newspapers complained and only one television commentator questioned the image of woman happy in her chains. The newsmagazine *L'Express*, in a paroxysm of liberalism, decided to serialize the novel.[38] Over at the secretariat for the status of women, Françoise Giroud stuck to her liberal guns. She saw no women's rights issue involved, and while she personally didn't like *The Story of O* she believed it to be a private matter. Giroud accepted the right to choice regarding sexual fantasies. Only a small group of MLF feminists challenged the marketing of O. Once an elitist fantasy worthy of the Marquis de Sade, O, willing slave, was being peddled to the masses. This was not a harmless fantasy but dangerous fuel to misogyny. The Ligue du Droit des femmes labeled such pornography "sexual fascism" and blamed it for rape and other crimes against women.[39]

They marched on the offices of *L'Express*. "Not only are immense profits realized on our bodies 'thanks' to porno films that invade the movie theaters, but l'*Express*, which has doubled its sales in Paris since the publication of *The Story of O* in its pages, defends the image of woman tortured and enslaved and, if we believe this weekly magazine for young bureaucrats in sexual distress, such is the way of our 'liberation.' No sirs, we want neither this 'liberation' nor to be woman, prudish, frigid, or confined to the home. It is for us to choose and to live our sexuality and our pleasure.''[40] Ten feminist organizations, including moderates UFCS and Choisir, the radical Pétroleuses and the Ligue du Droit des femmes of the MLF, and Femmes 2000 of the Socialists, signed a manifesto against the venerable magazine: ''When an organ of the great press, led by deliberately commercial imperatives, offers to a great public a show as degrading of women, we cannot be silent and by our silence allow pass as intelligent reflection what is only a great deviation of the needs and elementary rights of women.''[41]

Such actions as the protest against *The Story of O* gained some publicity for feminists, but probably had little effect other than to increase the take at the box office. In 1978 a demonstration patterned after the ''Take Back the Night'' campaign in the United States was held on International Women's Day. Shouting ''la rue est à nous,'' 2,500 women marched toward the sex shops and brothels off the boulevard St. Denis. The few who made it there trashed some pornographic books. This tactic of focusing on specific films, advertisements, and books that degrade women has had little success in winning support in the fight against pornography because it is too reminiscent of moralistic censorship and authoritarian book-burning. Feminists had to develop and win a new definition of this issue, one that would dispel the liberal view that pornography doesn't hurt anyone. In developing this position, they have concentrated on the question of power, not morality. Pornography tells of the triumph of males over females. Submission to the penis is symbolic of the submission of women to male power. Pornography is a form of patriarchal propaganda, condoning all means of control however violent. Seeing pornography as part of a larger system of repression has led feminists in recent years to concentrate on the broader issue of sexism and the legal means to combat it.

SEXISM AND THE ANTISEXIST BILL

Sexism is a concept new to the French vocabulary, borrowed, some say, from American feminists.[42] In the 1970s *Les Temps modernes* published a series of articles called *Le Sexisme ordinaire*. Simone de Beauvoir, one of the editors of the journal, called this series no small victory because "to name is to unveil, and to unveil is to act."[43] The failure or refusal to name the phenomenon had been a subtle way of perpetuating it by denying its existence. It was impossible to defeat something that did not exist. Making sexism a part of the language created a target—the ideology of sex exploitation. Analogous to racism, sexism was described as the justification of the elaborate pattern of discrimination against women in the family, economy, society, and politics.

The ideology of sexism denies women the right to define their own sexual pleasure and justifies for men a variety of attacks on female sexuality. Violence is not natural in men; they learn it from their cultural environment, where images of women submissive, in chains, and beaten reinforce dangerous myths. In a play on her own words, de Beauvoir wrote in *Le Monde*: "One is not born, but rather becomes, a man." Pornography is an extreme form of sexism. The fascination with overpowering and hurting women for the sexual pleasure of men perpetuates myths about the "normality" of rape and other violence against women. *Proxénétisme* is the practice of prostituting women to deliver in person what pornography promises in fantasies.

Fighting sexism became the primary concern of de Beauvoir's group, the Ligue du Droit des femmes. Their goal was to make sexism as illegitimate in society as racism. The analogy of sexism with racism offered some advantages. Sensitivity to racism had led to statutes outlawing public displays derogatory to racial minorities. Advertisers would not dare put degrading images of Arabs or Jews on every bus stop in the country. Such images of women were acceptable because they were considered sexy. The Ligue hoped to redefine them as sexist, as abhorrent as derogatory images of racial minorities. They proposed a statute modeled after the antiracist law of 1972. This 1972 law prohibits race discrimination in many areas: providing social rights, goods, or services, hiring, and firing. It also makes it a crime to provoke others to racial hatred and violence or to defame or insult a racial minority through the press. The law permits antiracist associations to sue the persons responsible for discriminatory acts. This means that interest groups can sue newspaper editors for derogatory statements published in their papers. In 1973 the Ligue advocated that the entire act be extended to apply to sexism. They especially wanted the right to file suit against sexism in the media and on the job. In 1975, Françoise Giroud added sex discrimination to the parts of this act dealing with employment discrimination (see chapter 6) but did not include the provision for interest groups to sue employers.

As the feminist campaigns against rape and pornography continued, Choisir and UFF joined the Ligue in advocating a comprehensive law against sexism. In 1980 a Socialist senator, Franck Serusclat, introduced the antisexist bill in the Senate. In the debate, Monique Pelletier supported the economic guarantees of the bill, even accepting in principle a role for feminist associations bringing cases against employers. But she reported, unequivocally, the government's disapproval of the amendments dealing with the media. Permitting feminist associations to sue editors of newspapers for sexist statements endangered the free press.

Although the Serusclat bill was defeated, it became part of the Socialist party program. In the 1981 presidential campaign Mitterrand pledged: "The dignity of woman will be respected, especially through the image that is given her in the textbooks, advertising, television. The associations for the defense of women's rights should be able to bring civil suit in cases of discrimination." [44] The Ministry of Woman's Rights included the antisexist bill in its original seventeen-point program. Roudy and Mitterrand repeatedly referred to the need for the legislation. It wasn't until 1983, however, that the Council of Ministers adopted the bill. Roudy announced the decision on 8 March, International Women's Day.

The antisexist bill was an exact copy of the antiracist law. Title I covered sex discrimination in employment, services, and social rights and meted out prison terms or fines. Title II permitted associations to make civil claims during trials for all these infractions except in case of firing. Title III amended the 1881 law on freedom of the press. It would apply to "public expression of [material] written or visual." Whoever, through those outlets covered by the 1881 press law, provoked discrimination, hatred, or violence on a person or a group of persons because of their sex would be subject to one year in prison and/or a fine of 2,000 to 300,000 francs. Also subject to sanction would be defamation and personal injury because of sex. Any association that had the official goal for at least five years of fighting discrimination based on sex would be able to file a simultaneous civil suit against any sexism in public expression that was prohibited by the law.

At her press conference, Roudy said that the intent of the new law would be to prevent attacks on the dignity of women. "Discrimination based on race differences has been condemned for a long time as racism; that founded on sex differences has continued in silence, which was a way of denying it existed."[45] The way to battle sexism would be to include it in the antiracist law. It was a necessary complement to all other action for women's rights, especially for employment opportunities. A woman would finally be able to fight back legally against the images in the media that showed her in a degraded position, were an affront to her dignity, and prevented her from full and equal participation in society.

In patterning their bill after the antiracist law, feminists had made an important choice. They had decided to define their issue, fighting the ideology of sex discrimination, in the same terms as race discrimination issues. There were potential advantages to this approach, not the least of which was a built-in official recognition of the evils of racism that could provide a reservoir of support for fighting sexism. But they were soon to learn that many people saw the two issues as very different.

The reaction to the antisexist bill was instant and virulent. For several weeks every newspaper and magazine covered the bill and most were very critical. "Caricature, derision, sarcasm, violence, all means, all forms are good in the polemic."[46] There were personal attacks on Roudy, calling her an autocratic ayatollah who shuddered at the sight of bare young breasts. She and feminists were pictured as Victorian prudes and the bill as an attempt at censorship based on an outdated morality. Especially critical were the advertisers. "This Victorian puritanism revolts me. This morality erected into the law makes me anxious. Tomorrow we can require women to wear the veil."[47]

Journalists accused Roudy of trying to rob men of their fantasies. Some saw the bill as a dangerous denial of freedom. Others predicted that half of the paintings in the Louvre would be vulnerable to lawsuits by feminist groups. Many wondered what feminists meant by sexism and feared they would apply radical man-hating emotions that would play havoc with the precious French culture. Women in the media were also critical. "We are adults," they cried, "we resent this assumption by the state that we need protection." They pointed out that it is women who most like the ads using female images to sell products. There were fears that France may become too much like America where "the feminists have gone too far and in order to fight the 'male chauvinist pig' they have made generations of homosexuals, powerless or terrorized by women."[48]

Roudy was shocked at the furor surrounding her announcement. Her bill for equal employment opportunity, which would have much wider effect in the society, had been greeted with enthusiasm and support. The contraceptive campaign was well received. Even the plan for reimbursement of abortion costs, though controversial, was popular. The reaction to the antisexist bill stunned the government and the Ministry of Woman's Rights. The *Journal du Parlement* observed that Roudy and her ministry were seriously damaged by the situation. "In likening sexism in advertisement to Hitlerian racism, Yvette Roudy has fallen in an excess that her friends in government today interpret as ridiculous. Even those Mitterrand Socialists who we know respect rights of women consider that she has gone too far and that she will end by doing a disservice to the female cause."[49]

What had gone wrong? The inadequacy of the policy process provides one explanation. The cabinet member in charge at the MWR assured Roudy's staff that it was just a simple matter of inserting sex in the antiracist law, accepting, in effect, the proposal originally put forward by the Ligue du Droit des femmes in 1973. The ministry therefore only consulted with a few feminist groups about the bill before it was presented. No one questioned the analogy between sexism and racism. They sought no reaction from those groups to be regulated: newspapers, reporters, magazines, editors, or advertisers.

If consulted, advertisers would have claimed the bill was unnecessary because they have self-regulation. The Bureau de Vérification de la Publicité (BVP) receives complaints against advertisers who violate their rule: "Woman must not be used as an object of advertising, especially if the image that is given of her has no relation to the use of the product or service that is the goal of the advertisement."[50] Critics charged the government with playing politics. The Conseil National de la Publicité described the whole thing as a clumsy effort to gain electoral support. The timing of the announcement of the bill, halfway through the two tours of the 1983 municipal elections, appeared to be politically self-serving for the Socialist party on its way to major electoral losses.

The feminists at the MWR argued that the violent reaction against their bill showed that they had hit sexism right on target: they threatened the male monopoly over female sexuality. The so-called sexual revolution had increased this control and in the consumer society had made a lot of money for the dominant class. Advertisers undisturbed by moral or legal restrictions have an enormous amount of influence and have manipulated women. The antisexist bill for the first time would give women the resources to strike back at images that surround them and degrade them, yet before which they are helpless. The reaction meant the feminists in government were finally doing something to undermine patriarchy and threaten the phallocrats.

The controversy demonstrated that more work had to be done to sell the bill in order to save it. Although Roudy's party had a majority in the National Assembly, she had to convince the legislative leadership to put a bill on the calendar and push it through. Since Socialists were facing mounting opposition on other economic and church-related policies, they wanted to avoid the ridicule that might be heaped on them for passing a bill opposed by the media. Roudy started her own publicity campaign. She argued that the critics had completely distorted her bill, making a caricature of it. It would give the government no powers of censorship; all it did was offer a legal remedy for women to fight back against sexism. Fighting sexism is not prudish or puritanical because sexism is not the same as sex. Sexism involves violence, hatred, discrimination. Like racism it provokes violence against a subject group; sexism leads to rape and battered women. Existing rules for advertisers were ineffective. An antisexist law, like the antiracist law, would be primarily dissuasive. The antiracist law has never been invoked because it has been effective in prevention. The threat of lawsuits and prosecution would cause people to think about the images of women they are putting out before the public.

Roudy gathered the feminist groups around her in a collective effort to save the bill. The Ligue, MFPF, UFF, and Centre Audiovisual Simone de Beauvoir all made public statements. L'AFI sponsored a public debate giving Roudy an opportunity to confront the opposition from the advertising industry. *Le Monde* gave her a good review. "The advertisers appeared ill at ease before a critical if not hostile public and had a hard time expressing themselves clearly. Madame Roudy, on the other hand, was at the best of her form, quick repartée, and never forgetting her role as minister of the rights of women (and not of feminists)."[51] Finally, the ministry started the long-overdue consultations with newspaper editors and advertisers.

Although feminists showed their public support throughout, many had reservations about the bill. Most welcomed an attack on sexism, and many were surprised by the extreme reaction in the media. Françoise Giroud and Monique Pelletier were sympathetic. As secretary for women, Giroud had expressed concern over the proliferation of sexist images. She still believes sexism, defined as an ''oppressive or condescending attitude in regard to one of the other sex'' should be fought. ''The battle will be difficult because women seem to like to see themselves half-naked in front of a stove'' and buy such products.[52] At the same time, Giroud criticized MWR's handling of the bill. At the 9 March press conference Roudy made an error by offering an example of what she thought was unacceptable sexism, an album cover showing singer Grace Jones in a cage. Many read this as moralism about sex and ridiculed the feminists for trying to censor the press. Giroud also had little hope for the analogy of racism; the antiracist law has not been effective and an antisexist one won't be either.

The decision to frame the issue of sexism in the same terms as racism has produced other problems. The most basic one is that the two beliefs do not have the same place in the culture.[53] Sexism is universalistic, deeply ingrained in culture, and closely related to basic human sexual identities. Racism is particularistic and limited in its effect on most people. Sexism is an entire social complex involving every sector from family to politics, while racism pertains to a minority. Men and women have always existed in a sexist relationship, while racial groups when separate have not always had master/slave patterns. Many feminists were not sure that a policy developed to fight discrimination against a minority could effectively address the problem of sexism in the culture. The 1881 law on freedom of the press had been designed to protect the dignity of the individual from defamation of character and of action. Later amendments sought to help protect members of specific minorities, especially Jews (1939) and Africans (1972). It was not framed to deal with large classes of people, let alone defamation against an entire sex. According to feminist attorney Odile Dhavernas, it was very unlikely that advertisers would ever be sued. What is needed is a bill drawn up specifically to deal with sexism and the media that focuses on the discrimination and violence against women.

In summer 1985, the antisexist bill quietly resurfaced and quickly passed the parliament.[54] It prohibits sex discrimination in hiring, fir-

ing, goods and services, or government benefits. Organizations registered under the 1901 law of association that have had the goal for a
least five years of fighting sexism can sue employers or public authorities for civil damages. The section dealing with the press had disappeared. Political and legal difficulties with the media had apparently
stifled the brave attack on sexist images made by the Ligue du Droit
des femmes and the Ministry of Woman's Rights.

Although American feminists applauded the intent and breadth of
the feminist struggle against sexism in France, they have had difficulty
developing a common theoretical position on sexism and sexuality,
much less offering concrete policy proposals. Women Against Violence Against Women (WAVAW) has protested specific derogatory
films and advertising. Women Against Pornography (WAP) has infil-
trated sex shops and movie houses on Times Square. The legal attack
has focused on providing civil remedies for women against violent
pornography.[55] Indianapolis enacted a statute that defines pornography
as sex discrimination and gives people the right to sue its sellers and
producers for violation of civil rights. The Supreme Court, however,
struck down the ordinance as a violation of the First Amendment.

Libertarian critics of the antiporn feminists denounce any effort to
regulate sexual expression as potentially more oppressive to women
than pornography. Women should demand the right to any consensual
sexual practice that brings pleasure. They are especially suspicious of
the coalition of feminists and the religious right that pushed through
the Indianapolis ordinance. Still other feminists criticize both the an-
tipornography and pro-sex feminists for failing to recognize that the
politics of sexuality is part of a seamless web of sexism and exploitation that pervades society.[56] The effort to find a constitutional antipor-
nography law goes on amid battles among feminists, civil libertarians,
and the new right over the definition of the issue.

DEFINITION OF THE ISSUE OF SEXUALITY

Feminists have broken the silence surrounding women and sexuality, a silence that persisted despite the sexual revolution. Rather than
offering a new definition of female sexuality, they have fought for the
right of each woman to determine it for herself. Winning this right
will enhance powers for all women, especially when confronting male
sexual demands. Feminists have challenged entrenched practices on

rape, prostitution, and pornography, issues that demonstrated the repression and exploitation of women's privacy and dignity. These practices are symptomatic of the widespread ideology of sexism. The greatest single step to freedom for feminists would be destruction of the underpinnings of sexism itself.

The battle is joined and a few successes have resulted. Feminists have made their greatest gain in the policy on rape and sexual assault. Rape has become a more serious offense and is officially defined as a crime against women. The new law has given direct power to some feminist interest groups to take action against their tormentors through civil suits. The notion that women secretly enjoy being forcibly taken by men has been officially squelched and the government has begun to try to improve criminal prosecution by moving trials to criminal court and hiring personnel to aid victims in making complaints to the police. There are also some public subsidies given to support groups for rape victims.

For the most part, the battle over control of the definition of the sexuality issue rages on. There is ambivalence toward prostitution: The general public and the government seem to accept it as inevitable. At the same time they disapprove of prostitutes and pimps and want some controls and limits. They consider the sex market to be a social problem like poverty or illiteracy and agree that services will help prostitutes to be "reinserted" into respectable society. Police frequently will treat public nuisance aspects of prostitution and control soliciting or pimping. A majority of feminists in and out of the government see prostitutes as victims of patriarchy who need help to get out of the "life." Many prostitutes themselves want to improve their status and working conditions. The discrepancies among views of government, police, feminists, and prostitutes point to the continuing conflict over what the problem is and whether it needs fixing. The result, therefore, is inaction. General controls on prostitution and pimping continue under the Mitterrand government but arrests have declined. Nevertheless, the legal basis for harassment of prostitutes remains. The efforts at reinsertion have been left to regional and local authorities whose slender resources are stretched already from dealing with other demands.

The issue of sexism and the image of women has been successfully brought to the public agenda but the conflict is immense. The feminists in government have opposed the version of woman created by man, especially the images that degrade or abuse her. They define this as discrimination so serious that feminist associations should have the power to fight these images in court. Others find this plan a threat to freedom of speech and the press. Despite some acceptance of the view that women have a right to control their sexuality, on this issue feminists have gone too far—they have threatened to encroach on the public display of private male fantasies.

NOTES

1. Michèle Sarde, *Regard sur les françaises* (Paris: Stock, 1983), 24.

2. Helene Cixous, "The Laugh of the Medusa," *New French Feminisms*, ed. Elaine Marks and Isabelle de Courtivron (Amherst: University of Massachusetts Press, 1980), 246.

3. Christine Delphy, "French Feminist Forum," *The Women's Review of Books* 3 (March 1986), 16. The argument over tolerance of heterosexuality divided radical feminists in the early 1980s. Militant lesbians and essentialist advocates of *néo-fémininité* (see chapter 1) not only rejected men, but purged women who refused to join them. Such a conflict affected the feminist journal *Questions féministes*. In 1981 there was a major reorganization to a feminist line eschewing the "Marxist stumbling block" and *néo-fémininité*.

4. "Viol de nuit, terre des hommes," in *Le Sexisme ordinaire*, ed. Simone de Beauvoir (Paris: Seuil, 1979), 174.

5. L'Agence femmes information, "Dossier: le viol" (octobre 1983).

6. Choisir, *Viol, le procès d'Aix-en-Provence* (Paris: Gallimard, 1978).

7. Annie de Pisan and Anne Tristan, *Histoires du MLF* (Paris: Calmann-Lévy, 1977), 197.

8. *Crie moins fort les voisins vont t'entendre* (Paris: Edition des femmes, 1975).

9. Pisan and Tristan, 197.

10. *Le Monde* (23 juin 1978).

11. *Journal Officiel*, Débats parlementaires (avril 1980), 326.

12. Ibid.

13. In Florida the sexual battery statute does not set the punishment for each type of felony. Judges follow a complex set of guidelines in tailoring the punishment to fit both the crime and the criminal. These guidelines permit sentences from twelve months in prison to life depending on the type of felony, the number of counts, the number of prior convictions, and the physical injury to the victim.

14. In France there are separate courts for civil and criminal cases. No civil action can take place in a criminal court without special provision in the penal code. Then, an association can bring an action called *partie civile* against the defendant in a criminal trial and the judge must make a decision on both the

criminal charge and the suit for civil damages. In the United States where courts handle both civil and criminal cases, there remains strict segregation of the procedure. A civil action against a rapist would be entirely separate from the prosecution for the crime. Further, only someone personally injured could bring the action, not feminists or any other association on the victim's behalf.

15. Ministère des Droits de la femme, *Les Femmes dans une société d'inégalités* (Paris: Documentation française, 1982), 130.

16. L'Agence femme information, "Viol: Quand une femme dit non, c'est non," *Bulletin* 185 (9–15 décembre 1985).

17. L'Agence femmes information, *Bulletin* (13 juillet 1983). Quote by Odile Dhavernas.

18. Ibid.

19. Maison des femmes, *Paris féministe* 17 (1–15 décembre 1985).

20. Jill Harsin, *Policing Prostitution in Nineteenth Century Paris* (Princeton: Princeton University Press, 1985), 81.

21. Quoted in Alain Corbin, *Les Filles de noce* (Paris: Montaigne, 1978), 15.

22. William Acton, *Prostitution* (London, 1857; New York: Praeger, 1968), 97.

23. Many contemporary policies regarding prostitution have counterparts in French history. Prostitutes and those who gave them lodging have been periodically banished since the reign of Charlemagne. They congregated and were tolerated in certain streets in the 1300s. In the 1600s was the first rehabilitation house (Maison de Bon Pasteur). Ever since venereal disease came to Europe from the New World in the sixteenth century, health has been a continuing factor in the treatment of prostitution (see Harsin, *Policing Prostitution*).

24. Colette Piat, *La République des misogynes* (Paris: Plon, 1981), 97.

25. "A Grenoble, des femmes prostituées accusent leur proxénètes," *Des Femmes en mouvement* (20–27 juin 1980).

26. Simone de Beauvoir, *The Second Sex* (New York: Vintage, 1952; 1974), 629.

27. Yvette Roudy, *La Femme en marge* (Paris: Flammarion, 1975; 1982), 128.

28. Benoîte Groult, Preface to *La Dérobade* by Jeanne Cordelier (Paris: Hachette, 1976); quoted by Sarde, *Regard sur les françaises*, 87, 220.

29. Gisèle Halimi, *Le Programme commun des femmes* (Paris: Grasset, 1978), 211–13.

30. Call Off Your Old Tired Ethics (COYOTE) is an advocacy organization for prostitutes. They provide legal services and lobby for changes in laws and police practices.

31. Ministère des Droits de la femme, *Les Femmes dans une société d'inégalités*, 126.

32. Ministère des Droits de la femme, *Citoyennes à part entière* (juillet–août 1982), 6.

33. *Journal Officiel*, Débats parlementaires (novembre 1981), 3894.

34. Pisan and Tristan, *Histoires du MLF*, 177.

35. Ibid., 179.

36. Eberhard Kronhausen and Phyllis Kronhausen, *Pornography and the Law* (New York: Ballantine, 1964).

37. Pisan and Tristan, *Histoires du MLF*, 184.

38. *L'Express* (1–7 Septembre 1975).

39. Kaja Silverman, "Histoire d'O: The Construction of a Female Subject" in *Pleasure and Danger: Exploring Female Sexuality*, ed. Carole S. Vance (Boston: Routledge and Kegan Paul, 1984), 320–49. A recent feminist analysis of the *Story of O* by an American scholar.

40. Pisan and Tristan, *Histoires du MLF*, 187.

41. Françoise Parturier, "La Liberté d'aimer et la pornographie," *Choisir* 16 (octobre/novembre 1975), 1.

42. Marie-Jo Dhavernas and Liliane Kandel, "Le Sexisme comme realité et comme représentation," *Les Temps modernes* (juillet 1983), 3–29.

43. de Beauvoir, *Le Sexisme ordinaire*, 7.

44. Proposition 68 of the Socialist party platform. See Ministère des Droits de la femme, *Citoyennes à part entière* (juin 1983), 12.

45. Quoted by Beatrice Slama, "Le débat continue: La loi anti-sexiste à travers la presse," *Les Temps modernes* 444 (juillet 1983), 32.

46. Ibid., 34.

47. Ibid., 36.

48. Ibid., 35.

49. "Les Fureurs d'Yvette" (30 juin–15 juillet 1983).

50. Rapport de la commission sur l'image de la femme dans la publicité, presenté à la press et à Françoise Giroud par M. Philippe Renaudin, Président, BVP (18 mars 1975).

51. *Le Monde* (24 juin 1983).

52. Interview with Françoise Giroud, 1983.

53. Dhavernas and Kandel, "Le Sexisme," 3–29.

54. Loi no. 85-772 du 25 juillet 1985.

55. Mary Kay Blakely, "Is One Woman's Sexuality Another Woman's Pornography?" *MS* (April 1985), 37–47.

56. Ann Ferguson et al., "Forum: The Feminist Sexuality Debates," *Signs* 10 (Autumn 1984), 106–35.

8

CONCLUSION

PUBLIC POLICY affecting women in France has changed dramatically in the past twenty years. Officially, women are no longer the overworked baby makers and servants for their husbands and the state; they now have equal rights as citizens, workers, and parents in their own right and are wooed by politicians for their opinions, votes, talents, and their decision to have children. The struggles to change both the laws and the underlying conceptions of women's place in society has engaged feminists outside and inside the government. Now the movement days are over. There will be no big court cases against the patriarchal system, no attack on the billboards, no demonstrations fueled by the energy of self-discovery. What is left is the *toilettage* (fixing) of laws—filling in the loopholes, adding specific provisions, overseeing the administration of hard-won reforms—and the small gesture, such as the "down with pornography" stickers glued to sexist advertisements in the *métro* and bus stops.

Feminists will be occupied with protecting their new rights in the uncertain atmosphere of *cohabitation*.[1] This is a time for them to take stock and consolidate their victories. From an American perspective the gains of French feminists have been remarkable. For a long time, France was among the countries, along with Spain, Greece, and Switzerland, where traditional legal inequalities persisted long after reforms had been won in the United States. It would have been a major achievement if twenty years of legislation had placed the rights of French women on a par with those of American women. Rather than making a case for parity, however, this study shows that in some areas laws in France are now more egalitarian than those in the United States, and new French policies go further toward achieving feminist goals.

This conclusion comes from analysis of the logic of policy reform in the two countries, that is, comparing the underlying definitions of the issues being addressed. As noted earlier, the crucial conflict in policymaking revolves around how to frame the problem that will be treated by policy. Winning control of the way the issue is perceived and defined by the government means determining the content of statutes and administrative regulations. Feminists have battled to control their issues and persuade the government to adopt their logic. The feminists pressed for several goals: to wrest from men the right of women to control and define their own sexuality; to replace separate sex roles with a pattern of shared sex roles in family and society; and to eliminate the cultural support for male dominance in society, the economy, and politics.

COMPARISON OF WOMEN'S RIGHTS IN FRANCE AND THE UNITED STATES

The French government has incorporated the feminist perspective in policies affecting reproduction, work, and rape and has begun to promote feminist goals in education. The logic of the policies regarding reproduction and work is more feminist than in the United States. In two areas, family and politics, the logic of the reforms is quite similar in the two countries. Both are based on role equity and fail to meet feminist demands for role change. French family law, however, has eliminated all remnants of patriarchy and provides formal equality with no classification by sex, while some laws in the United States continue to preserve male prerogatives and responsibilities. Finally, neither government has dealt much with sexuality issues other than rape.

Reproduction

Convincing the government to make abortion a woman's right was the first and most dramatic success for the French feminist movement. It was not a complete victory, however, due to protective and dissuasive administrative hurdles. Still, the French law is more feminist than the United States abortion laws, which have fewer formal restrictions. *Roe v. Wade* defines abortion as a medical matter and a right to privacy for a doctor and his or her patient, not in terms of a woman's right to control her sexuality.

On the question of contraception, reforms in the two countries started out based on a similar rationale—a recognition by the authorities that the pronatalist and moralistic laws were ineffective in the face of increasing public use of contraceptives. Official definitions have changed in France. Contraceptive information has become a woman's right and the government has the responsibility of providing it. The French administration advocates contraception and sex education as a way to help women, especially teenagers, avoid abortion. American public authorities, however, are moving away from relating contraceptive services and sex education to the prevention of abortion. In fact the New Right claims that contraception is a cause of abortion, both being connected to increased sexual promiscuity.

The different effect of the two perspectives on government action is striking. In France, the government runs a program of contraceptive information and services and pays for abortions; whereas, in the United States, the abortion issue itself is a barrier to government support for family planning. Abortion rates among teenagers have declined in France while they have increased in the United States. The conflict about the legalization of abortion in France is contained, settled, and cold; it is hot, contagious, and even fanatic in the United States, poisoning a wide range of other issues.

Work

The shift in the French government's attitude toward women, work, and the family has been the most important policy change in the last twenty years. For decades women workers were relegated to a special category for policy because of the belief that they alone were preoccupied with child rearing and homemaking. Special protection had to be provided for them, and since they were secondary earners there was little need to prepare them for lifetime careers or worry too much about their unemployment rates and low wages.

Since the mid-1970s, the official view of women, work, and family has changed. Three major propositions have been incorporated into the logic of French employment policy that render it more feminist than American equal-opportunity laws: (1) a career is considered essential for the personal dignity and independence of a woman as well as a man, and both have rights to job training and job opportunity; (2) generous maternity leave for all workers is compatible with equal opportunity; (3) both women and men have the right to special help in accommodating work and family responsibilities. The intent of the government policy in France (not yet fully accomplished) has been to encourage parents to share their family responsibilities so that women will be able to participate more equally with men in the work place.

In the United States, family responsibilities fall disproportionately on female workers and the government offers them little assistance.[2] The limited concessions made to maternity must conform strictly to a logic of equality. The effect is to perpetuate the separation of the sexes, with family burdens continuing to depress the status of women workers. Under American law a woman is equal to a man as an individual. Women, as a group, however, must still choose between families and careers, a choice men as a group are less likely to confront.

Rape

Reforms of rape laws have been the only new policies dealing with sexuality in either country and the logic behind the reforms is similar. Traditional rape laws have been changed to conform more closely to feminist concepts. The feminist perception of this issue focuses on the dignity of woman and her right to control her own sexuality. She has the right to a sex life and to choose her partners. She need not conform to the male-centered double moral standard that sees her only as a chaste virgin protected by a man or a loose harlot who is the property of every man. Rape represents the most extreme assault on women's sexuality, symptomatic of more ordinary male-and-female relationships idealized by pornographers and phallocrats. In both the United States and France rape is considered a serious crime primarily against women and not against the property of men. The expanded definition of rape in the new laws recognizes a range of sexual contact and directs attention to the assault on sexuality and away from virginity and penetration. Proof of the crime now involves the degrees of force, violence, and constraint actually used in the assault rather than attempts to divine whether or not the victim consented.

There are some differences in the reforms. In America, rape shield statutes protect victims from being excessively cross-examined about their personal sex lives and help preserve the idea of a woman's right to dignity and choice regardless of prior sexual behavior, even if she sold sex for a living. In France a victim can choose to have an open trial and identify herself to the press, accuse her attacker publicly, and shift the guilt for sexual assault away from herself to her attacker.

Although feminists see interrelationships among rape, prostitution, pornography, and other issues of sexuality, they have had little success in gaining control of the public controversy. They do not agree among themselves on the relation of prostitution to women's rights nor on the threat, if any, posed by pornography and sexist advertising. Some feminists in both countries have protested violent and sadistic films and books and tried to redefine pornography as a form of discrimination and violence against women. They have not, however, been successful in shifting the conflict away from the debate over obscenity and free speech.

Education

Despite the many differences in the structure of systems of public education in the United States and France, the place of women in them has been quite similar. Education opportunities have expanded, schools have integrated, and barriers have fallen. In spite of these reforms, however, tracking continues as the education system reinforces sex role separation. Limited educational experiences for girls lead to limited job choice, lower pay, and poverty. In France, government feminists urged changes in tracking, exposed sex role stereotyping in texts, and urged girls to think as hard about selecting a métier as boys do. They prodded the huge national education bureaucracy to tear down the tracking mechanisms—with the specific goal of improving women's rights. In the United States some local and state projects have made similar attempts but general education policy continues to follow more narrow individualist guidelines.

Family

Family law reform in France and the United States is based on a logic of equality that permits some role sharing. Motivated by trends toward modernization of civil law that have affected all Western countries, lawmakers have made the status of husband and wife equal, giving them joint responsibilities for children and property, and have reduced state controls on divorce. Equality does not challenge the sex role division of labor or the nuclear family structure but it does permit more variation in family relationships. Although reforms came later in France, they have gone further toward removing gender distinctions. In many states in the United States, the husband is still responsible for selecting the wife's domicile and bears larger legal responsibility for support of the family.

In the last few years, French government feminists separated the family, long considered uniquely a woman's issue, from the women's rights portfolio. This was consistent with changes in the definition of employment policy and linked role sharing in the home with equal opportunity on the job. This shift was especially important in France, where the family has been much more closely associated with women, than it has been in the United States, where family is defined primarily as a children's welfare issue.

Politics

Equal political rights came later in France than in the United States but they were based on a similar rationale: to bring the special talents of women to government, to modernize and expand democracy, and to reward women for service in a major war. The twenty-five-year head start on equal rights gave American women no special advantage over the French in gaining power, however. In both systems, women hold a tiny percentage of elected and appointed offices. The vote, despite hopes of the suffragists, did not bring women to power nor did it form a bloc of support for feminist issues. Removal of legal barriers to participation has little impact on the distribution of political resources, which are generally unavailable to homemakers and mothers. Political rights in both the United States and France have given women access to people in power through voting, organization, lobbying, and party work, but not power itself. Political power depends on other aspects of women's status discussed in connection with reproduction, family, work, and education.

In France the right to vote had an important effect on furthering other rights for women. It justified repeal of laws restricting opportunities for women in education, pay, and civil service. Long-standing feminist demands for *droit civil* for married women were finally realized only after the vote. Rejection of women's suffrage stalled these reforms. The government has since made up for the delay with the dramatic changes described in this book.

BACKGROUND TO UNITED STATES-FRENCH COMPARISON

Differences in the size, complexity, and politics of the United States and France make comparisons difficult. There are not enough common features in institutions or political processes to give credibility to alleged similarities or explain observed differences in policy outcomes. It is often difficult to find equivalent statutes to compare. The constitutions, though democratic, are quite distinct. The United States has a decentralized federal system, with complex interrelations among the national and the fifty state governments. France has a unitary and centralized system with one capitol, one legal system, and one government making policy for the entire country. In the United States many governments coexist and there's no ready way to know what the policies are at a given time in all the states. The provisions of any policy will be closely related to the legal system—common law in the United States and the code law in France. Common law is judge-made, is based on custom, and places severe limits on the state's power to interfere with citizen prerogatives and human rights. Code law is written law, is derived from abstract principles, and is an instrument of state power.

The political cultures are also distinct. For example, there is greater public acceptance of the welfare state in France. Proposals for government action to solve social problems such as contraception, health care, income maintenance, or job training are more compatible with overall policy. In the United States, feminists have to overcome popular beliefs in limited government and the separation of public and private functions in society in order to stimulate the government to more activity in providing services.

How have these differences in the two political systems affected this comparison of women's rights? The size, political complexity, and constitutional structure of the United States mean that oversimplification is inevitable in order to find an American policy to compare with the French unitary policy. For abortion, work, politics, and education, national laws exist, either as constitutional provisions, judicial decisions, or congressional statutes. In comparing these with French national policy, there is no intention to deny that variations exist among the fifty states but to find where possible those policies that speak for the entire country and are binding on all states. For issues for which there is no national direction, that is, in sexuality and family law, it is necessary to rely on an estimation of policies that prevail in a majority of states, or if not a majority, in those states where reforms have been enacted.

In this study, comparisons have focused, for the most part, on the logic that is the foundation for specific policies, rather than content of statutes. There are many similarities in the background of the conflict over the definition of the issues in the United States and France. When issues of interest to women arise, the conflicts over the meaning of those issues are likely to be similar. This is because both are advanced industrial societies with similar patterns of social and economic development. Over the years they have exchanged ideas, trends, and innovations. Statistically, the status of women in the two societies is parallel and all major policies affecting women have recently come up for reform. French and American feminists read each other's works and study each other's problems. In both countries they are free to organize, discuss problems, frame demands, and pressure governments.

Similar issues and controversies over their meaning have nonetheless led to different outcomes in the United States and France. Several factors help explain the differences in the rationale behind these reforms, especially why French policy has surpassed American in conforming with feminist goals. French women were late coming into their rights in politics and family law due to prolonged constitutional battles that continued into the 1950s. These political conflicts about the proper form of government lasted longer in France than the United States and were more frequent. There were long periods of various kinds of authoritarian rule. Despite the establishment of the democratic Third Republic in the 1870s it remained vulnerable to internal attack from both the Right and Left. Chronic political conflict led to *immobilisme* and delayed the resolution of many feminist demands.

When the constitutional battle was finally resolved with the establishment of the Fifth Republic, there was a lot of catching up to do. Rapid economic and social modernization after World War II brought an extraordinary push to modernize all aspects of French life. The political will to do this started with the strong presidency of de Gaulle

and has continued under his successors. Many areas of social, economic, and public life have been overhauled and laws changed to keep
up with and in some areas to anticipate future change. This commitment to long-overdue modernization accounts for the dramatic reforms
in family law, education, and the legalization of contraceptives. Rapid
modernization often meant quickly bringing laws up to date with changes
that had occurred gradually in the United States and other countries.
But it also meant that French leaders were able to adopt a more comprehensive approach to law reform. Instead of incremental revisions,
they redesigned the family code by replacing authoritarian theories with
contemporary egalitarian theories of the family. They have eliminated
all remnants of Napoleonic family law. Given the extreme male domination in the code of Napoleon, the new family law seems to be a
real break with the past. At the same time, the American incremental
reforms have left remnants of common-law inequalities in many states.

Different historical patterns do little more than explain the chronology of reforms in policies affecting women in the two countries. They
fail to account for differences and similarities in the way the issues are
defined and the logic of the policies adopted. These are the product of
the policy controversy itself and the interplay among the various interest groups and their ideologies. In both countries feminists have been
participants, although they are more active on some issues than others,
along with conservatives and labor leaders. The rosters show some
differences in the types of groups interested in women's issues. In
France there is a group not very important in the United States—pronatalists.[3] Often stronger than feminism and as ancient, pronatalism has
confronted feminism on most issues affecting women. Advocates of
the two ideologies have often supported the same proposals, such as
maternity leave and assistance to mothers with large families, although
for different reasons. More often they have clashed, especially recently, over family planning, legalization of abortion, and the relation
of family social policy to the rights of women workers. At the same
time, the fact that maternity benefits are more generous and widespread in France than in the United States can be traced in part to
pronatalists seeking ways to encourage women workers to have more
babies.

In the United States the most tenacious opponents of feminists are
religious activists. Religiosity continues to be important in American
politics, and fundamentalists confront feminists on several isssues.

Fundamentalists were responsible for outlawing contraceptives and abortion in the first place. They have fought to preserve the traditional sex roles in the family. Now their moral arguments endanger abortion rights and render the policy of legalized abortion tenuous and vulnerable. Informal coalitions between feminists and fundamentalists have occasionally arisen in the United States as they have between feminists and pronatalists in France. Both support policies to increase maternity leave and reduce discrimination against pregnant workers. They criticize the treatment of dependent wives by divorce courts. They join in opposing pornography. These odd alliances between feminists and their enemies belie great disagreements over the meaning of most issues.

It is an irony that religion is far less important to women's rights issues in France, a Catholic country, than in pluralistic America. The French church was historically significant in its opposition to equal education, political rights, and contraception. But in the Fifth Republic the church is almost unnoticed by feminists. Pronouncements of the bishops frequently conform to conservative traditions and church doctrine but they are virtually ignored. Polls show they have little effect on attitudes: In 1984 a majority agreed that the church should not interfere in sexual matters. Even among practicing Catholics only a minority saw the church law as binding.[4]

Antiracist or civil rights groups have been important allies for feminists in both France and the United States. The relationship has roots in the early campaigns. American women joined with the Abolition movement; later French women condemned racism in the Dreyfus affair. Parallels are especially striking in the recent period of reforms where feminists applied the antidiscrimination rationale of antiracist and civil rights laws to women. Congress belatedly tacked sex onto the employment title of the Civil Rights Act of 1964. President Lyndon Johnson ordered that affirmative action be applied to overcome both race and sex discrimination. Giroud sneaked through amendments to include sex in the employment provisions of the antiracist law of 1972. Roudy continued by incorporating sex into all but the press sections of the 1972 law.[5]

The antiracist logic envisions equality through the elimination of legal barriers. When it deals with underlying causes of inequality and discrimination it concentrates on class or economic disadvantages of minorities, not always pertinent to sex inequalities. Anne Zelensky of the Ligue du Droit des femmes has recently criticized "rights of equality which take as a reference the privileged category and try to extend the privileges to those discriminated against.'' Women must be treated in relation to their own situation.[6] French government feminists departed from the racist analogy by concentrating on special problems of sex discrimination, especially the impact of sex role separation on the economic and political rights of women. By forging their own policies on equality of opportunity in work and relating these to other changes in the conception of family policy, parental responsibilities, and work, the MWR promoted an antidiscrimination policy intended to lead to role change. With the exception of affirmative action, most policies for American women workers are based on equality of rights and do not go as far as the French ones toward envisioning substantive changes in woman's place in the work force and the family, let alone successfully dealing with burdens of maternity and child care.

Finally, the feminists themselves deserve credit for women's rights policies in France. They have been willing to promote a more radical definition of their demands and have had a more successful record of influence than Americans. Taking feminists as a whole both inside and outside the government, they demanded more and they got more. Their most daring success was in reproductive policy, specifically abortion. The story recounted here shows how the feminists took control of the conflict, expanded it, and determined the outlines of the statute. They rejected a reform that would have legalized abortion according to the conditions of pregnancy and only settled for a policy that based legal abortion on a woman's right to decide. On the rape issue they repeated the victory, convincing the government to define rape as a crime of power against women. These victories belong to feminist groups outside government. They used organizational, legal, and public relations resources to widen the conflict over abortion and rape and eventually persuaded the government to agree that reforms should further women's rights. Their standard was picked up by feminists in the government who went on to achieve other victories, notably in work, family policy, and education. The Ministry of Woman's Rights and its predecessors really made the difference between United States and French policy in the last few years. From within the government, Yvette Roudy and her staff held fast to their feminist vision: they evaluated all policy according to their goal of changing the patriarchal sex role pattern to achieve equal rights and participation of women in the economy, society, and politics.

Where are the government feminists in the United States? Some are found in every state as members of Commissions on the Status of Women (CSW). Although CSWs vary in composition, resources, and policy interests, most avoid controversial issues, especially those dealing with sexuality. Debra Stewart's study of CSW agendas revealed few links between employment and family issues.[7] Others in government are successors to the "woodwork" feminists that Freeman referred to—those women at the Departments of Labor or Health and Human Services who are feminists and who have from time to time been able to draw on resources of feminist groups outside the government to promote women's rights policies. For the most part they have concentrated on single issues and adhere to a conservative perspective of equality and anti-discrimination. While Yvette Roudy was promoting her feminist vision from the French cabinet, woodwork feminists in the United States were confronting Reagan appointees in top policymaking positions. Their idea is that pro-woman policies preserve sex role separation in the traditional mode. Under the Reagan administration American feminists have been on the defensive, trying to preserve the policy victories for equality and reproductive rights. They battle among themselves over tactics as they try to ward off attempts by opponents to redefine crucial issues such as abortion and employment. If Center Right parties gain control of both the presidency and the legislature in France, French feminists may find themselves in the same predicament as their American sisters under the Reagan administration.

FRENCH POLITICS AND WOMEN'S RIGHTS

The feminist movement in France arose outside the government, and for the decade of the 1970s provided the energy for social, political, and legal change. Fueled by self-discovery and rage over phallocratic control of their private selves, the Mouvement de Libération des Femmes forced the public to consider subjects long-hidden: abortion, rape, and sexism. These were powerful issues, heavy with the symbolism of primitive male domination; they provoked instant media interest and piqued the curiosity of a public recently set free from moralistic controls over sex. For a few years, the feminist movement had more political resources to affect these issues than the government. Giscard used some of this energy toward his own vision of a modern France and appointed several women to his executive. These government feminists spent much of their time reacting to the demands of MLF and Choisir, while trying to control and channel them. As the political resources of the government feminists increased after 1978, they successfully put the brakes on the feminist movement and were able to promote their own moderate agenda. Feminists savored their victories on abortion and rape but began to change in reaction to government leadership. The move by Psych et Po to incorporate as MLF-*déposé* and the resulting battle among feminist groups began the trend toward a more formal organization of feminism. Activists learned that "to avoid being registered by others it was necessary to register oneself."[8]

Other factors encouraged trends toward formal organization of the women's rights groups. In the first place, new laws gave feminist and antipimping associations the right to sue their enemies in court. The proposed antisexist bill promised to allow organizations to sue employers, public agencies, and even pornographers. Only groups that were formally registered with the state for at least five years as declared opponents of rape and *proxénétisme* could use the new rights. In the second place, the new ministry established in 1981 had its own budget and Roudy was eager to subsidize feminist projects for education, shelters for battered women, and job-training programs. To receive money, groups had to prepare proposals that fit government guidelines and submit to regular bureaucratic procedures. Confronted with these opportunities and constraints, many groups either disbanded or formed formal associations under the law of 1901.

With this trend toward institutionalization, the radicals joined moderate and socialist feminists in the joys and tribulations of Annual General Meetings, constitutions, selection of officers, newsletters, and the rest. Nevertheless, the balance of power continued to shift in favor of the government feminists at the MWR. Between 1981 and 1986, the Ministry of Woman's Rights became the most important political and organizational resource for women's rights in France. The ministry recruited many feminist leaders as members of the ministerial cabinet or to staff committees for special projects. Although there was no permanent women's rights bureaucracy, they enjoyed traditional prerogatives of state power. As a government minister, Roudy automatically attracted media attention. Skilled at producing the quotable slogan and passionately attached to a comprehensive pro-woman philosophy, she was the subject of many magazine features, television talk shows, and news stories. The leaderless feminists tried to compete for attention with public demonstrations. Their first effort after the 1981 election did draw the journalists, but what the journalists wrote about was the Ministry of Woman's Rights.[9]

Especially important are the political resources the MWR enjoyed as a member of the political executive. Never before had feminists been able to lay claim to a sympathetic majority in the National Assembly. Roudy was fond of commenting on how fortunate feminists are in the Socialist party, which unlike other parties is committed to the principle of change and equality. She did not always prevail with her Socialist colleagues. Yet even the defeats demonstrate the strength of the MWR compared with women's rights associations. During the controversy over the reimbursement of abortion, for example, the associations were used as a resource by the ministry. When Roudy lost her battle in the Council of Ministers, the associations took to the street, convincing Mitterrand that he must keep his campaign promise. Such demonstrations alone would not have forced the government to act without the MWR on the inside. Later, the MWR took up the antisexist bill originally drafted by the Ligue du Droit des femmes. When the opposition swamped government feminists, the crucial provision to control sexism in the media succumbed. Throughout the two years that the bill awaited its fate in a National Assembly committee, the associations were unable to take the initiative to save what had originally been their own bill. Their only rally against sexism in late 1983 was even funded by the MWR. When the death notice for the provision appeared, those outside the government circles knew little and could do nothing about it.

The MWR brought about important changes in the definition of government policy affecting women. The sexuality issues were expanded. Contraception and abortion were linked as essential rights of women and the state assumed the responsibility of providing information services. Nearly every other item on the women's rights agenda was addressed: remaining inequalities in the family law, the quota for municipal councils, sexism and tracking in the schools, single mothers and the feminization of poverty, the reinsertion of prostitutes, and the rights of the wives of farmers and small businessmen.

The priority of MWR—woman's right to work and the improvement of the economic and professional status of women workers—was its greatest success from a feminist perspective. Until Roudy took office, feminist agendas routinely listed equal pay and jobs but rarely gave these goals much attention. Roudy set up enforcement of a new equal-opportunity law and also made important new linkages among the issues of family, work, and sexism. Her ministry represented the formal acceptance of the belief that simple legal equality is not enough to improve woman's lot and there must be role change through redefinitions of family policy, maternity and parental leave, job training for the young, flexible time, and the shortened workweek. Roudy and her staff promoted a comprehensive vision of how all these factors must fit together to further women's rights. They were not equally successful in controlling the conflicts in government on all these issues, but they introduced the feminist perspective on role change at the highest levels of policymaking. For the first time women workers became a high priority because government feminists viewed work and job training as the keys to independence, dignity, and equality for women.

The feminists in the Mitterrand government represented the special culture of socialist feminism. There is a long history of antagonism between socialism and feminism and only a minority of socialists have historically accommodated women's rights into their ideology. The two movements have been repeatedly drawn together, only to rediscover the old tensions and conflicts. In the 1960s, several women attracted to the Left vowed to reconcile the two "isms." Feminists in the unions, such as Christine Gilles of the CGT and Jeannette Laôt of the CFDT; the group around Mitterrand, including Marie Thérèse Eyquêm, Collette Audry, and Yvette Roudy; and the leaders of the UFF and the women of the Communist party, all studied the questions, consulting leftist intellectual traditions along with the new feminist writings. For Laôt, this period was "the richest of my adult life." [10] Like Roudy, she had to fight the Proudhonians in her midst whose misogyny relegated women to two roles: housewives or harlots.

Roudy recalls that the feminists in the Socialist party, inspired by the neglected works of Bebel, Engels, and Simone de Beauvoir, wove their goals for women into the reformed Socialist platform in 1978. "With patient and daily work we were able to introduce into the texts— that is, into the law of the party, into the 'bible'—the feminist theme; socialists recognized feminism as a political fact. Poor Proudhon had to be turning over in his grave!''[11] In the Socialist party manifesto on women, primary place was given to their economic status. But more important was the statement of interrelations:

The women's struggle against inequalities and discriminations is a global struggle, which touches on all sectors of private and public life. As such, each demand must be examined and appreciated as a function of all the others. Otherwise, either we will perpetuate the inferiority of women with protective measures, or divide women (housewives and workers) or aggrevate the opposition between male and female workers.[12]

The Socialist victory in 1981 brought a government to power pledged to support a strong feminist program. The years after 1986 will show how much women's rights in France depends on the parties of the Left. In her recent biography, Roudy voiced some worries about the future. She acknowledged that while her government's actions to promote women have been popular, the gains remain fragile, endangered by traditional biases and ordinary sexism that lurk beneath the surface in all aspects of life. Women, she pointed out, don't have any real power and few are willing to brave the "brutality and violence in the circles of power" even to fight for their own rights.

So, despite conclusions that French policy conforms closely to feminist goals because of the strength of feminists in the government, the next few years promise change. The 1986 parliamentary elections brought a Center Right government to power to govern with a Socialist president. After the 1988 presidential elections the executive will change again. No one knows what the long-term role of feminists will be. The MWR's plan was to set goals, provide legal tools, and prod women to meet it halfway in making use of the new rights and opportunities. It was a very partisan agency with a staff and regional delegates recruited because of their loyalty to Yvette Roudy and her particular vision of feminist socialism. A more conservative government will bring in an executive less concerned with inequality and role changes. Although the new legislation should survive, a Center Right government will take a less active stance, in general. Feminists in the Center and the Right advocate equality and nondiscrimination yet preserve the idea of a choice for women between working outside the home or being full-time homemakers. Whatever form the administration of women's rights policy takes, it will be less active in prodding bureaucrats, publicizing new laws, or promoting pilot projects. In Chirac's first government of 1986, no successor to Yvette Roudy was appointed. Responsibility for the status of women was assigned to a delegate in the Ministry of Social Affairs and Employment.

UNRESOLVED ISSUES

Two new women's issues, female homosexuality and surrogate motherhood, are developing and may soon reach the public agenda. Both challenge feminist ideologies.

Female Homosexuality

Love between women was first a linguistic rather than a political problem. For years, guardians of the French language searched for the right word to name this relationship. Finally, in the dictionary of 1762, the Académie Française settled on *tribade*, derived from a Greek word meaning a woman with an abnormally large clitoris. They defined woman-love as an unnatural act based on a sort of rare anatomical pathology that could neither be understood nor helped. Later, the dictionary warned: "One avoids using this word."[13] While male homosexuality was considered a clear threat to civil society and the moral code, and premarital sex and adultery presented a threat to the family and the state, female homosexuality was barely recognized, and it remained on the fringes of communities. The *tribades* were not feared but seen as misfits, similar to cripples and people who heard voices. Evelyne Le Garrec describes the unusual couples in her hometown; women with short hair and tailored clothes who lived in houses with drawn shades. "They have special morals," her mother's friends agreed.[14]

Lesbians have suffered little active abuse; rather, they have endured the oppression of silence. Their nonexistence continued even into the 1970s and the rise of the new feminism. While the movement fostered much discussion of separation, gynoculture, and female-centered sexuality, there was little attention to the special demands of lesbians and their relation to women's rights and feminism. An MLF lesbian group, Les Gouines Rouges, formed in 1971 but lasted less than a year. The problematic relationship between feminism and homosexuality has continued into the 1980s.

Homosexual rights has been a public issue in France since 1979, and lesbians have joined with gay men in breaking the silence and pressing for the right to live openly without fear of reprisal. The Comité d'Urgence Anti-repression Homosexuelle (CUARH) attracted both men and women to fight discrimination based on sexual preference in the economy, society, and government. In April 1981 occurred the first major public demonstration for gay and lesbian rights. Homosexual activists took an interest in the presidential campaign and endorsed Mitterrand after he endorsed them: "Homosexuality should not involve either inequality or discrimination in any form, and concrete measures should be taken on all issues you so justly raise." [15] The president partially kept his promise by removing the last vestiges of legal discrimination, including a provision in the penal code that made it a crime to have a homosexual encounter with a person under eighteen (whereas the age of consent to heterosexual contact is fifteen). Gisèle Halimi, who led the debate on this amendment, indicated that Socialist deputies did not want any repression or discrimination regarding sexuality. "The law must not intervene in the sexual choices of males and females in this country." [16] The CUARH and other gay rights groups now seek laws to protect them against discrimination in work and housing and guarantee them the right to form homosexual families on the same bases as heterosexual couples. [17]

Is homosexuality a feminist issue? Among lesbians there is disagreement. Those involved in the CUARH believe they have more in common with male homosexuals because both want to remove discrimination against sexual preference. They share the desire to live openly, to have job security, and to retain custody of children or adopt children. Lesbian feminists on the other hand consider they have special problems as women. They complain that while there is a complete subculture for gay men, including hundreds of bars, restaurants, saunas, a radio station, and a press, women do not enjoy such cultural support. Some lesbian groups such as the Mouvement d'Information et d'Expression des Lesbiennes (MIEL) and Collectif Lesbien de Recherche et d'Action (CLRA) meet at the Maison des femmes in Paris. Still other lesbians reject both gay males and regular feminist groups. For them, homosexuality is a political choice. Radical lesbians broke with feminists in 1981 to create the Front des Lesbiennes Radicales. They argue that feminists, by advocating the right of sexual choice, accept the male-dominant heterosexual system as legitimate. Evidence of the feminists' commitment to heterosexual issues is their belief that the right to abortion is the key to liberation. To the radicals this is a compromise with male dominance; for them the only way to liberation is to reject heterosexuality altogether. A woman is always defined in relation to a man; therefore the lesbian is the only female who escapes being a woman.[18]

Surrogate Mothers

The increase in sterility and new technologies of reproduction provides another new issue for French feminists. Social and medical practice has outdistanced the cultural and political response. In 1983, the National Assembly recognized the issue by appointing Choisir president Gisèle Halimi and other deputies to a special investigative committee. Monique Pelletier and Yvette Roudy have convened colloquia, just a few of many held throughout the country on the advances in the science of reproduction—including in-vitro fertilization and frozen embryos. Some feminists fear that in the future women will lose control of reproduction to male-dominated science. "Under cover of a new science of reproduction in what ways are they transforming the female body into the biological laboratory of the future? The logical end of all this is to take away from women not only control of reproduction, but reproduction itself."[19]

Of more immediate concern, however, are the rights of the woman engaged to give birth to a child for a sterile couple, the *mère porteuse* (surrogate mother). Three definitions of the problem have been formulated. Pelletier views the practice in terms of its effect on the dignity of the woman. Hiring surrogate mothers devalues the place of woman as the giver of life. She is viewed more and more as a receptacle for producing babies. "When woman becomes the glass jar in which scientific experiments are conducted, it's necessary to weigh the meaning of the word [dignity]."[20] Halimi has warned that the indignity of surrogate motherhood will fall disproportionately on the poor. In a statement before the National Assembly in 1983, she opposed the practice because it created two classes of women: the rich who order and pay for the children and the poor who produce them. She went on to call it a form of American-style free-enterprise prostitution, where anything is for sale, even the wombs of the poor.[21] Rather than encourage such a dreadful business, the sterile woman should look to either the new technologies of in-vitro fertilization or adoption to help her form a family.

At the MWR, Roudy sponsored her own colloquia on the new technologies of reproduction. She did not frame the issue of surrogate motherhood in as serious terms as Pelletier and Halimi. She spoke first of all about the strong desire of sterile women to have children. "What would be the effect of prohibiting this procedure, when we know the strength of the desire of sterile couples for a baby."[22] And how, she added, could she forbid them to do so if they find a woman who is willing to help? Instead of condemning, Roudy warned that the rights of the pregnant woman must have top priority, including the rights to abortion or to keep the child after birth. The best way for the government to prevent surrogate motherhood is not by regulation, but by attacking the problem of sterility through research and the prevention of sexually transmitted diseases.

New issues arise, technologies innovate, cultures adapt, and sex roles change; all converge to challenge policymakers. For several years, feminist values were strongly represented in the government of France and changes in public policy have been dramatic. The new laws enforce sex equality and in some cases prepare for comprehensive role change. The meaning of all this in the daily lives of ordinary women depends on the importance of laws, statutes, and constitutions in society as a whole. Pragmatists argue that the content of these documents means little, that what is really important is how the laws are carried out, in other words, the final outcome of the policy. Many of these changes are too new to have had an effect, but determining the impact of policy on everyday lives will be difficult even after the passage of time.

This study is based on the view that policy processes and the resulting definition, values, logics, and rationales of government action have significance in their own right. Some changes in procedures show immediate results, for example, in adding grounds for divorce or legalizing contraceptives. Other revisions of laws affect official symbols. The stance a government adopts in one area affects values and policy positions of other governmental as well as nongovernmental structures and processes. Giving women the right to vote, for example, led to changes in education and family law. Sometimes the controversy over an issue has an impact without going so far as changing the law substantively, especially if feminists gain control of the definition of the issue. The quota for women in municipal elections, although struck down as unconstitutional, seemed to provoke the political parties to include more women candidates on their lists. Perhaps the campaign portraying pornography as degrading to women and perpetuating male dominance through sexual violence will encourage women to reject the images that surround them along with the men whose fantasies they portray.

NOTES

1. In March 1986, the French government embarked on untested waters: a popularly elected president of the Left and a political executive representing a coalition of rightist parties. This bipartisan government is called *cohabitation*.

2. Sylvia Ann Hewlett, *A Lesser Life: The Myth of Women's Liberation in America* (New York: Morrow, 1986).

3. Pronatalism in France is closely related to nationalism. In the United States the "right to life" activists are pro-birth, but they do not talk of the need to increase the birth rate in order to strengthen the economy and society. Theirs is a moral and religious argument.

4. SOFRES, *Opinion publique: 1985* (Paris: Gallimard, 1985), 310.

5. Organizations such as Les Nanas beurs have begun to form to promote the special needs of immigrant women. They have the same problem of identity and priority facing black women in the United States: Which is the more serious discrimination, race or sex?

6. Anne Zelensky, "Des Droits nouveaux pour les femmes," *Citoyennes à part entière* 43 (juin 1985), 12.

7. Debra Stewart, "Institutionalization of Female Participation at the Local Level: Commissions on the Status of Women and Agenda Building," *Women and Politics* 1 (Spring 1980), 37–63.

8. Françoise Picq, "Quelques étapes dans la constitution des associations féministes," *Pénélope* 11 (automne 1984), 202.

9. International Women's Day, 8 March 1982, was marked by the first official observance by the government. Nongovernment activities were overshadowed by the announcement of the seventeen-point program for women's rights by the Mitterrand government.

10. Jeannette Laôt, *Stratégie pour les femmes* (Paris: Stock, 1977), 63.

11. Yvette Roudy, *A Cause d'elles* (Paris: Albin Michel, 1985), 119.

12. Parti socialiste, "Féminisme–Socialisme–Autogestion" (février 1979), 8.

13. Marie-Jo Bonnet, *Un Choix sans équivoque* (Paris: Denoël, 1981), 73. "On évite d'employer ce mot" found by Bonnet in the 1790 edition of the Académie Française dictionary.

14. Evelyne LeGarrec, *Des femmes qui s'aiment* (Paris: Seuil, 1984).

15. Ibid., 251.

16. *Journal officiel*, Débats parlementaires (21 juillet 1982), 4626.

17. French law has established a status called *concubinage* defined as a man and woman who live maritally under the same roof continuously and publicly. These couples become eligible for certain benefits if there are children, but so far the government has refused to recognize homosexual couples in this category.

18. Monique Wittig, *Questions féministes*, no. 8. Quoted by LeGarrec, *Des femmes qui s'aiment*, 262.

19. Anne Marie de Vilaine, "Nouvelle méthods de procréation—pour qui, pourquoi," *Citoyennes à part entière* 44 (juillet–août 1985), 16.

20. L'Agence femmes information, *Bulletin* 155 (mai 1985).

21. "Mères porteuses," *Le Nouveau Choisir* (février–mars 1985), 11.

22. "Yvette Roudy au colloque de Marseilles," *Citoyennes à part entière* (mai 1985), 15.

BIBLIOGRAPHY

PUBLIC DOCUMENTS

Comité du Travail féminin. *Bilan de l'application de la loi du 22 décembre 1972 sur l'égalité de rémunération entre les hommes et les femmes*, mars 1976.

———. *L'Etude des salaires masculins et feminins*, 1971.

———. *L'Evolution de la situation des femmes dans la société française*, 1975.

———. *Rapport sur les inégalités de rémunération*, 1971.

Journal Officiel de la République Française, Débats parlementaires. Assemblée Nationale, Sénat. Compte rendu intégral des séances, 1922–85.

———. Edition des Lois et Décrets.

Ministère-délégué à la Condition féminine. *Bulletin de la Condition féminine*, 1979–81.

Ministère des Droits de la femme. *Citoyennes à part entière*, 1981–1985.

———. *Les Femmes dans une société d'inégalités*, 1982.

———. *Guide des droits des femmes*, 1982–85.

Ministère de l'Education nationale. "Action éducative contre les préjuges sexistes." Arrêté du 12 juillet 1982.

———. "Orientation des jeunes filles." Circulaire no. 82-182 du 29 avril 1982.

Ministère du Travail et de la Participation. *Les Discriminations et les disparités dans le travail féminin*. Rapport remis à Robert Boulin et à Nicole Pasquier par Jacques Baudoin, octobre, 1979.

Secrétaire à la Condition féminine. *Les Inégalités entre femmes et hommes dans le droit social français*. Rapport du groupe de travail nommé par F. Giroud, 1974.

PRESS CLIPPING FILES

L'Agence Femmes Information. Avortement; Ministère des Droits de la femme; loi anti-sexiste; Yvette Roudy; égalité professionnel, 1979–83.

Bibliothèque Marguerite Durand. Françoise Giroud; Monique Pelletier; Nicole Pasquier; travail; éducation des filles.

Bureau d'Accueil des professeurs universitaires étrangers. Women's rights and feminism, 1981–1983.

Centre Audiovisuel Simone de Beauvoir, Videotape collection.

CEVIPOF, Campaign literature, 1974, 1978, 1981.

ARTICLES

L'Agence femmes information. *Bulletin* (1983–85); *Nouvelles* (1986).

"L'Avortement, 1975–85." *Le Monde aujourd'hui* (10–11 février 1985).

Bachrach, Peter, and Baratz, Morton S. "Two Faces of Power." *American Political Science Review* 56 (December 1962), 947-52.

Beauvoir, Simone de. "La Femme revoltée." *Nouvel Observateur* 379 (14 février 1972), 47–54.

Bellescize, Diane de. "Le Statut de la femme dans la fonction publique: bilan des réformes les plus récentes." *Revue administrative de l'est de la France* 8 (hiver 1977), 17–32.

Blin-Sarde, Michele. "L'Evolution du concept de différence dans le mouvement de libération des femmes en France." *Contemporary French Civilization* 6 (Fall/Winter 1982), 195–202.

Brown, Bernard E. "The French Experience of Modernization." *World Politics* 21 (April 1969), 366–91.

Catala, Nicole. "Activité professionnelle des femmes et évolution du droit." *Revue Française des affaires sociales* 35 (Décembre 1981), 167–72.

"La Cause des femmes." *Regards sur actualité* (novembre 1974), 40–44.

Charraud, Alain. "Travail féminin et revendications féministes." *Sociologie du Travail* 16 (juillet–septembre 1974), 291–318.

Clark, Linda L. "Socialization of Girls in the Primary Schools of the Third Republic." *Journal of Social History* 15 (Summer 1982), 685–97.

Clerc, Christine. "Trois femmes d'action à suivre." *Réalités* 384 (février 1978), 16–17.

"La Condition de la femme en 1975." *Promotions* 98 (1975), numéro spécial.

Coombs, Fred. "The Politics of Educational Change in France." *Comparative Education Review* 22 (October 1978), 480–503.

Coulon, Colette. "Femmes: Le parti communiste français propose . . . " *Economie et politique* 8 (décembre 1977), 29–33.

Decrocq, Françoise. "The Liberation Movement in Socialist France." *Feminist Studies* 8 (Fall 1982), 676–82.

Delphy, Christine. "French Feminist Forum." *The Women's Review of Books* 3 (March 1986), 16.

Devaud, Marcelle. "La Situation de la femme au travail en 1973 et le role du CTF." *Vie Sociale* 7–8 (juillet–août 1973), 381–89.

Devaud, Marcelle, and Levy, Martine. "Women's Employment in France." *International Labour Review* 119 (November/December 1980), 739–54.

Devreux, Anne-Marie, and Fernand-Picard, Michèle. "La Loi sur l'avortement, chronologie des événements et des prises de position." *Revue française de sociologie* 23 (1982), 503–18.

Dhavernas, Marie-Jo, and Kandel, Liliane, "Le Sexisme comme realité et comme représentation." *Les Temps modernes* 40 (juillet 1983), 3–29.

"Dix ans de féminisme en France." *Politique aujourd'hui* 3–4 (été 1981), 87–102.

"Les Droits des femmes." *Revue practique de droit social* 436 (août–septembre 1981), 277–268.

Dumont, Yvonne. "Condition féminine et réformisme." *Cahiers du Communisme* 54 (août–septembre 1978), 50–60.

"Education des filles, Enseignement des femmes." *Pénélope 2* (printemps 1980), entire issue.

"Education, Occupation and Earnings." *European Economic Review* 13 (January 1980), 103–27.

"Féminisme en famille." *Informations sociales* 7 (1983), 2–79.

"Féminisme international: Reseau contre l'esclavage sexuel." *Questions féministes* 8 (hiver 1984), entire issue.

"Femmes." *La Nouvelle Critique* 82 (mars 1975), 11–53.

"Femmes, droit et justice." *Actes* 16 (automne 1977), numéro spécial.

"Les Femmes en France." *Le Monde, dossier et documents: Vie social et politique* (22 juin 1975).

"Femmes et associations." *Pénélope* 11 (automne 1984), numéro spécial.

"Femmes et féminisme." *Les Cahiers d'éducation civique* 45–46 (juillet 1978), numéro spécial.

"Les Femmes et la prostitution." *Dialogue de Femmes* (1981–82), 86–105.

"Femmes et Mondes." *Revue du mouvement du Nid* (1985).

"Femmes, mouvements de femmes." *Que faire aujourd'hui?* 8 (octobre 1980), 10–67.

"Les Femmes s'entêtent." *Les Temps modernes* 333–34 (avril–mai 1974).

Ferguson, Ann et al. "Forum: The Feminist Sexuality Debates." *Signs* 10 (Autumn 1984), 106–35.

Fodor, Regina. "Day-Care Policy in France and Its Consequences for Women." *International Journal of Urban and Regional Research* 2 (October 1978), 463–81.

"La France misogyne." *Le Nouvel Observateur* 904 (6 mai 1982), dossier spécial, 7 pages.

Garnier, Maurice, and Hout, Michael. "Inequality of Educational Opportunity in France and the United States." *Social Science Research* 5, 225–246.

Giolotto, Pierre. "Côté fille, côté garçon." *L'Education* (17 décembre 1981), 9–13.

Glendon, Mary Ann. "French Divorce Reform, 1976." *American Journal of Comparative Law* 24 (Spring 1976), 199–228.

Gozard, Claudine. "Le Nouveau Divorce, un bien ou mal pour les femmes?" *Antoinette* 128 (1975), 28–31.

Halperin, Monique. "Travail des femmes et 'condition féminine' ou les limites d'une frontière qui n'existe pas." *Revue française des affaires sociales* 35 (décembre 1981), 231–34.

Jensen, Jane. "The Modern Women's Movement in Italy, France and Great Britain: Differences in Life Cycles." *Comparative Social Research* 5 (1982), 341–75.

Kandel, Liliane. "Journeaux en mouvement: La presse féministe aujourd'hui." *Questions féministes* 7 (février 1980), 15–36.

Kesselman, Mark. "Overinstitutionalization and Political Constraint, the Case of France." *Comparative Politics* 3 (October 1970), 21–44.

Lesbia 26, 27 (mars–avril 1985).

"La Loi anti-sexiste: Remédie ou placebo?" *La Revue d'en face* 11 (automne 1981).

Loos, Jocelyne, and Louis, Marie-Victoire. "Femmes, travail et temps partiel." *Les Temps modernes* 39 (décembre 1982), 1150–66.

McLaren, Angus. "Abortion in France, Women and the Regulation of Family Size 1800-1914." *French Historical Studies* 10 (Spring 1978), 461–85.

———. "Sex and Socialism: The Opposition of the French Left to Birth Control in the Nineteenth Century." *Journal of the History of Ideas* 27 (1976), 475-92.

Maison des femmes. *Paris féministe* (1985-86).

Mossuz, Janine. "La Regulation des naissances, les aspects politiques du débat." *Revue française de science politique* (octobre 1966), 913–39.

Mossuz-Lavau, Janine and Sineau, Mariette. "Les Femmes et la politique." *Revue française de science politique*(octobre 1976), 929–56.

Mouvement de Libération des Femmes. *Le Torchon brûle*, (1971–73).

Northcutt, Wayne, and Flaitz, Jeffra. "Women and Politics in Contemporary

France: The Electoral Shift to the Left in the 1981 Presidential and Legislative Elections.'' *Contemporary French Civilization* 7 (Winter 1983), 183–198.

Ollivier, Olympe. "Une Femme, un ministère, des projets." *Pourquoi* 173 (mars 1982), 8–19.

Parturier, Françoise. "La Liberté d'aimer et la pornographie." *Choisir* 16 (octobre–novembre 1975), 1.

Pelletier, Madeleine. "Feminism and the Family, the Right to Abortion." Translated by Marilyn J. Boxer. *The French-American Review* 6 (Spring 1982), 3–26.

Pelletier, Monique. "La Promotion des femmes dans le secteur publique." *Administration* 107 (mars 1980), 109–24.

Picq, Françoise. "Droit de la femme ou droits des femmes, le ministère, ses lois, et le sexisme." *La Revue d'en face* 14 (automne 1983), 5–22.

"Quel féminisme aujourd'hui?" *Economie et humanisme* 244 (novembre–décembre 1978), 4–63.

Segers, M. C. "Equality, Public Policy and Relevant Sex Differences." *Polity* 11 (1979), 319-39.

Silver, Catherine Bodard. "Women and the Professions in France." *American Journal of Sociology* 78 (January 1973), 836–51.

Slama, Beatrice. "Le Débat continue: La loi anti-sexiste à travers la presse." *Les Temps modernes* 444 (juillet 1983), 31–61.

"Status of Women in France." *American Journal of Comparative Law* 20 (Fall 1972), 647–61.

Stewart, Debra. "Institutionalization of Female Participation at the Local Level: Commissions on the Status of Women and Agenda Building." *Women and Politics* 1 (Spring 1980), 37–63.

Thebaud, Annie, and Lert, France. "Emploi, travail et santé des femmes: La legislation et les recherches face aux mouvements sociaux en France." *Droit social* (décembre 1982), 781–92.

"Le Travail des femmes." *Revue française des affaires sociales* 35 (décembre 1981), 7–282.

Verdes-Leroux, Jeannine. "Le Travail des femmes." *Les Temps modernes* 337–338 (août–septembre 1974), 2700–22.

Vincent M. "Condition féminine: Une autre politique est nécessaire." *Cahiers du communisme* 51 (mars 1975), 30–40.

"Vivre au féminin." *Les Cahiers français* 171(mai–août 1975), numéro spécial.

Vorenberg, Elizabeth and James. "The Biggest Pimp of All, Prostitution and Some Facts of Life." *The Atlantic* (January 1977), 27–38.

Weitz, Margaret Collins. "An Interview with Evelyne Sullerot." *Contemporary French Civilization* 2 (Spring 1978), 451–62.

————. "The Status of Women in France Today: A Reassessment." *Contemporary French Civilization* 6 (1981–82), 203–18.

BOOKS

Acton, William. *Prostitution*. London, 1857. Reprint. New York: Praeger, 1968.

Adams, Carolyn Teich, and Winston, Kathryn Teich. *Mothers at Work*. New York: Longman, 1980.

Albistur, Maïté, and Armogathe, Daniel. *Histoire du féminisme français, du moyen age à nos jours*. Paris: Des Femmes, 1977.

Alliot-Marie, Michele. *La Décision politique, attention! une république peut en cacher une autre*. Paris: Presses Universitaires de France, 1983.

Alzon, Claude. *La Femme potiche et la femme bonniche*. Paris: F. Maspero, 1973.

Anderson, Charles. "The Logic of Public Problems: Evaluation in Comparative Policy Research." In *Comparing Public Policies: New Concepts and Methods* edited by Douglas Ashford. Beverly Hills: Sage, 1978.

Andrews, William G. *Presidential Government in Gaullist France, A Study of Executive Legislative Relations 1958-1974*. Albany: SUNY Press, 1982.

Ardagh, John. *France in the 1980s*. Hammondsworth: Penguin, 1982.

Ashford, Douglas E. *Policy and Politics in France, Living with Uncertainty*. Philadelphia: Temple University Press, 1982.

Audry, Collette. *Les Militants et leurs morales*. Paris: Flammarion, 1976.

Baer, Judith A. *The Chains of Protection, the Judicial Response to Women's Labor Legislation*. Westport, CT: Greenwood Press, 1978.

Banks, Olive. *Faces of Feminism*. Oxford: Martin Robinson, 1981.

Barry, Kathleen. *Female Sexual Slavery*. Englewood Cliffs, NJ: Prentice Hall, 1979.

Beauvoir, Simone de. *The Second Sex*. Translated by H. M. Parshley. New York: Vintage, 1952, 1974.

Beauvoir, Simone de, ed. *Le Sexisme ordinaire*. Paris: Seuil, 1979.

Berger, Henry. *L'Avortement, histoire d'un débat*. Paris: Flammarion, 1975.

Bernard, Jesse. *Women and the Public Interest*. Chicago: Aldine-Atherton, 1971.

Bidelman, Patrick Kay. *Pariahs Stand Up! The Founding of the Liberal Feminist Movement in France, 1858–1889*. Westport, CT: Greenwood Press, 1982.

Billon, Bernard. *Viol et violeurs*. Paris: CNRS, 1984.

Blanquart, Louisette. *Femmes: l'âge politique*. Paris: Editions sociales, 1974.

Boneparth, Ellen, ed. *Women, Power and Policy*. New York: Pergamon, 1982.

Bonnet, Marie-Jo. *Un Choix sans équivoque*. Paris: Denöel, 1981.

Boons, Marie Claire. *C'est terrible quand on y pense.* Paris: Galilée, 1983.

Bouillaguet-Bernard, Patricia; Gauvin-Ayel, Annie; and Outin, Jean-Luc. *Femmes au travail, prosperité et crise.* Paris: Economica, 1981.

Breton, Denise. *Histoires Ordinaires du féminin présent.* Paris: Temps actuels, 1982.

Brimo, Albert. *Les Femmes françaises face au pouvoir politique.* Paris: Montchristien, 1975.

Callet, Christine, and du Granrut, Claude. *Place aux femmes.* Paris: Stock, 1973.

Callu, Marie-France. *Le Nouveau Droit de la femme.* Lyon: Edition l' Hermès, 1978.

Carroll, Joseph T. *The French, How they Live and Work.* 2d ed. Newton Abbott, England: David & Charles, 1973.

Charzat, Gisele. *Femmes, violence, pouvoir.* Paris: J. E. Simoen, 1979.

Charzat, Gisele. *Les Françaises sont-elles des citoyennes?* Paris: Denoël/Gonthier, 1972.

Choisir. *Avortement: Une loi en procès, l'affaire de Bobigny.* Paris: Gallimard, 1973.

————. *Quel président pour les femmes, réponses de François Mitterrand.* Paris: Gallimard, 1981.

————. *Viol, le procès d'Aix-en-Provence.* Paris: Gallimard, 1978.

Chroniques d'une imposture: Du mouvement de libération des femmes à une marque commerciale. Paris: Association Mouvement pour les Luttes Féministes, 1981.

Clark, Linda L. *Schooling the Daughters of Marianne.* Albany: SUNY Press, 1984.

Cobb, Roger W., and Elder, Charles D. *Participation in American Politics: The Dynamics of Agenda-Building.* Boston: Allyn & Bacon, 1972.

Cohen-Tanugi, Laurent. *Le Droit sans l'état, sur la démocratie en France et en Amérique.* Paris: Presses Universitaires de France, 1985.

Collective Works. *Rights of Women and the EEC.* London: Rights of Women in Europe, 1983.

Conseil national des femmes. *Etats généraux du féminisme.* Paris, 1929.

Contraception et avortement, dix ans de débats dans la presse 1965–1974. Paris: CNRS, 1979.

Coquillat, Michelle. *Qui sont elles?* Paris: Mazarine, 1983.

Coquille, Sylvie. *Naissance du mouvement de libération des femmes en France 1970–1973.* Memoir de Maîtrise. Nanterre: Université de Paris X, 1980.

Corbin, Alain. *Les Filles de noce, misère sexuelle et prostitution.* Paris: Montaigne, 1978.

Cordelier, Jeanne. *"The Life": Memoirs of a French Hooker.* Translated by Henry Mathews. New York: Viking Press, 1978.

Council of Europe. *The Situation of Women in the Political Process in Europe*. Vols. 1–3. Strasbourg, 1984.

Dagnaud, Monique. *L'Elite rose*. Paris: Ramsay, 1982.

Darling, Martha. *The Role of Women in the Economy*. Paris: OECD, 1975.

Daune-Richard, Anne-Marie. *Travail professionel et travail domestique, étude exploratoire sur le travail et ses représentations au sein de lignées féminines*. Aix-en-Provence: CEFUP; Paris: Ministère du Travail, 1984.

David, Rene. *French Law, Its Structures, Sources and Methodology*. Baton Rouge: Louisiana State University Press, 1972.

Davisse, Annick. *Les Femmes dans le fonction publique*. Paris: Ministère de la Fonction public et Reformes administratives, 1983.

Decaux, Alain. *Histoires des françaises*. Paris: Librairie académique Perrin, 1972.

Decroux-Masson, Annie. *Papa lit, maman coud, les manuels scolaires en bleu et rose*. Paris: Denoël, 1979.

Delmas-Marty, Mireille, and Labrusse-Riou, Catherine. *Le Mariage et le divorce*. 2d ed. Paris: Presses Universitaires de France, 1978.

Dhavernas, Odile. *Droits des femmes, pouvoir des hommes*. Paris: Seuil, 1978.

Dogan, Mattai, and Narbonne, J. *Les Françaises face à la politique*. Paris: A. Colin, 1955.

Données sociales, 1981. Paris: INSEE, 1981.

DuBois, Ellen Carol. *Feminism and Suffrage, the Emergence of an Independent Women's Movement in America 1848–69*. Ithaca: Cornell University Press, 1978.

Duverger, Maurice. *The Political Role of Women*. New York: UNESCO, 1955.

Dworkin, Andrea. *Pornography: Men Possessing Women*. London: The Women's Press, 1981.

Epstein, Cynthia Fuchs, and Coser, Rose Lamb. *Access to Power*. London: Allen & Unwin, 1981.

Fargier, Marie-Odile. *Le Viol*. Paris: Grasset, 1976.

Faure, Christine. *La Démocratie sans les femmes*. Paris: Presses Universitaires de France, 1985.

Faure, E. *L'Education nationale et la participation*. Paris: Plon, 1968.

Femmes, féminisme et recherches, Toulouse—décembre 1982. Toulouse: AFFER, 1984.

Floriot, Rene. *La Réforme du divorce*. Paris: Flammarion, 1975.

Fraser, W. R. *Reform and Restraints in Modern French Education*. London: 1971.

Feeman, Jo. *The Politics of Women's Liberation*. New York: Longman, 1975.

Fuchs, Rachel G. *Abandoned Children: Foundlings and Child Care in Nineteenth Century France*. Albany: SUNY Press, 1984.

Gallup, George, ed. *The Gallup International Public Opinion Polls: France 1939, 1944–1975*. Vols. 1–2. New York: Random House; Westport, Conn.: Greenwood Press, 1976.

Garcia Gaudilla, Naty. *Libération des femmes: Le M.L.F..* Paris: Presses Universitaires de France, 1981.

Gelb, Joyce, and Palley, Marian Lief. *Women and Public Policies*. Princeton: Princeton University Press, 1982.

Gianini-Belotti, E. *Du côté des petites filles*. Paris: Des Femmes, 1974.

Giroud, Françoise. *Cents mesures pour les femmes*. Paris: Documentation française, 1976.

———. *La Comédie du pouvoir*. Paris: Fayard, 1977.

Glendon, Mary Ann. *State, Law and Family: Family Law in Transition in the United States and Western Europe*. Amsterdam, New York, and Oxford: North-Holland Publishing Co., 1977.

Gordon, Linda. *Woman's Body, Woman's Right; a Social History of Birth Control in America*. New York: Grossman, 1976.

Gramont, Sanche de. *The French, Portrait of a People*. New York: Putnam, 1969.

Groult, Benoîte. *Ainsi soit-elle*. Paris: Grasset, 1975.

Halimi, Gisèle. *Le Programme Commun des femmes*. Paris: Grasset, 1978.

———. *The Right to Choose*. Brisbane: University of Queensland Press, 1973.

Halls, W. D. *Education, Culture and Politics in Modern France*. Oxford: Oxford University Press, 1976.

Hanley, D. L.; Kerr, A. P.; and Waites, N. H. *Contemporary France; Politics and Society since 1945*. London: Routledge & Kegan Paul, 1979.

Hans, Marie-Françoise, and Lapouge, Gilles. *Les Femmes, la pornographie, l'érotisme*. Paris: Seuil, 1978.

Harsin, Jill. *Policing Prostitution in Nineteenth Century Paris*. Princeton: Princeton University Press, 1985.

Hause, Steven C., with Kenney, Anne R. *Women's Suffrage and Social Politics in the French Third Republic*. Princeton: Princeton University Press, 1984.

Hewlett, Sylvia Ann. *A Lesser Life: The Myth of Women's Liberation in America*. New York: Morrow, 1986.

Huston, Nancy. *Mosaïque de la pornographie: Marie-Thérèse et les autres*. Paris: Denoël/Gonthier, 1982.

Iff, Simone. *Demain la société sexualisée*. Paris: Planning familial; Calmann-Lévy, 1975.

Jones, Charles O. *An Introduction to the Study of Public Policy*. 3d ed. Monterey, CA: Brooks/Cole, 1984.

Kergoat, Danièle. *Les Femmes et le travail à temps partiel*. Paris: Documentation française, 1984.

Krislov, Samuel, and Rosenblum, David H. *Representative Bureaucracy and the American Political System*. New York: Praeger, 1981.

Laôt, Jeannette. *Stratégie pour les femmes*. Paris: Stock, 1977.

Leclerc, Annie. *Parole de femme*. Paris: Grasset, 1974.

LeGarrec, Evelyne. *Des femmes qui s'aiment*. Paris: Seuil, 1984.

Leger, Danièle. *Le Féminisme en France*. Paris: Editions Le Sycomore, 1982.

Lemeunier, Francis. *Comment fonder et administrer une association loi du 1er juillet 1901*. 2d ed. Paris: Delmas et Cie, 1983.

Levy, Darlene Gay; Applewhite, Harriet Branson; and Johnson, Mary Durham, eds. *Women in Revolutionary Paris, 1789–1795; Selected Documents with Notes and Commentary*. Urbana: University of Illinois Press, 1979.

Marks, Elaine, and de Courtivron, Isabelle, eds. *New French Feminisms: An Anthology*. Amherst: University of Massachusetts Press, 1980.

Martin-Fugier, Anne. *Les Indépendantes*. Paris: Grasset, 1985.

Maruani, Margaret. *Les Syndicats à l'épreuve du féminisme*. Paris: Syros, 1979.

McMillan, James F. *Housewife or Harlot: The Place of Women in French Society 1870-1940*. New York: St. Martins, 1981.

Michel, Andrée. *Le Féminisme*. Paris: Presses Universitaires de France, 1981.

Michel, Andrée, and Texier, Genevieve. *La Condition de la française d'aujourd'hui*. Vols. 1–2. Paris: Gonthier, 1964.

Moody, Joseph. *French Education Since Napoleon*. Syracuse, NY: Syracuse University Press, 1978.

Moreau, Gisèle. *Libres et égales*. Paris: Editions sociales, 1982.

Moses, Claire Goldberg. *French Feminism in the Nineteenth Century*. Albany: SUNY Press, 1984.

Mossuz-Lavau, Janine, and Sineau, Mariette. *Enquête sur les femmes et la politique en France*. Paris: Presses Universitaires de France, 1983.

———. *Les Femmes françaises en 1978, insertion sociale, insertion politique*. Paris: le CORDES, 1980.

———. "France." In *The Politics of the Second Electorate*, edited by Joni Lovenduski and Jill Hills. London: Routledge & Kegan Paul, 1981.

———. "Women and Politics in France Today." In *Comparative Women's Rights and Participation in Europe*, edited by Gisbert H. Franz. Dobbs Ferry, NY: Transnational Publishers, 1983.

Mouvement française pour le planning familial. *D'une révolte à une lutte: 25 ans d'histoire du planning familial*. Paris: Tierce, 1982.

Ouston, Philip. *France in the Twentieth Century*. New York: Praeger, 1972.

Ouvrage collectif. *Les Mutilations du sexe des femmes aujourd'hui en France* Paris: Tierce, 1984.

Parti socialiste. *Féminisme-Socialisme-Autogestion—Les Grands Themes du manifeste du parti socialiste sur les droits des femmes*. Collection directed by Collete Audry. Supplement to No. 71 of Combat socialiste, 1979.

Pelletier, Monique. *Nous sommes toutes responsables*. Paris: Stock, 1981.

Piat, Colette. *La République des misogynes*. Paris: Plon, 1981.

Pisan, Annie de, and Tristan, Anne. *Histoires du MLF*. Paris: Calmann-Lévy, 1977.

Prost, Antoine. *L'Enseignement en France 1800–1967*. 2d ed. Paris: Colin, 1968.

Poulain de la Barre, François. *De L'Egalité des deux sexes, discours phisique et moral*. Paris: Antoine Dezallier, 1673; Fayard, 1984.

Rabaut, Jean. *Féministes à la "Belle Epoque."* Paris: France-Empire, 1985.

————. *Histoire des féminismes français*. Paris: Stock, 1978.

Randall, Vicky. *Women and Politics*. London: Macmillan, 1982.

Réage, Pauline. *The Story of O*. New York: Ballantine Books, 1973.

La Recherche des femmes. Paris: SNCS, 1981.

Reigel, Robert E. *American Women, a Study of Social Change*. Rutherford, NJ: Fairleigh Dickinson University Press, 1970.

Rheinstein, Max. "The Code and the Family." In *The Code Napoleon and the Common Law World*, edited by Bernard Schwartz. New York: New York University Press, 1956.

Roudy, Yvette. *A cause d'elles*. Paris: Albin Michel, 1985.

————. *La Femme en marge*. 2d ed. Paris: Flammarion, 1975; 1982.

Ruggie, Mary. *The State and Working Women: A Comparative Study of Britain and Sweden*. Princeton: Princeton University Press, 1984.

Sanger, Margaret. *An Autobiography*. Reprint. New York: W. W. Norton, 1938; Dover Publications, 1971.

Sarde, Michèle. *Regard sur les françaises*. Paris: Stock, 1983.

Schattschneider, E. E. *The Semisovereign People*. Hinsdale, IL: Dryden Press, 1975.

Silver, Catherine Bodard. "France: Contrasts in Familial and Societal Roles." In *Women's Roles and Status in Eight Countries*, edited by J. Z. Giele and A. C. Smock. New York: Wiley, 1977.

————. *A Sociological Interpretation of the Position of Women in French Society*. Mimeo. New York: Center for Social Studies, Columbia University pre-print series no. 55.

SOFRES. *Opinion publique: 1985*. Paris: Gallimard, 1985.

Sousi, Gerard. *Le Fonctionnement des associations: étude jurisprudentielle*. Lyon: Edition l'Hermès, 1980.

Sowerwine, Charles. *Sisters or Citizens? Women and Socialism in France since 1876*. Cambridge: Cambridge University Press, 1982.

Spengler, Joseph J. *France Faces Depopulation*, postlude ed. 1936–76. Durham, NC: Duke University Press, 1979.

Sullerot, Evelyne. *Les Françaises au travail*. Paris: Hachette, 1973.

————. *Pour le meilleur et sans le pire*. Paris: Fayard, 1984.

Tilly, Louise, and Scott, Joan. *Women, Work and Family*. New York: Holt, Rinehart and Winston, 1978.

Weiss, Louise. *Ce que femme veut; souvenirs de la IIIe République*. Paris: Gallimard, 1946.

Wilson, Elizabeth. *Women and the Welfare State*. London: Tavistock, 1977.

Zeldin, Theodore. *The French*. New York: Pantheon, 1982.

Zephir, Jacques J., with Zephir, Louise B. *Le Néo-féminisme de Simone de Beauvoir; trente ans après Le Deuxieme Sexe: Une post-scriptum*. Paris: Denoël/Gonthier, 1982.

INTERVIEWS

Elizabeth Berger-Suet, Association femmes libertés, November 1983.

Marie-France Cavallon, Union des Femmes Françaises, November 1983.

Michelle Coquillat, Chargée de mission, Ministère des Droits de la femme, November 1983.

Jacques Courbin, Directeur de cabinet, Ministère des Droits de la femme, December 1983.

Marcelle Devaud, former Senator, November 1983.

Janie Deveze, Déléguée régionale, Ministère des Droits de la femme, December 1983.

Odile Dhavernas, author and lawyer, December 1983.

Nicole Dromard, Vice-President, Union Française Civique et Sociale, November 1983.

Jacques Durand, former Directeur de cabinet, Ministère des Droits de la femme, October 1983.

Paulette Girard, Conseiller technique, Ministère des Droits de la femme, November 1983.

Françoise Giroud, former Secretaire d'Etat à Condition féminine, November 1983.

Jeannette Laôt, former officer of CFDT, Elysée Palace, November 1983.

Martine Levy, Chargée de mission, Ministère des Droits de la femme, December 1983.

Henri Maurel, Conseiller technique, Ministère des Droits de la femme, November 1983.

Christiane Papon, Femmes Avenir, November 1983.

Yvonne Pelat, Mouvement Jeunes Femmes, November 1983.

Monique Pelletier, former Ministre à la Condition féminine, November 1983.

Monique Petit, Choisir, November 1983.

Claire Poisignon, L'Agence femmes information, November 1983.

Yvette Roudy, Ministre des Droits de la femme, December 1983.

Christiane Scrivener, Member, European Parliament, November 1983.

Mireille Segrétain-Maurel, Conseiller technique, Ministère des Droits de la femme, November 1983.

Evelyne Use, Union Française Civique et Sociale, November 1983.

Anne Zelenski, Ligue du Droit des femmes, November 1983.

INDEX

About the Author

DOROTHY MCBRIDE STETSON is Professor of Political Science at Florida Atlantic University. She is the author of *A Woman's Issue: The Politics of Family Law Reform in England* (Greenwood Press, 1982) and has contributed to the *Journal of Comparative Family Studies* and other journals.